IN THE BELLY OF THE BEAST

HOLDING YOUR OWN IN MASS CULTURE

D0005118

SEVAK EDWARD GULBEKIAN

HAMPTON ROADS
PUBLISHING COMPANY, INC.

for the evolving human spirit

Cover design by Tiffany McCord
Cover image © 2004 Creatas/Stockbyte

Hampton Roads Publishing Company, Inc.
1125 Stoney Ridge Road
Charlottesville, VA 22902

434-296-2772
fax: 434-296-5096
e-mail: hrpc@hrpub.com
www.hrpub.com

If you are unable to order this book from your local
bookseller, you may order directly from the publisher.
Call 1-800-766-8009, toll-free.

  Library of Congress Cataloging-in-Publication Data

Gulbekian, Sevak.
  In the belly of the beast : holding your own in mass culture / Sevak
Gulbekian.
      p. cm.
Includes bibliographical references and index.
  ISBN 1-57174-305-7 (pbk. : alk. paper)
  1. Religion and culture. 2. Materialism--Religious aspects.
3. Popular culture--Religious aspects. 4. Spirituality. I. Title.
  BL65.C8G84 2004
  299'.932--dc22
                                            2003018517

ISBN 1-57174-305-7
10 9 8 7 6 5 4 3 2 1
Printed on acid-free paper in the United States

Table of Contents

Part 3
Concepts: Signposts for the Weary Traveler

A Personal Note

Ever since I can remember I have been fascinated by popular culture. As a youth I was obsessive about soccer, and later pop and rock music. I went to the games; I went to the concerts. Although never an avid television viewer, I have always wanted to know what that medium produces, what is going on, what is popular and why. I am intrigued by celebrity culture. I like to know about people: what they have achieved and how they are known in the world. I want to be aware not only of what is in the news, but also how it is presented; what passes for news in the tabloid papers, and what is left out. When it comes to film, my interest does not stop at art-house movies, but I like to know what people are watching in the multiplexes. And so on . . .

During my early twenties, after I left college, I became interested in spirituality—or, it seemed, it became interested in me. Either way, I knew this more complete perspective on life was what I had been looking for, and I could not get away from it even if I wanted to. I began to follow various spiritual interests and gradually refined my outlook and understanding. But then I was faced with a dilemma. How could I relate my new life to my ongoing absorption in contemporary and popular culture? At first it appeared as if the two didn't connect. I felt instinctively, however, that it was wrong to abandon one for the other. And then it slowly dawned on me that one had the ability to illumine the other. In other words, my spirituality could help me really *understand* modern life. A marriage between the two was called for. I soon realized that this was a task, and that it was not being accomplished much elsewhere. And so, slowly and painfully, this book was born.

Given this, the ideas in this book are built on my own experience: They reflect my path, yet I am sure they reflect those of many others today. I am but one of millions who, increasingly, want a spirituality that is not apart from everyday life. For many, spirituality is still over *there* (in the church, mosque, synagogue, etc.), and life over here; the two things bear little relation to each other. The following pages represent my struggles to bring spirit into life, to integrate them fully, and show that in essence spirit *is life*, and life *spirit*.

But why "*In the Belly of the Beast*"? As I see it, we are all in a sense living within "the Beast." By the Beast I mean materialism, and by materialism (as I will explain later) I am not just talking about consumerism and the desire for material wealth. For many people today materialism is a philosophy of life, one that is often unconsciously lived. It is our culture's leading paradigm, and many of our judgments and convictions are borne from it; from the way we approach religion and art to the practices of mainstream medicine, education, agriculture, and so on. Thus, like it or not, we are all resident within the belly of this particular Beast.

But as I see it we should not be content with that situation. This book is about working from the inside out. It is about transformation and metamorphosis: getting within the skin of the dragon and changing it from the interior. I don't think it is wise to delude ourselves by pretending that we are living a beautiful spiritual existence when we are surrounded by the hard-edged and often ruthless reality of twenty-first-century life. The path I describe here is about bringing change within our present situation: transforming materialistic culture through spiritual practice.

However, the book's title also refers to the Manichean spiritual approach, which I discuss in chapter 1.4. As I see it, the modern Manichean path tackles destructive and evil tendencies by attempting to bring the light of *understanding* to them. As I will elaborate, spiritual

Manichaeism is about transmuting evil to good through esoteric practice and discipline. In the present context, this means applying one's thoughts, feelings, and will to a particular phenomenon and trying to comprehend it—to get "within its skin" so to speak. To transform the destructive aspects of materialistic culture, we have to get our metaphorical hands dirty, to work within the belly of the Beast itself. Sometimes it may even be necessary to take an interest in and study things which seem distasteful, unspiritual, and even degenerate. I will describe this path more fully in the following pages.

Introduction:
The Task

You're awake! Don't be afraid of your own time!

—Osip Mandelstam[1]

Anyone who chooses to take up personal development will at some point in their lives become aware of an inwardly deepening sensitivity to other people and to life in general. Things that may once have been overlooked become more noticeable, awareness is generally enhanced, and a greater sense of wakefulness evolves. This is an experience any person can have—providing that their spiritual path is built on good foundations.

Ultimately, personal development is about extending and developing consciousness. But while such an increased consciousness may have many positive advantages—allowing, for example, for the development of greater understanding toward the actions of others—it can also create difficulties. Whereas before the individual may have been unaffected by the relentless barrage of opinions and facts conveyed by the media, the omnipresent advertising and marketing strategies of which we are all targets, or the crude materialism and consumerism of twenty-first-century life, now all these things become an irritation. They reveal their potential to be oppressive and suffocating. In the worst case, this experience can lead to a desire to find a means of total escape from the modern world.

Here humanity is faced with a great paradox and perhaps our greatest challenge. We are, apparently, given the task as human beings of treading a *spiritual* path in a very *physical* world—a world which has become loaded with more material riches and distractions than ever before.

So how is it possible to walk a spiritual path in modern life while maintaining sanity and balance? The aim of this book is to put forward a way of healthily and constructively *engaging* modern culture and grappling with it from a spiritual perspective. By this I do not mean agitating against twenty-first-century culture, or even crudely rejecting it. Rather, the goal is consciously to meet materialistic civilization with enriched thoughts, feelings, and will—to absorb it, transform it, metamorphose it even—through clear and heightened consciousness and spiritual insight. I will show that ultimately we can only effectively do this by truly understanding modern culture, and—crucially—by taking an interest in it. I will also argue that this is something we are compelled to do in our time if we intend to follow a fully sound and contemporary spiritual way.

For the majority of people today it is no longer realistic or even healthy to live their lives in a secluded Shangri-La—whether a monastery, commune, ashram, or something similar. It is my conviction that we are here on Earth at this time to face all the horrors and joys of the modern world. From a higher perspective, it is possible that this is something we have *chosen* to do, and the real challenge is to do it with soul: to shine with a living consciousness amidst the spiritual darkness (despite all humanity's technological advancements) of modern times. I will show how this path of engaging with the contemporary world is not simply a path of individual personal development, but can have a critical significance for humanity's evolution as a whole.

In part 1, I describe this spiritual path in some detail, and present a background philosophy to it. I discuss why a person might want to do this work, the challenges they face in doing it, and the development and strengthening of the inner self which is a natural consequence. As is demonstrated in the pages which follow, mass culture is manipulated by hidden forces that depend on our being unaware of them. In this regard, consciousness is the key. I discuss the historical and contemporary spiritual movement associated with the metamorphosis of such backward forces.

In part 2, I present some studies of modern and popular culture which take us right into the *phenomena*. These chapters represent my endeavor to awaken to a spiritual understanding of our time. I have tried to observe aspects of contemporary culture objectively, allowing spiritual ideas and concepts to emerge through the process which throw light on them. This is an attempt to reunite spiritual practice with everyday life. These essays are a beginning—a starting point—in my own path, and I hope they will be of use to you as an illustration of the path outlined in the first part of this book.

The essays are all based on things which I have personally been drawn to or become interested in. My starting point was always a desire to understand something more fully. In this sense, the subjects of these essays are intimately related to my own path. If some or all are not of interest to you, I apologize in advance, but they are intended as nothing more than a stimulus for your own work.

In chapter 2.1, for example, we enter into the shady world of "gangsta" rap. How and why did the promising and highly inventive street art form of rap or hip-hop turn into such a bleak and baleful commercial commodity? I study the distorted spiritual/social archetypes which are intimately related to this question. In the next essay, I look at the tragic situation of the young boy who is born as a high spiritual leader of Tibet but is presently missing and is either dead or abducted by the Chinese state. His case relates to a very similar attempt by dark forces to subvert the spiritual mission of another very spiritually gifted child in the 19th century, Kaspar Hauser. In chapter 2.4, I look at contemporary Hollywood movies and offer some perspectives on screen violence and certain trends in science fiction. Later in the book, I make studies of remarkable individuals and their life-paths, such as the British royals Lady Diana and Prince Charles, the black radical Malcolm X, and the underground author and speaker David Icke.

Sometimes, as in the case of Charles and Diana, I have sought simply to give different perspectives on issues which are presented in a very black-and-white form by the media. As we will see in chapter 1.6, there are various "layers" of reality. Simply getting the truth on the factual level—let alone attaining higher spiritual insight—is often a challenge today. But it is a more than worthwhile pursuit. In the case of Prince Charles, I describe the fascinating and deeply spiritual philosophy of the man, and suggest that consistent attempts to discredit his character are related to sinister "occult" forces in the shape of secret societies.

Finally, in part 3, I present three spiritual concepts which form a backdrop to the rest of the book and help give a context to the other sections. The three sections do not necessarily have to be read in the given order. Those readers especially interested in an analysis of modern cultural phenomena, for example, could start reading at part 2. But it should be borne in mind that the philosophical framework and background are given in part 1.

I believe that the most profound understanding of modern culture comes through the ability to research it using heightened capacities of perception—"clear sight," or clairvoyance. By this I do not mean mediumship, channeling, vague visions, etc., but the extension and expansion of clear consciousness developed through individual esoteric endeavor. Throughout the ages, the most advanced spiritual teachers and initiates of humanity have been able to practice this ability. Although the vast majority of people are not able to exercise "clear sight" at the present time, I am convinced that our capability to evolve as a human race requires each of us to begin developing this capacity.

There are many sound ways to do this, and the reader will be aware of many books and practices which are readily available today. But the path outlined in this book is not dependent on spiritual vision. It is a path that anyone with the right attitude and application can follow. In essence, it involves a meditative approach to life that enables the reading and interpreting of events at deeper levels than that of "everyday" or "consensus" reality. This, I suggest, is also the first rung of the spiritual ladder of higher consciousness, and an important preparation for any future personal development.

Meditation is commonly understood to be a solitary activity of concentration and centering. But it does not need to be restricted to a five minute slot at the end of the day. Each of us can make life itself a meditation by continually widening our consciousness to include invisible, spiritual dimensions. This is a lifetime journey of discovery— of finding the full reality and meaning of existence.

Part I

Orientation:
Clearing a Spiritual Path
through the Morass

1.1 The Situation: Facing Up to the Problem

Snakes blowing up the line of design
Trying to blind the science I'm sending them

—Public Enemy[1]

Truth, Faith, and Knowledge

The essential purpose of all genuine spiritual and religious paths is to lead the individual to one thing: *truth*. But there are many different paths in the modern spiritual supermarket, and there are also many degrees of truth. What distinguishes all true esoteric or inner paths is that they lead the student to *knowledge* of the truth, as opposed to simple faith or belief. Most religious systems present a set of teachings invested with a higher authority. Sometimes the teachings are contained in a book (the Bible or Koran, for example) or an oral tradition, or in other cases they are given by a living person (note the many religious sects in existence today). The extreme example of this principle of authority is the modern-day "cult," where people are forced to adhere to a decreed truth and from which it is difficult to leave once you join. In the worst case, people are led to their deaths by fanatical and deranged leaders (for example, Jim Jones, leader of the People's Temple, who led hundreds of his followers to commit suicide in northwestern Guyana in 1978).

3

The *esoteric* spiritual path, in contrast, calls for intense personal activity leading to an individual perception—cognition—of truth. The individual must learn to distinguish reality from illusion, truth from falsehood, in everyday life. The student cannot be a passive follower, but on the contrary needs to an active participant and must struggle to come to truth through understanding and knowledge.

In any age, treading such a path of inner knowledge is profoundly difficult, and produces many challenges. But in our twenty-first-century world—surrounded as we are by a multitude of media pouring out a mass of information, messages, images, and pictures—the task of telling reality from illusion is increasingly complex.

Never before in history has the human race been saturated by so much "content" in the form of words and pictures. Newspapers and magazines, televisions and DVDs, radios and CD players, advertising boards and posters, e-mail and the Internet—they all provide us with a cascading torrent of "information." Who can possibly digest all this? Who can know what is real and unreal to create meaning from it all?

Even the remarkable technologies themselves, which are the catalysts for this incessant flow, constantly challenge us to tell reality from illusion. Special effects in film can be so dazzlingly convincing that they draw us into a world of fantasy where we smile with pleasure or gasp with fear at the actions on the screen. The crystal-clear sound quality of digital recordings and the "sensesurround" effect of modern CD players can emulate the experience of real live music so we no longer know whether what we are hearing is "real" or not; and the increasing sophistication of computer images can draw us into an obsessive and addictive counter-world of illusion. In fact, for many people today, the fake but seductive domain of modern media can be more comfortable and inviting than everyday reality.

Truth and Illusion in Modern Media

But quite apart from the allure of technological tricks, one of our biggest challenges today is deciphering—on the simple level of fact—

the truth of the content poured out from the massive reservoir of media "information." I would like to give an example here which relates to the presentation of the Gulf War of 1991. Through studying this particular case, it is possible to learn not only how information is selectively and subjectively relayed, but also how it is "consumed" and accepted by a large section of the population.

Before going into detail, however, let me stress that I have no interest in making political points for one side or another, or even to enter the shadowy world of "conspiracy theory." I intend, rather, to use the case of the Gulf War as something of an archetypal example of how our perception of truth can be distorted by media translation. This is a useful case because it requires only an observation of the actual facts, and is not dependent on "political theory" or any other type of subjective analysis.

From the point of view of media history, the Gulf War represented something of a watershed. It was, quite simply, the most televised war up to that point in time. While all recent conflicts have been reported publicly to varying degrees—the Vietnam War, for example, left a legacy of graphic images which cannot easily be forgotten—the Gulf War was the first CNN war, featuring 24-hour live media coverage. You could switch on night or day and get the latest! It was a bit like watching sports, except it wasn't. It was war, and not surprisingly thousands of people were killed. But you wouldn't have known that from the media pictures.

The presence of so many reporters and television crews in the Gulf during Operation Desert Storm gave us, the public, the impression that we were being given much more access to events than, say, our parents and grandparents had of earlier wars. But that simply wasn't the case. In fact, the Western allies treated this war as a prototype for public relations that has since served them well (for example in the NATO/Serbia/Kosovo conflict of 1998).

The remarkable pictures of pinpoint-accurate bombing raids relayed from the Gulf gave the impression of a precision war. In a press briefing, Colin Powell pointed proudly to a video screen which showed a vehicle scrambling over a bridge moments before an allied bomb blew it to pieces. Powell famously referred to the driver as the "luckiest man in Iraq." He may as well have been pointing to the screen of a giant video game. And, like all good video games, nobody seemed to get hurt. There was no blood, no bodies—just startling images of targets getting bombed by seemingly deadly accurate laser-guided missiles.

But despite the impressive technology—which in retrospect turned out to be much less accurate than we had been led to believe—the Gulf conflict was, basically, another good old-fashioned war, although the full horror of it was carefully concealed from the public by expert manipulation of the news media. So, for example, most people were not aware of the bulldozers employed on the front line to bury alive (or mash to death) enemy soldiers in trenches. It is estimated that up to 2,000 Iraqi soldiers died in this way.[2]

The advanced technology of laser-guided bombs did not preclude the use of napalm, more usually associated with Vietnam. Several hundred napalm bombs were dropped by U.S. marines on trenches. Further, traditional blanket bombing by B-52 bombers killed more than 30,000 soldiers on the ground, many of them retreating conscripts killed in the so-called "turkey shoot" of the Basra road. But, not surprisingly, images of all these bloody events were carefully kept off television screens.

Another rather insidious example shows how complicit the media was in manipulating public perceptions of the war. In November 1990, the Kuwaiti side was provided with a key news story via the public relations firm Hill & Knowlton, which it had hired for millions of dollars to help in its battle to control public perceptions of the conflict. The PR firm, retained by Citizens for a Free Kuwait, distributed much footage on behalf of its client for TV stations around the world, utilizing the satellite and video services of Medialink, a company that usually distributed material to promote new products to the public.

The story they released went as follows: In the first days of the invasion Iraqi troops had entered a Kuwaiti hospital and removed sick babies from incubators, leaving them to die on the cold floor. This highly emotive story had a major effect on the direction of the war—in fact, George Bush referred to it six times in one month. It also featured in an influential Amnesty International report. Most compellingly, an apparent eyewitness to the event, one Nayirah, gave a moving public testimony in which she broke down in tears. But, remarkably, the story was a complete fabrication. As a final twist, the *New York Times* revealed that the key witness Nayirah was the daughter of the Kuwaiti ambassador to the USA.

Let me emphasize that in relating the above I am not interested in being politically partisan, "anti-Western," or anything similar. It would be equally possible to reel off negative facts associated with the Iraqi handling of the war (see, for example, their brutal treatment of ethnic groups). It should also be kept in mind, of course, that propaganda and misinformation have been used in war by all sides throughout history. They can be a critical—and, some would argue, legitimate—tool in getting a population behind its battling armed forces. But what is shattering about the example of the Gulf War is the scale of deception—or, to put it more mildly, "illusion"—that was made possible by the media.

No doubt the Iraqi state also expertly controlled and manipulated its media to give a certain perception of events to its own population. But, in a sense, that was to be expected. After all, the Iraqi Baath party, under Saddam Hussein, led a totalitarian government. It should be more surprising to us, however—living as we do in a society that is largely free to all outward appearances—to what extent our own media can feed us a "story."

I am not suggesting that the media are part of some great overarching conspiracy or even that they are deliberately seeking to mislead. But we are left with the indisputable fact that in many situations the public is presented with a partial view or perception of events that does not constitute the full reality. Simply bearing this in mind is essential to today's spiritually striving individual. This does not mean that we should develop a cold cynicism in relation to what we hear through the media, but rather that we should carry a questioning attitude, patiently testing all information and withholding judgment until a sense for the truth is reached. (I will develop this theme later in chapter 1.6.)

"Interpreting" Reality

In developing such a questioning attitude of mind as described above, we face a yet greater challenge than that of trying to decipher reality from illusion on the level of simple external fact. From a wider, more philosophical perspective, it can be said that much of what we hear and see from media such as advertisements, television, radio, newspapers, and computer technology, represents a particular version or *reading* of reality. "Reality" is not simply reflected back to us through these media. Rather, so-called reality is continually undergoing an *interpretation*. Take, for example, the way a book is written or a film is scripted. The writers who create the narratives or texts for these media are actively translating their ideas and experiences on the basis of their understanding or view of the world—literally their "worldview." Their perception of reality is individual, and this is reflected in how and what they write. In this sense, the "content" of all media is based on subjective assessment—someone's personal perspective, or, as stated earlier, their interpretation of reality.

In our increasingly fragmented society—multiethnic, multifaith, multisexual persuasion, etc.—such personal philosophies are many and varied. The buzzword today is "pluralism," i.e., we all pursue our own personal truth, our own mythology, our own reading of reality. So runs the theory, but there exists a powerfully influential, hegemonic philosophy in modern Western society, which dominates all others. Especially in the twentieth century, it was believed that this particular philosophy had begun to solve all the problems of its time. We know this worldview under many different guises: sometimes it is simply referred to as "science," at other times as "rationalism." But the most truthful name is "materialism," or literally "matter-realism": the philosophy that matter is real. More accurately, materialism as an outlook holds that *only* matter is real.

With the advent of modern science and more exact instruments of measurement, such "real" matter could include very subtle manifestations such as gases, X-rays, radiation, etc. As these things are ultimately all physically quantifiable, they fit materialism's definition of reality. What materialism wholly rejects, however, is any notion of soul or spirit. These cannot be measured materially, and therefore they cannot—and do not, according to the philosophy—exist. (This is reflected in our language. We say "It doesn't matter," meaning literally it is not matter and therefore not important!) Materialism is also, aptly, sometimes referred to as "reductionism," because it reduces everything to physically measurable paradigms (for example, the notion that human thought is solely the result of biological processes in the brain).

Although materialism is the leading paradigm of our time, I am not suggesting that the content of everything we receive through the various forms of modern media is based on this philosophy. However, it is the most influential worldview, and, as can easily be experienced today, determines the understanding and the underlying assumptions of much of modern life. In fact, a very large portion of what we encounter in the way of ideas and modern thinking, whether in the sphere of politics, economics, religion, or general culture, is actually based on this often unconscious, but continual *interpretation* of reality. (In becoming conscious of it, we soon become aware that it takes increasingly subtle guises, and so can even be found in various manifestations of religion and the most seemingly sublime philosophies.)

Although our Western culture is permeated by this philosophy of materialism, its dissemination is relatively indirect. Most of our political leaders still go to church, and our societies are still established on declarations of religious belief. Outwardly, a lot of people pay lip service to "God" and religion (although many of our "rational" leading scientists, educationalists, and others from the *intelligentsia* [the elite intellectual class] do not inwardly entertain such fictions). Also, we live in a society which, in an outward sense, is largely "free"—there is relatively little external political repression of spiritual or religious life. In contrast, during the 72 years of Communist rule in the USSR, materialism as an outlook was explicitly and officially venerated as a "science." Spirituality and religion, regarded by the authors of the *Communist Manifesto,* Marx and Engels, as "the opiate of the masses," were carefully restricted and controlled.

The Communist regimes, which at the time of this writing have mostly disappeared (with the obvious exception of China), adhered to what Marx and Engels referred to as "scientific materialism"—an atheistic philosophy which purports actually to prove that spirit does not, and cannot, exist. It could be argued, ironically, that the Communists turned materialism itself into a belief, a faith! After all, is it really possible for the theory of materialism to be a science? Can any scientist prove that the entire spiritual dimension does not, or cannot, exist?

It is well known that in science it is very difficult, if not impossible, to prove a negative. Most honest thinkers would accept the notion that to try to prove that entire worlds or dimensions, which in any case are immeasurable through materialistic means, *cannot* exist is ludicrous and presumptuous in the extreme. What's more, it is totally unscientific. The true scientist remains open-minded at all times and waits for evidence to prove or disprove a hypothesis. All scientific statements should be based on an objective, unemotional observation of the facts as they reveal themselves through investigation.

Like the materialist, the atheist states that God does not—and cannot—exist. But again, an atheist cannot prove such a notion scientifically. Most people who think honestly about this will accept that proving such a negative is impossible. (Agnosticism is a more truthful and scientific position, as the agnostic keeps an open mind and waits for evidence to prove or disprove the existence of God.) In reality, then, atheism presents us with the extraordinary phenomenon of "faith" in the notion that God does *not* exist (or that spirit does *not* exist). The atheist is, bizarrely, a believer!—a believer in the theory that God does not exist. Both atheism and materialism are, ultimately, positions of faith. The materialist *believes* spirit does not exist. The atheist *believes* God does not exist. Such belief is wholly naïve, and bears a closer resemblance to the simple faith in God of the uneducated peasant than that of a truly scientific, modern mind.

At the beginning of this chapter, I spoke about the individual on the modern spiritual path seeking to develop personal knowledge rather than simple belief. Science itself means, literally, knowledge. So if, as concluded above, "scientific materialism" and atheism are thoroughly *unscientific*, what then *is* a more complete scientific way of viewing the world?

This chapter began with the problem of distinguishing truth from illusion, and it has been shown that the greatest illusion is the philosophy of materialism. In the next chapter it will be necessary to speak of the concept of evolving human consciousness, in order to see materialism in its context and to understand its true purpose. I will also present a scientific, yet spiritual view of the world as an antidote to a "science" of materialism.

1.2 The Background: Understanding the Context

[The modern human] stands upon a peak, or at the very edge of the world, the abyss of the future before him, above him the heavens, and below him the whole of mankind with a history that disappears in the primeval mists.

—C. G. Jung[1]

In seeking to develop a scientific and truly holistic perspective, one cannot be content with established systems of belief and set dogmas. On the other hand, it would be foolish to ignore the wisdom of past traditions and assume, somewhat arrogantly as modern science often does, that people of foregoing generations were all deluded and/or irredeemably superstitious. Looking back to the dozens of cultures that have preceded our own—African, American, Chinese, Arabic, Asian, European, etc.—it can be seen that all of them have been spiritually based. In fact we know from historical records that all developed cultures and societies preceding the 19th century venerated a higher force of some kind. Could it be the case that, in the space of a couple of hundred years, mankind suddenly superceded the "childlike" knowledge of its ancestors? Were people of the past unintelligent and intellectually inferior to us?

This is surely not the case if one considers the spiritually venerating minds who designed and built the physical wonders of the pyramids. Or the brilliant but deeply religious Greek philosophers with their powerful logic and methods of deduction. Or even the relatively contemporary genius of Einstein. All of them, in their own ways, were extraordinarily intelligent, yet each experienced a higher spiritual force as a reality.

Humanity's Spiritual Heritage

Taking account of all the anthropological and historical evidence, it is evident that the vast majority of all the people who have *ever lived on the Earth* have believed in or had knowledge of spiritual worlds. Common sense would therefore dictate the studying of past traditions, religious systems, and ancient wisdom for what they might reveal.

But were the people of the past correct in their beliefs? Some sociologists would argue, somewhat crudely, that the ruling classes of all cultures have perpetuated spiritual and religious ideas in order to suppress people and keep them in their place. There is no doubt that over the years organized religion has in certain cases been used politically, and people have committed unspeakable atrocities in the name of their faiths. But other acts of inhumanity have also been committed in the name of racial theory and tribalism (Nazi Germany, Rwanda) or political ideology (Soviet Russia, Cambodia).

This indicates only that when people gather together under a certain banner they have the capacity to do terrible things to others—and religious groups are no exception. But this phenomenon does not prove the nonexistence of spirit. Likewise, the exploitation of religion for socially repressive purposes is not evidence for the inherent untruth of religion itself.

Where social and political arguments against spirituality stumble is in their assumption that spiritual ideas are imposed from above. The evidence, however, points to the contrary. The further back we go in studying ancient cultures, the more it becomes evident that there have been many people who knew of the existence of spiritual dimensions from their own experience. (In these cases, we can rightly speak of "spiritual knowledge" as opposed to "spiritual belief.") Different peoples and cultures have used differing means to obtain such information, but much spiritual knowledge was simply part of people's common culture.

Up to the present day there remains so-called "folk wisdom" in parts of the world, for example in Ireland where in rural areas many still speak of the "little people" or "fairy folk." These notions do not derive from the spiritual teachings of the Catholic Church, which is dominant in southern Ireland; rather, people speak of such elemental spirits from local tradition as well as their own perception. Likewise, in primal societies—for example, the remaining Aborigines of Australia—we still find a widespread spiritual tradition (known as "the Dreamtime") and knowledge among the ordinary people.

Taking a broad view of past cultures, it becomes apparent that religion as a phenomenon (or "organized religion") appears externally when the mass population begins to lose its instinctive, inner knowledge of spirit. As this process occurs, societies begin instead to focus on individuals who are able for different reasons to keep the connection: people who have come to be known as prophets, seers, initiates, priests, etc. Such individuals act as intermediaries between material and spiritual worlds, but their function is fulfilled in different ways, according to the context within which they work.

In ancient times, for example, certain women known as sibyls acted as the mouthpiece of a god or gods at special oracles or temples. The sibyl went into a trance and spirits would speak through her. In other cultures there was the shaman or "witch doctor" figure, who retained magical methods and means of communing with higher powers. In some tribal societies knowledge of the use of herbs or drugs was preserved by special individuals and used in ceremonial situations to create an intense "out-of-body" experience. In the mystery cultures of ancient Egypt, a neophyte—the one to be initiated—would embark upon elaborate preparation and training by a priest and would then experience spiritual sight through specific rituals. Many more examples could be given of individuals who retained the link between spiritual and material worlds.

Perhaps surprisingly, the figure of the present-day priest, or minister of religion, emerges as the modern representative of this rich background. From the old mystery temples of Ephesus to the Druids of ancient Britain to the modern-day Christian churches, the role of the priest is to act as mediator between God and man. In the past the position of "priest" was based on a person's ability consciously, actively, and with firsthand perception, to mediate between the earthly and spiritual worlds. Today, however, in the majority of cases, the priest has lost his or her direct perception of spirit and their role has become largely symbolic.

Evolving Human Consciousness

So if people once commonly had a knowledge of spirit, why did they lose it? What happened in the interim, and why did external religion and its representatives need to fill the gap? Rather than present a dogmatic answer, I will put forward what can be taken as a hypothesis. The concept I will describe is sometimes referred to as "the evolution of human consciousness." When applied to understanding the past, it can unlock the secrets of human history. But, if preferred, the following account can be approached as a kind of myth.

Imagine a time in distant prehistory, when human beings lived in harmony with their God. (The biblical story of the Garden of Eden can be seen as one figurative representation of this period.) This harmony existed because people knew of the spiritual dimension; they lived in the knowledge of spiritual entities and higher forces because these were visibly present to them through their capacities of spiritual sight. As a result of this primeval consciousness, people lived in a dreamlike state. And being not so connected to the Earth and matter, their bodies were also more pliable and less dense than present-day human bodies.

Over the millennia, as clear rational consciousness came to the fore, the wider perceptions of these ancient ancestors were lost. People became intellectually clever and sharper in their thinking, and likewise their bodies became harder and more defined, but their spiritual vision slowly disappeared. This descent into matter reached a culmination in recent times, when it became possible for people to entertain the notion that God or spirit did not exist (which would previously have seemed absurd). Because people no longer knew of spiritual worlds from their own perceptions, the atheistic contention could be made without it seeming ridiculous. However, intuitive knowledge of spirit was still retained by many people. As people forgot their heavenly origin, so came the necessity of "religion," and the human intercessors—priests, prophets, etc.—spoken of before. (The word religion, from the Latin, means literally "reestablishing the connection," implying of course that a connection once existed.)

If this "myth" offers an explanation as to *how* people came to lose their instinctive connection to God and spirit, it is also necessary to ask *why* this had to happen. Why the descent into matter? The following explanation can also be taken as a hypothesis.

Through the process of becoming separated from knowledge of spirit, human beings reached a stage equivalent to adolescence. As with the child who eventually leaves parents and home, so humanity had to grow independent of its heavenly parents and leave home. This process led to individual consciousness and the ability to think, reason, and—potentially—be free. Materialism as an existential philosophy was a critical part of this development, allowing people to separate temporarily from their spiritual dwelling, so within this context it played an important role in human progress.

But the evolution of human consciousness does not stop at this point. The goal, the endgame, is for people to reconnect with spirit. Whereas before this connection was instinctive and therefore lacked freedom, in the future it is to be based on individual knowledge and perception. Previously, the "infant" human being could not be other than part of the world of spirit, but now the "adult" human being finds his way home in full consciousness, knowledge, and freedom. Like the grown-up person who freely chooses to visit her parents, likewise the spiritually mature human resolves independently to rediscover her own spiritual heritage. But as an integral part of this process, humanity has undergone a transformation: Our individual consciousness has developed and evolved, and we have become far more independent of our spiritual source than was possible previously.

Developing a Science of Spirit

These changes in human consciousness are significant. We are dynamic, changing beings. Our approach to the world, therefore, also has to be dynamic. With this in mind, it is possible to return to the earlier, central question: What is a truly scientific way to approach the world today? It has already been concluded that atheism and scientific materialism are naïve and unscientific—although the theory of evolving consciousness goes some way to explaining their role and purpose in human history. On the other hand, simple faith and belief have been shown to be inadequate for the truly modern mind. The answer to the question, I suggest, is for individuals to develop a *scientific approach* to spirit—a technique of exploring the world which extends the methods of natural science to include dimensions which so far have not generally been explored via scientific means.[2]

For a new way of viewing and understanding the world to be effective, all existing dogmas—including scientific ones—have to be set aside. There is no doubt that the conventional scientific method has produced tremendous external results and we all benefit from its gifts: from the technology which drives our motor vehicles and allows for labor-saving devices such as washing machines and computers, to developments in surgery and medicine. But it has also led us to a cul-de-sac of knowledge.

Having an increasingly intimate understanding of the physical, material world has not in itself been enough, for example, to solve critical social problems in our societies. It has not enabled humanity to overcome illness and disease; with each virus which is "defeated" by vaccination such as smallpox, a new disease such as AIDS appears, or older ones such as cancer become more prevalent. Our highly developed technologies have led to environmental problems: Use of fossil fuels has resulted in climate change and environmental effects which cannot easily be reversed by human ingenuity; modern farming methods have leeched the soil, producing food which lacks vital forces, and so on. Despite its benefits, conventional science has produced a trail of problems which it cannot solve, and a whole set of other problems cannot even be addressed by it.

All this points to the conclusion that humanity now needs to think "outside the box" of conventional science in order to enter the next stage of human development. As long as our thinking is constrained by inflexible paradigms, we are constrained as well.

Speaking of humanity's heritage, it is apparent that humanity has always—in different ways and to varying degrees—interacted with divine worlds and spiritual entities. These have provided a source of wisdom—spiritual wisdom—and guidance when called upon. So how can people call upon such spiritual guidance today in a way consistent with modern consciousness?

Rather than abandoning conventional science, a science of spirit can take scientific methodologies and research techniques and apply them to gain knowledge of metaphysical dimensions. But first the *premises* on which we base our research will need to be enlarged. A critical difference between the conventional scientific method and the spiritual scientific method is that the former relies on the five known human senses of sight, touch, smell, taste, and hearing. A spiritual approach suggests that human beings have the capacity to develop other modes of knowledge and perception.

Although these are as yet largely unknown, the evidence indicates that there have been many people—and there are many alive today—who have capacities which extend beyond the limits of conventional science. In the language of modern culture, these qualities are sometimes referred to as extra-sensory perception (ESP), clairvoyance, channeling, remote viewing, psychic ability, etc. Others have been given glimpses of higher worlds through near-death experiences (NDEs), visions of angels, and other spiritual experiences. But to speak of a *science of spirit* is to refer to a quite specific method and capacity of experience, in contradistinction to all of the above.

As described earlier, according to the theory of the evolution of human consciousness, a time existed when all people had an instinctive knowledge of spirit. Later, when this general perception of spirit was lost, many individuals continued to retain the link between spiritual and physical worlds. But qualitatively their perception was not always the same; people experienced the spirit in different ways at different times in human history. To speak in very general terms, the experiences of the past were characterized by a passive quality—they were "given" to special individuals who graciously received them—or in other cases were sought through the mediation of drugs. The ancient sibyls, for example, spoke out of a trance state and were therefore not conscious of what messages passed via their lips. They were a medium for whatever worked through them.

It is possible today to repeat these methods of the past. Many a modern channeler, for example, is unconscious of either the source or the content of what is passing through them. (For a more detailed discussion of methods see chapter 2.9.) However, given the fact that we have a different and more evolved mode of ordinary consciousness today, encompassing the quality of individual awareness of self and the possibility for clarity of thought, likewise our methods of connecting with spirit need to be different. The scientific mode of research, with its basis of knowledge as opposed to faith, is right and true in this context.

The goal, then, is to develop a perception of metaphysical dimensions while retaining clarity of consciousness: to be able, inwardly, to raise oneself up to spiritual levels in full wakefulness and to research and gain knowledge from these other dimensions. Also, to be of use to humanity, the information gained needs to be translated and brought back to the physical world in a form so that it can be of practical value. In order to do this in a strictly scientific sense, it is necessary to be able to differentiate between the entities and many dimensions that can be experienced in those other worlds, as well as being able to discriminate between truth and illusion. This is no easy task.

As C. G. Harrison, a mysterious spiritual teacher of the nineteenth century, said, it is one thing to "see" in the spiritual world, but it is another to *understand* what one sees and to be able to make sense of it. As an analogy, he likened the former process to being able simply to see the printed word with physical eyes, and the latter to being able to *read* the words and understand their content.[3] Harrison calls spiritual vision "clairvoyance," and the ability to comprehend what one sees "initiation."

Clairvoyance in itself, therefore, is only a first stage. True initiation enables a person to use spiritual perceptions in a meaningful way, particularly in the sense of developing systematic methods of research so that the results can be useful to human progress.

It is not the purpose of this book to describe techniques of gaining clairvoyance or initiation. There are many paths and methods available today. I will mention briefly, however, the three main approaches:

1. *Meditative exercises and/or study of spiritual literature.* These are recommended as the safest and most reliable means, particularly when practiced together with protective exercises to strengthen the human qualities of thinking, feeling, and will.[4] The exercising of inner effort and work is a sign that a spiritual path is healthy and appropriate for modern times.

2. *Various types of outer, physical manipulation, which can involve subtle methods such as the use of audio tones, or breathing techniques and body movements.* These methods can often catapult an unprepared person into spiritual experience, and so caution should be exercised. Some types of physical manipulation such as certain forms of yoga may be quite unsuitable for contemporary individuals, designed as they were for people of different cultures and times. Other methods involving the use of technology could have long-term effects which are at present unknown.

3. *The use of drugs, particularly hallucinogenic ones.* This path is definitely not recommended. Apart from the fact that

society has deemed such drugs illegal, they are also "spiritually illegal" in that they provide an inappropriate and
unprepared entry into other worlds. In addition they give a
chaotic and untutored spiritual vision, and can lead to
destruction of the spiritual organs and to serious mental
and physical problems.

It was necessary to speak of the evolution of human consciousness
in order to see materialism in its context and to understand its purpose. It was also necessary to understand how a science of spirit is the
antidote to a "science" of materialism. With the next chapter, we will
come closer to the specific purpose of this book: to develop a healthy
path for approaching modern culture from a spiritual perspective.

1.3 Finding a Solution: Preparing to Respond

Keep you doped with religion, sex, and TV
And you think you're so clever and classless and free
—John Lennon[1]

As we have seen, the philosophy of materialism had a particular mission to accomplish: to completely separate human beings from spirit for a short period, so that we could evolve individual consciousness in full freedom. But does it still have a role to play today?

There is no doubt, as stated earlier, that materialistic science forms an integral part of our culture and that we all benefit from its accomplishments. But a lifestyle focused solely on materialism can engender a great deal of dissatisfaction. For example, recent research[2] has shown that people whose primary aim is to acquire material wealth are likely to feel "depressed, angry, and dissatisfied." The purchasing of a particular consumer item may provide a transient fulfillment, although in the long term it leads to "frustration and feelings of helplessness." The conclusion of the research was that materialistic people were more likely to be unhappy.

But the desire to acquire consumer goods is not the only problematic aspect of materialism. Materialistic *thinking*, denying the existence of spiritual dimensions, creates limitations and difficulties in all areas of life.

I will give a specific example to illustrate this point. Modern Western medicine, with its intricate knowledge of biology, is based on the "germ theory" of disease—a hypothesis which has been continually developed and refined through heavily funded research. According to this theory, people get ill because bacteria, viruses, or other microorganisms attack them. (It is now claimed that even illnesses such as diabetes and cancer are caused by such microorganisms.) However, while germ theory may appear to be true on the surface—there is little doubt that the modern understanding of hygiene has saved many a life in medical contexts—there are still many questions about its validity. While we know that specific micro-organisms become present in larger numbers in sick people, we cannot be sure that it is the micro-organisms which actually *cause* illness, or whether they appear as a result—an *effect*—of the person being sick in the first place.

Samuel Hahnemann, the eighteenth-century founder of homeopathy, asserted that illness is a result of individual susceptibility.[3] It is well known that while many people may be exposed to a flu virus, only some will get ill. Why is that? If illness is caused by micro-organisms, it would follow that equal exposure to them would result in consistent effects. Hahnemann's thinking suggests, on the other hand, that the people who contract flu are susceptible to the virus because they are already in a weakened state at the time. This susceptibility may be a result of poor nutrition and sanitation, but it could also be because a person is under great stress or that mentally and emotionally they feel weak and exposed.

The materialist, then, only sees what is manifest on the material level—the micro-organisms—and naturally assumes, according to the only principles the materialist knows, that they must be the cause of the disease. The possibility that other processes may be going on at metaphysical levels of the organism is discounted, or not even considered.

If Hahnemann's objection to the germ theory is accepted as valid, then Western medicine's approach to health would have to change. It would of course be foolish for a person to expose themselves deliberately to viruses—and it is certainly not being suggested that a healthy individual would not be susceptible to types of sexually transmitted diseases. But if the general principle that micro-organisms do not cause illness but appear as a result of it holds good, then prevention of illness would need to be connected to issues of lifestyle, such as nutrition, hygiene, exercise, and mental and spiritual health, rather than the avoidance of bacteria and viruses.

As a result, methods of treatment revolving around the administering of strong drugs would be called into question. The chief aim of these drugs is negative, i.e., to eradicate the "guilty" predators, rather than to strengthen the human organism in a positive way. Often these drug treatments are crude and can cause serious damage, while other approaches might have produced better and healthier results.

Approaching Contemporary Culture

This example serves to show that materialistic thinking is often diametrically opposed to a more holistic, spiritual approach, and can be extremely restricting and often damaging in its view of life. Dozens of other examples could be given (see the second part of this book) to indicate that the crude, base aspects of materialistic thinking no longer serve a purpose in our culture today. In fact, I explained in chapter 1.1 that materialism as a *belief system,* which is what it has been shown to be, is a spent force and acts destructively in our time. The doctrinal adherence to materialism is now retrogressive, and as a philosophy has nothing to contribute to human development.

Thankfully, materialistic thinking no longer has a monopoly on Western culture. There are increasing signs that many people are sensing that something important is missing from modern life. The ecological and antiglobalization movements are significant signs of this questioning attitude. There is also an enormous and growing interest in "new age" ideas, esoteric teachings, and alternative types of spirituality, indicating a yearning for deeper values and spiritual truths.

Despite their shortcomings, what distinguishes these paths from traditional forms of spirituality is that they are often based on the individual gaining personal, firsthand experience of spiritual truths. People want to find the deeper meaning today, but do not appear to be satisfied with *belief*. They want to *know* for themselves. Organized religion still provides answers for many seekers, but it is significant that the churches in the West which are growing are those which offer an experiential, active participation, rather than those based on traditional forms and intransigent dogmas.

An impartial review of recent times would suggest that, since the middle of the twentieth century, a culture of conscious spirituality is slowly, painfully, being born. It is small, and like a baby needs nurturing to grow strong, but it has the potential to develop as a genuine complement to our intimate knowledge of the material world, to be the missing half that creates the whole. However, the weeds of materialistic thinking, if allowed to take over the garden, could still stifle the delicate blossom of spirituality that wants to flower.

If it is accepted that this is true, that crude materialism is a harmful influence, even acting as an "evil" force in the world today, then we face a fundamental question which needs tackling. How should the spiritually striving individual react to the materialistic culture of our time? This basic and very contemporary problem takes us back to the beginning of chapter 1.1 and the problem of how a modern person can digest the saturated content of modern media. How is it possible to tell truth from illusion given the avalanche of materialistic opinion, misunderstanding, misinformation, and untruth which most people find themselves confronted with? What should our attitude be to all this?

I will speak of two possible responses to this situation. These characterize extreme, polar positions. On the one hand, there are many people today who feel at home in the world. They are absorbed by materialistic culture and, to varying degrees, want to identify with its thinking. They are seduced and comforted by the consumer products and rewards of materialistic society, and are content to collaborate with the culture as they find it. These people wholeheartedly embrace materialism.

On the other hand, there are people who react to materialism by feeling so overwhelmed by it that they seek to escape all its manifestations.

This can mean, for example, the avoidance of all technology (radio, television, the Internet), media (such as newspapers and magazines), and corporate-produced consumer products and services. Such people try to create a bubble within which materialistic culture does not exist. In the most extreme cases, this type of reaction can lead to an attempt to escape modern life altogether, to live in a secluded place with only the most basic requirements for existence.

Neither approach need be based on a lack of intelligence. For example, the anti-technologist-turned-terrorist Ted Kaczynski (popularly known as the "Unabomber") was a Harvard graduate with a doctorate at the University of Michigan and once an assistant professor at the University of California at Berkley. His "manifesto," published in the *Washington Post*, is a highly articulate and well-argued piece of writing. Although undoubtedly bright, Kaczynski's dislike of industrialized society and technology had him lead a rudimentary, isolated existence, and ultimately resulted in a murderous campaign of parcel bombs which he orchestrated from his hut in the woods.

General Secretary of the Communist Party of the USSR for over 30 years, Joseph Stalin was at the other extreme. An atheist and hater of religion, Stalin embraced the philosophy of materialism wholeheartedly, demolishing and desecrating churches, and forcing radical industrialization on the whole of the Soviet Union in an attempt to transform a God-fearing peasant culture into an urban working class saturated with materialistic propaganda. In the process, millions of people were killed. Yet Stalin was no fool. As a young man he excelled in his studies, winning a scholarship to further his education. He was cunning and clever in his political maneuverings, and proved to have a commanding grasp of military strategy.

Of course, these two are extreme examples. The two types of reaction to materialistic culture outlined above need not be violent or dramatic. The examples of Kaczynski and Stalin give a vivid illustration of the two polar responses, but people also embrace or reject materialistic culture in ordinary, everyday ways, and to varying degrees of intensity.

The common dangers of embracing materialism are self-evident. Individuals can become so hardened in their thinking that they lose the possibility of entertaining even the most basic spiritual concepts. They become lost in a corporeal prison, a dark world of reductionist thinking which denies whole dimensions of reality, or they get caught in endless competition to acquire material possessions and wealth in a fruitless search for happiness.

But the other way of reacting to modern culture is also dangerous. In seeking to avoid all forms of contemporary culture, a people can become lost in an illusory spiritual fantasy, denying their destiny as part of the modern world, and rejecting the challenge of engaging with it in a constructive way. Instead, individuals can become increasingly caught up in an escapist mentality, losing touch with themselves and their contemporaries.

In between the two extremes there are many more moderate and balanced positions. To be fair, that is actually where most people stand today. But the individual on a conscious spiritual path need not be content with one or another intermediary position. The central idea put forward here is that there is another way to *respond* to modern culture: a positive, conscious spiritual approach. It is a genuine third option or middle way. This path offers a constructive response and can bring about transformation and a metamorphosis of materialism itself.

Approaches to Evil

But before such a response can be elaborated in more detail, a fundamental issue needs to be addressed. Earlier the statement was made that materialism *as a philosophy* has no further constructive role to play, and that it is even a kind of "evil." Supposing that were true, how should one respond to such an evil? How do people deal with other evils? Essentially, when society views something which it perceives to be bad or harmful and wants to be rid of, it tends to counter it in one of two contrasting ways:

1. An attempt is made to fight and defeat the evil.

2. An attempt is made to reform or transform the evil.

These two methods are illustrated in society's approach to law and order. The jail system is based on the former principle, that evil has to be crushed and punished. The evil (the criminal) is defeated by the "good" forces (the system of law and order), which teach it a lesson through confinement and deprivation. In theory the criminal will leave prison and not reoffend out of fear of further punishment. The evil has thus been opposed and defeated. The ultimate expression of this principle is capital punishment. The individual is believed to be so far beyond redemption that extermination becomes the only option. This is the logical (but tragic) conclusion to this type of thinking.

A second approach, which also exists in parts of the criminal justice system (depending on the country and its political makeup), seeks to reform the criminal through education. Methods differ, but in general terms the criminal is confronted with the consequences of crime through counseling and group discussion, and is shown other ways of using his energy constructively, i.e., through art, crafts, or study. The individual finishes the internment with new skills, understanding, and purpose. Through this approach, the evil behavior of the criminal has been reformed and metamorphosed into something constructive through education and example. (It is well documented that people emerging from such regimes based on reform have a much lower record of reoffending than those who are released from justice systems based on punishment. Only politics and people's primal desire for vengeance stop the most practical method being the one most widely practiced.)

These two approaches of crushing evil or transforming it can be traced back in human history. Perhaps one of the most dramatic examples is that of the early Christian Church in its opposition to schools of thought it considered heretical and evil. During the period of consolidation of the early Christian church, before Constantine's Council of

Nicea, many schools of thought existed within Christianity. With the establishing of the Church of Rome came the need for official doctrine and a recognized Creed and Sacraments. As part of this process, those who believed in different approaches were branded as sectarians and heretics, and when they refused to reform or capitulate to the official Roman Church, were often mercilessly exterminated. The church preferred to crush those it presumed to be evil, rather than tolerate conflicting views.

The culmination of this policy came in the 13th century when Pope Innocent III began a crusade against the various Christian sects in the south of France, known collectively as the Cathars (meaning "the pure"). Thousands of people including women and children were massacred in the Church's attempt to eradicate this rival teaching. Before the capture of the town of Beziers, the Papal Legate was asked how Catholics could be distinguished from Cathars. "Kill them all, God will recognize his own" he is reported to have replied.[4] The Church evidently believed that the best way to deal with the Cathars' "evil" heresy was to eradicate its proponents.

The Cathars, however, had a different philosophy. Theirs was a quiet life of nonviolence, fasting, prayer, and poverty. They were vegans and for the most part celibate, and rejected the worldly power of the established church and its ritual forms. In particular they sought to transcend the world of matter, which they perceived to be under the control of the dark powers. Although the Cathars thought of themselves as Christian, they disputed key aspects of Christian theology, including the doctrine that Christ had incarnated into a physical body.

The Cathars' outlook echoed that of a far older teaching, the Manichean religion of the third century. The Manichaeans, likewise persecuted by the fledgling Church, also preached nonviolence. As we shall see in the next chapter, the Manichaeans represent an esoteric movement which continues to work spiritually in our time for the transformation and metamorphosis of evil.

1.4 Transforming Evil: Tackling the Problem

Ye have heard that it hath been said, An eye for an eye, and a tooth for a tooth. But I say unto you, That ye resist not evil: but whoever shall smite thee on thy right cheek, turn to him the other also.

—Matthew 5:38–40

The words quoted above are among the most difficult and challenging in the Bible. But their message of nonresistance to evil is crystal clear. At the end of the last chapter, two ways of responding to evil were spoken of: fighting and destroying it; or reforming and transforming it. In this quote, the second approach is indicated. These words are an explicit call for outer nonresistance coupled with an (implied) inner attitude of redemption, transformation, and metamorphosis.

Few people who call themselves Christians even attempt to practice this noble teaching. Certainly no nation state does so today (although Mahatma Gandhi attempted it during his years as political and spiritual leader of India, up to his assassination in 1948). In recent times it has become common for even the "Christian" Western countries to respond to an evil action such as a terrorist outrage with more violence and even vengeance. Words such as "massive retaliation" and "retribution" are commonplace. While the Old Testament law of an "eye for an eye" called for revenge to be *limited* to one eye for one eye, the modern law of the political jungle often regresses to the taking of ten "enemy" eyes for the loss of one "innocent" eye.

Given the belligerent state of twenty-first-century civilization and culture, it is remarkable to learn that many hundreds of years ago there were groups and individuals who attempted sincerely to live by the teaching of nonresistance to evil. The Manichaeans were key among them. Incredibly, their teaching spread far and wide without the use of violence, forced conversion, or coercion of any kind. Originating in Babylonia, Manichaeism eventually gained adherents across North Africa, Europe (as far south as Italy), and east as far as China. It is no exaggeration to say that at one time Manichaeism was a major world religion.

Mani's Life and Teaching

Mani was born in A.D. 216 in the region of modern-day Iraq. The context within which he grew up was one of vigorous religious and spiritual debate. He would have come across various types of Christians as well as Zoroastrians, Buddhists, Jews, and adherents to pre-Christian "mystery" religions and sects. But Mani had his own inspiration—a spirit being he called the Twin—who told him that he had a personal mission to fulfill. According to an ancient Coptic text, this Twin revealed to him the hidden mysteries of existence, including "the mystery of light and darkness, the mystery of the contest, the war, and the great battle caused by darkness."[1]

On the basis of his spiritual revelation, Mani began a great spiritual movement which has come to be known as Manichaeism, although Mani and his followers thought of themselves simply as Christians. For many years Mani enjoyed the royal patronage of the Iranian king Shapur I, but one of his successors eventually imprisoned, tortured, and executed Mani. He died in the city of Gundeshapur in 277 A.D. at the age of 60. Despite many attempts to physically exterminate the movement, Manichaeism survived and eventually inspired other Gnostic-Christian sects such as the Cathars, Albigenses, and Bogomils.

In the past hundred years or so, many Manichean writings have been discovered, and quite a lot is now known of Mani's philosophy and teaching. A fair bit is also known through the writings of his enemies, such as the Christian Saint Augustine, who was once a Manichean but later wrote many polemic tracts attacking his former beliefs.

Apart from being a spiritual teacher and leader, Mani was also a distinguished artist, and is said to have communicated spiritual truths through his paintings. This is significant because at the very heart of his so-called "dualistic" teaching are the themes of light and darkness. Mani is said to have withdrawn to a cave for a year, emerging with a scroll of pictures of extraordinary beauty. One can imagine that his teachings of light and dark were dramatically illustrated in his paintings.

Good and Evil

Traditional interpretations of Manichaeism have suggested that it was a philosophy which feared and shunned matter, and that Manichaeans wished to escape the "evil" physical world. Manichaeism is spoken of as a dualistic religion, which sees good and evil, or light and darkness, in eternal conflict and as forever separated. The world, which is evil, is a place of sin that has to be transcended as quickly as possible. While it may be true that many Manichaeans and later Manichaean-inspired sects such as the Cathars had beliefs based on these ideas, another understanding of their philosophy is possible, as can be seen from the intricate Manichean creation legend, told in many versions in the surviving literature.

In essence, Mani speaks of three periods of cosmic history:

- A time in the distant past when light and dark, or good and evil, were separate.

- The present time, when good and evil have combined within human beings.

- A future time when good and evil will no longer be mixed together.

What is given here in my words is a greatly shortened, composite picture, encompassing only the most important points:

In the beginning was the Father of Greatness, who lived in his Kingdom of Light. Light was separated from the dark depths, where the evil forces were active. In their interminable strife, these destructive forces arrived one day at the borders of the territory of Light, where they glimpsed a few beams of it. The dark forces wanted to control the Light, and set about to do battle with the Kingdom of Light. The great Father, aware that his kingdom was about to come under attack, prepared to defend it—but what could he do? His kingdom only constituted goodness, so he could only fight evil with goodness; punishment and force could not be considered. Consequently, he allowed the Mother of Life to emanate from him, who in turn gave birth to Primal Man. This primal human being (the "soul"), armed with elemental forces, descended into the darkness to do battle.

A great war then took place, in which the forces of darkness tore apart and devoured the Light. The result was that, for the first time, a mixture of light and dark was created. But the primal human soul was still caught in the darkness. So, the forces of Light raised up the human being to the Light, but its soul was left behind in the darkness. The world was then created by the good forces as a mechanism for liberating the remaining light. But in a desperate attempt to keep the light, the dark powers created the earthly human being, in order to imprison within human bodies the Light (the human soul) which they had seized.

So, according to the Manichean legend, the human body belongs to the dark powers while the human soul is of the light. The human is a mixture of light and dark. We have become enmeshed in the evil powers, yet we carry the seed of redemption, the light of the soul, within us. In uniting itself with evil, the good gives the possibility for metamorphosis. The lower nature is redeemed by the higher nature; the dark is transmuted by the light. In this sense, Manichaeism can be understood as a spiritual system which seeks to transform evil, rather than one which simply shuns it.

Another important theme that emerges from the legend is the idea that the good can only combat evil through its own nature. It cannot fight it with aggression or violence, but can use only its qualities of goodness. In relation to the ideas presented in the last chapter, it becomes apparent from this legend that Manichaeism belongs to the second approach to evil described there: the approach that seeks to reform evil. Its relevance to our theme is now revealed. Far from being the preserve of dusty history books, the ancient teaching of Manichaeism can be seen as a spiritual impulse which is alive today in the approach to evil which works for its transformation into good. In relation to our main theme, this means the metamorphosis of the destructive aspects of materialism into a spiritual culture.

The Esoteric Movement of Manichaeism

But first, it is important to distinguish between the *historical* manifestations of Manichaeism as they have been documented by academics and historians, and the *spiritual archetype* of Manichaeism itself.

The historical study of Manichaeism can only tell us about the past, of the many different forms that this spiritual movement has taken on the stage of world history, which includes the Cathars, the Albigenses, the Bogomils, and of course the original Manichaeans themselves. The spiritual archetype of Manichaeism, however, has to be differentiated from these past manifestations. This "archetype" is the pure ideal which has not yet appeared in its fullest, truest sense on Earth.

By means of explanation, an analogy can be made with Christianity. Over the past two thousand years since Jesus Christ appeared on Earth, many different churches, sects, and groups have been founded in his name. Many of the practices of these various Christian groups differ greatly, and their teachings and interpretations of Christianity often contradict each other. Frankly, in an objective sense, they cannot all be "true." Yet most of these Christian groups believe that only they practice the "true" form of Christianity, and that the others are at best seriously misguided, and at worst doomed. For example, Catholics, Mormons, and Jehovah's Witnesses, all of whom subscribe to the New Testament, hold radically different positions on basic aspects of Christian teaching.

Another view of this problematic situation is that the different interpretations of Christianity represent stages or elements of Christianity's gradual process of incarnation, i.e., its revelation and establishment on Earth. None is wholly right or wrong, but rather each embodies a step along a path, a lengthy process of evolutionary development, which may yet take many thousands of years to come to fulfillment. The archetypal, esoteric, spiritual form of Christianity exists independently of this outer developmental process, hidden from view as a shining light one can aspire to.

If we apply this thinking to Manichaeism, it is conceivable that it, too, has an archetypal form which likewise can only reveal itself in stages. As with Christianity, its earthly, physical manifestation is in evolution. Therefore, its essential nature should not be judged from its past history. This is not to say that Manichaeism has not been a great force for good in the past, but that its true revelation and inner mission are yet to find their complete fulfillment.

The concept of spiritual evolution was put forward by the Austrian spiritual teacher and philosopher Rudolf Steiner (1861–1925). A highly advanced seer, he was able to research and study the spiritual facts connected with the Earth and humanity from his own direct perception of higher dimensions. Steiner spoke of Manichaeism as a spiritual movement with a great task for the future: the transformation of evil.

The Manichaeans, Steiner said, understood that evil was to be allowed to peak according to a cosmic plan. This culmination of evil was permitted by the good powers in order that people should over-come it through inner forces, and ultimately be strengthened in the process. The final result would thus be a greater good. In this sense, evil plays an important part in the drama of human life by providing the necessary resistance for the good to be challenged and invigorated.

But this process of transformation, said Steiner, was only to begin in a small way in our time. In the distant future, when more highly evolved forms of evil would show themselves on Earth, the clash between good and evil would intensify and the good forces would have to develop new qualities to be successful in their task. But Steiner was insistent that true initiation in Manichean spirituality had to remain hidden from the majority for a long time to come.[2]

How are we to understand all this? What does "transformation of evil" mean today? There is little doubt that many people already work in the front line of the fight against evil. One only has to think of those who counteract child abuse, the dealing of hard drugs, criminal mafias, and violence. But I suspect that most of the people involved in this work do not see it as their task to "transform" the evil they confront. Their job is simply to try and stop the perpetrators of evil and to hand them over to the "justice" of the legal system. In relation to the two ways of confronting evil spoken of earlier, this process represents the fight against evil, a fight which seeks to crush and defeat it.

Some people involved in similar types of work *do* see it as their task to try to transform criminal behavior in others. The methods they use are many and varied, and might typically include counseling and ther-apy of different kinds. While there is no doubt that such a direct meet-ing with the outer manifestations of evil is noble work, regrettably it is not something which everybody is able to do in our time. Such work would simply not be appropriate for many people.

For example, trying to reform a murderer who suffers from deep psychological disturbances requires in-depth training, specialist tech-niques, and great skill. This is an important vocation for certain indi-viduals, and is a pointer to the type of meeting with evil which will increasingly be called for in the future, but it is not one that is generally applicable today. Wonderful as it is that people undertake these important societal roles, it is not the purpose of this book to speak of this type of immediate confrontation with evil.

But there is something which all human beings *can* do today to take part in the process of transforming evil. It is something we can do right now, and does not necessarily call for an outer confrontation with evil. It is hinted at by Rudolf Steiner in the notes he wrote on Manichaeism to his friend, the French writer Edouard Schuré. The Manichean goal, said Steiner, consists of "the true understanding of the nature of evil."[3]

This may at first seem an enigmatic phrase, but can be readily understood. One of the most direct and intimate experiences of evil that human beings can have is in connection with our own inner nature. We all know how it feels to experience jealousy, spite, hatred, fury, and so on. These human characteristics, related to our passions, emotions, and thoughts, can be addressed, although it may take a lifetime to inwardly transform them. But nevertheless it is possible through great self-discipline and force of will to have a personal experience of metamorphosing destructive and negative aspects of our nature.

However, other types of evil manifesting outside of ourselves also exist. Over such evils it is much more difficult to have an effect. Here we can think of many cultural phenomena, such as wars, media disinformation, mass starvation, and environmental destruction. In relation to the central theme of this book, the philosophy of materialism with its many negative influences has also been considered a kind of evil. Such evils work insidiously and in many ways are greater than any one person who promotes them. While individuals or groups can confront these evils through political activism, it is more difficult to influence them in an outer sense, let alone to begin to "transform" them.

But there is a way of having a direct influence on these evils. This method can stand alone, or it can complement external action. It entails a sincere and sustained effort to *understand* evil. Such understanding is not meant as a purely intellectual, brain-oriented exercise.

True cognition at deeper levels—understanding of the essential nature of what is being observed—is a spiritual tool. This form of thought becomes, in itself, a redemptive force.

Thought as a Spiritual Force

This idea may appear absurd to a person who reduces the human to a biological entity. If thinking is merely a physical process connected to the sending of messages via neurons (a process traditionally believed to be fundamentally similar to the way electronic computers work), then surely it cannot have any wider effect. Of course, a thought which is voiced, written down, or transmitted via electronic media, may have an effect on other people and the world. But if thinking is seen to be merely a physical process of the body, then in itself without external communication it cannot have any wider impact.

Another view of thinking, however, is that it is a tangible spiritual process with a physical counterpart. According to this conception, thoughts comprise an actual spiritual force. This force has at least as much effect on the world as outer, physical actions. Seers, such as the Theosophist C. W. Leadbeater, have written about how thoughts appear and what effect they can have on other people.[4] Individuals who have spiritual perception speak of how a negative thought directed against a fellow human is equivalent to physically striking that person.

Most people, whether clairvoyant or not, have some inkling of this. Many of us have had the experience of walking into a hostile place and feeling the malicious thoughts of the people there. Other times we might go somewhere and feel immediately at home among the "good vibes" or pleasant atmosphere. It is common to sense when a person is angry with us, or conversely to feel great love and warmth emanating from a close friend or partner. Many spiritual teachers, from the Buddha onwards, have spoken of the value of "right thinking" or "positive thinking." Good thoughts, it is said, shine spiritually like a beacon of light, whereas negative, ugly thoughts appear dark and dirty.

Picture for a moment a person deep in thought. Whereas previously we may have seen that individual as a self-enclosed entity locked in inner brain activity, with this new perspective we can picture the thoughts expanding beyond the person's head, radiating into the world.

If it can be accepted, in theory at least, that thoughts have an impact on the world, then the challenge of transforming evil becomes more approachable. Qualities of insight, clarity, understanding, and cognition take on a new significance. When we think in a spiritual way about a problem connected with evil, our thoughts are not only restricted to ourselves, but have an incisive effect on the human drama taking place around us. If individuals aspire to understand the truth behind the negative manifestations of materialistic culture, their efforts will have a powerful effect in counteracting its dangerous and degenerate external aspects.

1.5 Developing the Self: Strengthening Within

Then the beautiful Anfortas, who had been seated next to him, said, "Sir, do you see the Grail lying there before you?"
—Wolfram von Eschenbach[1]

As stated earlier, the chief aim of this book is to put forward a technique for approaching materialistic culture with spirit. In the next chapter, I present this method, based on the development of clear thought and cognition, but before leaving behind the theme of Manichaeism, I would like to delve into its esoteric core and suggest why this spiritual movement is increasingly relevant today.

Manichaeism has very old roots, deriving from the third century A.D. But it also has strong connections to recent history and the present. The twentieth century had a particular significance for the unfolding of the Manichean spiritual impulse.

The Twentieth Century as Birthplace for the Self

Now that humanity has fully crossed the threshold into the twenty-first century, it is possible to begin reflecting on the chaotic twentieth century with some distance and objectivity, and even tentatively to interpret some of its hidden aspects. Whatever else it may have been, outwardly the twentieth century was a time of extreme change. Technological development moved at breakneck speed, so that by the end of the century hyper-fast communication and transportation appeared to speed up time itself. Socially, at least in the Western world, there were also many changes: the emancipation of women, the introduction of the liberal ideas of multiculturalism and pluralism, tolerance of nonconformist types of sexuality. On the international stage, wars of unprecedented ferocity and destruction took place, and weapons of enormous destruction were unleashed. Humans discovered that their actions could affect the very environment in which we live, threatening our ability to survive on Earth.

The radical advances in science did not bring about the utopian society that some at the beginning of the twentieth century had imagined. Rather than freeing people from drudgery and work, technology made our lives busier, more stressful, and left us with seemingly less rather than more time. Neither did scientific development improve the moral standing of the human race. Instead, the process of killing became more clinical and detached, and was frequently justified intellectually and "scientifically." Two of the twentieth century's most monumental—yet polar—political regimes perhaps best characterize this insidious tendency for pseudoscientific ideology. Marxism and National Socialism, so-called extreme left and right movements, were responsible for the deaths of millions of people.

National Socialism, under the leadership of Adolf Hitler, was based on the principle of blood and race. Hitler, inspired by racist thinkers such as Houston Stewart Chamberlain, sought to create a pure race of *Übermensch*—pure-blooded Aryans who would ultimately achieve their rightful place as rulers of the world. In the process, those who were perceived to be subhuman—Jews, Romanies, Poles, the disabled, homosexuals, Communists—were deported, imprisoned, or exterminated.

Although Hitler's ideas can be traced back to "scientific" theories of race deriving largely from the nineteenth century, ultimately his vision of a pure race harks back to a principle of "blood" which comes from the distant past. Hitler wished to re-create a mythical pure-blooded race. According to his thinking, the principle of race, of the inherited physical body, determined the nature of the human being. Based on this idea, human value is defined essentially by our inherited physical constitution. Human consciousness becomes dependent on the physical principle of genetics and biological makeup. Hitler's thinking thus took humanity back to primitive instincts of a tribal nature.

Marxism, founded by Karl Marx and Friedrich Engels and developed by Lenin, Trotsky, Stalin, Mao, and others, was based on a diametrically opposed ideology. Marx theorized that people's nature was largely determined by the political and economic system within which they lived. The principle of social class, arising from industrialized, capitalistic societies, became the overriding influence. The capitalist, or bourgeois, class had to be overcome and defeated by the working class through revolution. A new state based on communistic ideas would be set up in which private property would be abolished and the state would provide work and subsistence for all.

Although other similar social ideas, going back to the French Revolution and beyond, had already been in existence, Marx's formulation and expression of Communism proved to be the most appealing to political radicals. Marx's philosophy, in which people would live in an egalitarian way out of a respect for their fellow human beings, had at its heart an idealistic aspect. Although in practice it caused untold misery, death, and destruction to millions of people in the twentieth century, nevertheless it contained a seed of truth. In the slogan "workers of the world unite" is the idea of brotherhood and sisterhood across nations, races, and states. A new society is sought based on a human principle that unites rather than one which divides.

But the failure of Marxism in practice betrayed the fact that the idea was brought before its time. Such a utopian, socialistic society may be possible in the future but was not possible in the twentieth century, and hence lower human qualities of corruption, power-mongering, and greed soon took over. New oligarchies were created with some people becoming "more equal than others" (to quote George Orwell's *Animal Farm*, a satire of the Soviet Union).

While National Socialism dragged humanity back to a tribal, racial society, Marxism tried to pull humanity forward, prematurely, to a future for which it was not yet ready. The society based on the principle of blood had a role to play in former times, but brought into the present it became an evil. Likewise, a communistic society is a goal for the future, but enforced on humanity in the present it also becomes an evil. And so the Nazis and the Communists, packaging their wares with the gloss of scientific justification, were responsible for enormous suffering in the twentieth century.

What was the effect of all the radical change and the extremes to which humanity was subjected in the last century? Seen from a higher vantage point, the twentieth century can be viewed as a stage for a vast initiation of mankind. The twin ideologies of National Socialism and Marxism offer the best illustration of this. The Nazis sought to drag humanity back to its past history, while the Marxists tried to bring forward a goal from the future. As a metaphorical picture, the human being can be seen as standing between these two extremes, pulled by retarding forces on one side and precocious forces on the other. This pulling from two sides leads to an awakening, with the individual struggling to find his own destiny in the balance of these excesses. Amidst the chaos and rapid movement of the century, quietly and almost imperceptibly, something new was created.

The Birth of the Self through Adversity

The new principle that was born in the twentieth century is discernible in the many sociological and psychological phenomena in recent history. For example, within the few decades following WWII, the role of women in the West has radically transformed. From being wives, homemakers, and child bearers, women entered the work place and gained access to the highest positions. Within a relatively short time in terms of human history, women's position in society changed completely. It became generally recognized that women have the capacity to do virtually everything that men can, including jobs previously the preserve of men—fighting wars, driving trucks, working in laboratories.

Another example can be found with race. Whereas racist thought and practice were once thoroughly acceptable, in the twentieth century the idea of equality was introduced and embraced, at least in theory, by most Western societies. It was no longer legal to segregate people or to discriminate on the basis of ethnic origin. In the U.S., African-Americans won the right to enter colleges from which they were previously barred. In South Africa the policy of apartheid or "separate development" (one of the most systematized regimes of racial segregation) collapsed under the weight of its own unpopularity.

A final example relates to the notion of social class. At one time, particularly in Western European countries, a person's life and career were determined by his social class. A clear hierarchy existed from the aristocratic upper class to the middle and lower classes. A person's economic means were also closely related to their position within the social system. In recent times—at least within Western societies—this structure has begun to break down. An individual is no longer constrained in the same way within their class; mobility up or down the system has become more possible. Economically, also, class no longer has the same meaning. A "blue-collar" worker—a plumber or builder—may earn much more than a "white-collar" office worker; a teenage pop star may become a multimillionaire while a highly educated teacher earns only a modest living, and so on.

So what is this new principle that was born amidst the upheaval and flux of the twentieth century? As humanity grows beyond tribe, nation, and race, and as gender and social class begin to be less significant, something else takes center stage: the universally *human* element. The twentieth century shows us that as a human race we have a common denominator, an individual autonomous self which ultimately is neither male nor female, black nor white, upper- nor lower-class. This spiritual self gives us the possibility of making decisions and choices, of determining individual destiny, of rising above family, tribe, nation, race, gender, and class.

Beyond the ravages of National Socialism and Marxism we see this noble human self as the balance between extremes, as the self-determining principle which does not wish to be swept away by the ancient blood-ties of race and nation, or the fanatical dogma of class war and rigid social systems.

Looking back at the tumultuous twentieth century—with its millions of murdered souls, its wars and battles for freedom, its conflicts and struggles—it becomes apparent that the birth of the autonomous spiritual self came at a price. At numerous points throughout those hundred years, real friction in the shape of outer conflict and disaster challenged and awakened this new human consciousness. The delivery of this new principle, like the birth of a human child, was painful. But nevertheless, within these struggles for individual human rights—be they the rights of women, people of color, the working classes, or individuals' battles against oppressive political and social systems—a strengthening and awakening of the human spirit, an *initiation*, took place.

One thing we can conclude from all this is that triumph over adversity is never meaningless. Forces which counter human evolution, such as these retrogressive social factors, can, within a wider context, lead to greater leaps in development. Forces which seek to hinder, distort, or derail human development often lead ironically to stronger progression.

What are these forces that seek to hold back human development? In traditional theological language they are the forces of *evil*. But accepting this definition leaves us with a paradox concerning good and evil. For these forces which seek to disrupt human evolution potentially lead to greater development through awakening and energizing the individual, spiritual self. Resistance calls forth greater hidden strength.

To use an analogy, a person seeking to develop their bodily muscles might lift weights—fighting the forces of gravity that pull the weights down. The effect of the struggle against gravity is to increase the strength of the muscles. Likewise, the evil forces which counter humanity act as a catalyst, allowing humanity to move forward. To take this a step further, it can be said that the presence of evil on Earth facilitates the awakening of the human self.

Manichaeism and the Mystery of the Self

In the previous chapter the Manichean relation to the transformation of evil was discussed. It is now possible to make another important connection. The meeting of evil, its overcoming, and ultimately its metamorphosis, is linked to the awakening of the spiritual self, the human being's individual, higher nature. The following belong together:[2]

- The fundamental task of the Manichean spiritual movement is the transformation of evil.

- The overcoming and metamorphosis of evil awakens and strengthens the spiritual self.

- Manichaeism as an approach to life stands for the mysteries of the individual higher self.

This insight helps explain why Mani called himself "The Son of the Widow." In esoteric traditions the soul is referred to as the feminine principle, while the divine element—or God—is spoken of in the masculine form, "the Father." Throughout human history, the "Mother" (the human soul) receives spiritual nourishment from the divine world (the Father). But with the advent of the "Dark Age," when humans lost their spiritual sight and their natural connection to the divine world, this feminine principle became separated from the masculine. The mother or soul was thus "widowed."

But the widowed mother carried the divine seed of the Father, and this seed can be nurtured; the soul can birth "the Son" (or Child), the spiritual individuality, or higher self. Because Mani represented this higher human principle, he designated himself and his followers "the Sons of the Widow," i.e., those who had given birth to the higher self.

It is relevant to note that this theme of the higher self can be detected in the history of Manichaeism, in particular in the Church

Father Saint Augustine's writings and recorded debates with representatives of the Manichean movement, some of the most vivid and lively representations of all the extant records of Manichean teaching.

Augustine was born in 354 A.D. in North Africa. As a young man he was an adherent of Manichean philosophy and later Neoplatonic mysticism, but by 396 he had become the Christian bishop of Hippo, a post he kept for the rest of his life, thus representing the fledgling Church. Having converted to Christianity, Augustine viewed Manichaeism as a dangerous heresy alongside many others, and devoted much time to written and oral disputations with its representatives. In one exchange with his former teacher, Bishop Faustus of Mileu, Augustine defends the truth of certain accounts in the Bible. The Manichean Faustus, who is questioning Augustine's devoted faith, exclaims: "But what escape from this difficulty can there be for you, who receive everything without examination, condemning the use of reason, which is the prerogative of human nature, and thinking it impiety to distinguish between truth and falsehood, and as much afraid of separating between what is good and what is not as children are of ghosts?"[3]

Bishop Faustus's main line of argument is that, in the final analysis, Augustine accepts the dogma and teaching of the Church on the basis of faith alone. There is a certain amount of truth in this contention. For while Augustine displays a razor-sharp intellect in his many writings, reasoning and arguing numerous points exhaustively, his absolute faith in the authority of the Catholic Church as an institution ultimately overrides any personal doubts or questions he may have. Thus, in another anti-Manichean tract, Augustine states that he would not believe the Christian gospel if it were not decreed to be true by the Catholic Church.[4]

This is indeed a remarkable statement, implying that the earthly establishment of the Church commands greater spiritual power for him than the Christian gospel itself. On the other hand, the Manichean Faustus maintains that individual thought, reason, and argument should take precedence over blind faith. To go further, it could be argued that Faustus represents the qualities of individual freedom, judgment, and discernment—qualities connected to the spiritual self—while Augustine holds to a more primitive group-consciousness which is gratified to believe in a given structure and teaching.

To put all this in context, and to be fair to St. Augustine, the Manichaeans of Faustus's time represented some very unorthodox views on Christianity which flew in the face of biblical accounts and Church teaching. For example, they did not accept that Christ incarnated on the Earth, let alone that he was crucified, and they wholly rejected the Old Testament. It could be argued also that Augustine was carrying out the historical mission of establishing the Christian Church and creating a coherent Christian theology and teaching. But regardless of his historical task, the development of Augustine's thought in defense of his Church led him to some bizarre conclusions symptomatic of his general state of mind.

Toward the end of his life Augustine advanced the doctrine of "predestination." He concluded that the human race is so imprisoned by the effects of original sin that the individual human will is free only to commit sin. Humanity, he believed, is divided into two parts, of which the greater is eternally doomed. The smaller group is to be spared, but they are only saved because of the grace of God. Indeed, Augustine makes it clear that without this grace given by God to the chosen few—and it is "predestined" to be given—it is impossible for a human being *not* to sin and be doomed.

If you think Augustine's ideas through to their logical conclusion, it is clear that in practical terms he could not have believed in free will. Rather, he saw humans as being closer to automatons, some predestined to be saved, but most predestined to be doomed. Our lives on Earth are scripted and we play out our parts with little real involvement on the part of our true selves. The Manichaeans, on the other hand, despite their unconventional and unorthodox spiritual views, foreshadowed a new consciousness of the "I," or spiritual self, which was only truly birthed in the twentieth century. This spiritual, inner core of the human being has the power to determine destiny, to act independently of dogmas and institutions, and to find a direct connection to the divine through its own inner striving.

1.6 Seeing the Reality: Heightening Perception

> We can begin right now to practice calming our anger, looking
> deeply at the roots of the hatred and violence in our society and
> in our world, and listening with compassion in order to hear and
> understand what we have not yet had the capacity to hear and to
> understand.
>
> —Thich Nhat Hanh[1]

So how does a modern Manichean deal with contemporary civilization? How is it possible to approach our culture with all its retrogressive materialistic aspects in a way which allows for transformation? In chapter 1.4, *thought* was spoken of as a spiritual force, as a tangible, dynamic, living energy which has a profound effect on the world, and that bringing knowledge, understanding, and cognition to the modern world begins the process of metamorphosis of our materialized culture.

In struggling to understand an aspect of modern life, whether it is a book, news report, or fashion trend, our goal is to distinguish truth from illusion. This is easier said than done, but what is important is our continual striving in this direction. In this chapter, I will explore some of the practical aspects of doing this.

The presented method, ideally combined with other spiritual practices such as meditation, is relevant to every spiritually striving person today who wants to have a positive effect on the world. Of course, there are many ways to contribute to humanity's well-being, and what is described here is but one path among many. But I am convinced that increasingly it will be difficult for an individual on a modern spiritual path to avoid this approach, or one which is similar, if they wish to remain grounded and connected with real life.

Responsibility

As has already been discussed, we cannot avoid the modern world or contemporary culture. Recognizing that, we can take practical measures to respond to its negative traits in a positive way. But it is also important that we feel ourselves to be responsible for the culture as we find it. It is easy to criticize the crude aspects of Western civilization, the fast-food culture and base entertainments, what the Romans called "bread and circuses," which keep the masses content (although generally not truly happy). But it is quite another thing to accept the modern world as part of *our* culture, our destiny, our karma even.

From a perspective which includes knowledge of reincarnation, it is possible to say that each of us chose to be on Earth at this time, and hence also chose the responsibility of dealing with the world as it is. If past lives are taken as fact, then we have to accept that we are at once individually and collectively responsible for what we find here. In our many past lives on Earth we have contributed to and helped cause the culture around us, whether for good or ill, and it is therefore also our task now to metamorphose it to a higher spiritual level.

Interest, Enthusiasm, and Love

Following on directly from this, it becomes apparent that the first step in transformation is actually taking an *interest* in modern life and culture. However spiritual or unspiritual we may think ourselves to be, it is critical that we take a real interest in all that is going on around us in everyday life, from family and work surroundings to the worlds of politics, economics, art, science, and religion, even if we perceive much of this to be degenerate and materialistic.

We should actually endeavor to develop our interest to the level of *enthusiasm*. By this I mean a lively and positive approach to the whole of life. After all, this is a remarkable time to be alive. Despite the destructive aspects of materialism, modern life is rich and fascinating. With unprecedented access to various forms of information, from books and computers to the highest levels of spiritual perception, we have the potential and capacity to learn more about the outer and inner worlds than our predecessors could ever have hoped.

Finally, this enthusiasm can become *love*—love for our culture, our world, and our own time. Without real love, which is not meant in a sentimental sense, but as an absolute commitment and devotion to humanity, there can be no metamorphosis. If we truly live with the thought that we have helped create the culture into which we are born, then feelings of responsibility and love will develop naturally. This does not mean that we become satisfied with contemporary civilization as it is—quite the contrary—but that we have sufficient energy and good will to participate in the process of helping humanity reach the next level of evolution.

Research and Study

Out of this mood of interest, enthusiasm, and love comes the capacity to develop what can be referred to as "research consciousness." This is an approach to life in which we seek to discover, examine, and investigate. If we are serious about becoming seekers of truth, we should accept at the outset that there are no easy answers. Truth is extremely complex, and it takes hard work to come close to it. We should therefore approach life and the modern world with the open mind of a researcher who is spiritual and scientific. This involves study and a meditative state of mind.

For example, you may see a film which has a powerful effect on you. It may disturb or delight you. At the same time, you may wish to understand how such a film was inspired and created—what lies behind it. To research this, you will need to do the obvious: read various materials such as interviews with the filmmaker. But you can also carry questions in your consciousness about the spiritual forces behind the film. How does this film affect people? Is it generally beneficial or damaging to our understanding of the human condition? What is the tendency behind the thinking in the film? The process of reaching an answer could be very slow, and the questions may need to be held inwardly for a long time. But the important thing is that you have a genuine striving for truth.

It should be added that while we might work to develop an interest in all that takes place around us, we cannot study and ponder everything. Our efforts would only become too diffuse. Each person will find different issues and questions which they can more readily relate to, and these become individual "research questions" for that person.

Eliminating Prejudice and Developing Objectivity

When approaching a particular phenomenon with the intention of understanding it, it is critical that all prejudice is eliminated from one's consciousness. Prejudice means literally to "pre-judge." This does not mean that in each and every situation we are expected to extinguish all previous knowledge and experience from our minds. It is natural and right that we learn from the past and bring forward what we have gained in order to help us comprehend the present. Being unprejudiced means not judging a situation in advance or jumping to conclusions. Rather, we seek to study the phenomena as they present themselves. This calls for a scientific consciousness.

Overcoming prejudice is not easy. Apart from the obvious prejudices that exist in society, such as racial or sexual prejudice, we all carry an often hidden layer of cultural prejudice (such prejudice can be based on a particular spiritual teaching or view of the world). This can manifest as a tendency to pre-judge something based on what we know from our own background, and how we expect things should be. To work against such built-in prejudice requires profound and continual self-examination. The moment we believe we have achieved lack of prejudice, we are often challenged by a life situation which shows us how much more we actually still need to accomplish in this respect.

Intimately related to overcoming prejudice is the quality of objectivity. Developing objectivity is a life-long task, so it is important to start as soon as possible. Objectivity means, literally, the ability to perceive the object, rather than being lost in one's own subjective being. In its purest sense, it is seeing *what is real*. This can only come about through disciplined inner work and self-development. After all, by imposing our thoughts based on past judgments, it is we who stop ourselves from seeing what is actually there.

True Judgment

The path I am presenting here does not involve the elimination of all thoughts and ideas as some other spiritual disciplines teach. In this activity we *should* think about what we see and experience. The intention here is to develop a critical faculty to enable crystal-clear judgment. "Critical" in this sense does not mean fault-finding or censoriousness, but rather it implies an intention to *understand* what is perceived. Also, the term "judgment" in this instance does not mean passing judgment in the sense of a court. Quite rightly, the biblical maxim "judge not that ye be not judged" asks us to avoid condemnation of the deeds of others. No individual can ever fully understand the plethora of circumstances and causes behind any person's actions. But "judgment" can also mean the process of consideration and assessment necessary to reach clarity and understanding. Absolute conclusions are not important; what is significant is the process of thought—the honest energy and will to understand deeper levels of truth.

Another obstacle to seeing reality is the tendency to intellectual theory, i.e., the construction or spinning of ideas to explain something, or the imposition of an abstract interpretation on what is perceived. One way of avoiding this is to approach the object of study with the enthusiasm spoken of earlier: Learn what we can about it and allow related questions to be inwardly alive. The process of this engagement, providing it is accomplished with sincerity and right intention, will begin to provide answers and insights. Such answers are not an imposition of intellectual theory, but rise out of the process of observation itself. They are objective in the sense that we are perceiving *what is already there.*

Gaining Spiritual Concepts

An important aid to the process of understanding deeper levels of truth is the study of spiritual literature. In normal life, unless we have been given the gift of spiritual vision or have consciously developed it, we only perceive the outer aspects of reality, i.e., we cannot delve beneath the outer semblance. But we *do* have access to written reports of other people's spiritual experiences, research, and teachings. There are also many religious texts, both ancient and modern, which are freely available. From these writings and teachings we have the opportunity to gain concepts which can help us to understand our perceptions.

The following story gives a useful explanation as to why such study is important: A person from a secluded tribe is one day brought into contact with the developed world and is shown a tractor. The tribesman is confronted with perceiving the tractor for the first time, but because he has no concept of what a tractor is—he has never been told that they exist and has no idea how they are made or what they are used for—he interprets the tractor as a huge monster or dragon. This is not because the tribesman is stupid, but simply because he has no concept for what he is seeing.

Likewise, a person who has no spiritual concepts will not be able to understand or perceive spiritual phenomena when they come into contract with them. For this very reason, it is important for the spiritual seeker to study spiritual literature and teachings in order to understand spiritual concepts. Such a penetration into new worlds of concepts unavailable through everyday perception will enable an expansion of consciousness. (However, as stated earlier, these concepts are not to be applied in an intellectual manner through theory or speculation, but are to be *read* in the phenomena studied.)

It is not my intention here to be prescriptive or dogmatic about what type of spiritual literature to study. The point is not that we all believe in or adhere to a particular spiritual understanding of the world. The important thing is that we strive for a spiritual understanding as part of a holistic thinking, in contrast to a materialistic one. It is my conviction that any sincere person who is seeking true spiritual guidance will be given the book which is *right for them at the right time*—i.e., according to their particular understanding and the twists and turns of their individual destiny. The path to truth is long and involves the building of layers of knowledge and understanding. There is no quick fix. What is important is the effort exerted in gaining new perspectives. In this sense, the process is as important as the end result.

From Symptom to Reality

I would like to mention an aspect of the work of Rudolf Steiner which relates to a particular training of perception in relation to external events. Steiner gave many talks to his followers around the time of the First World War. As a spiritual teacher he was understandably troubled by the events taking place on the world stage, and sought to explain the deeper causes behind them.[2] He asserted that an important key to such understanding is overcoming the illusion that events and phenomena on the physical plane are the results of purely material factors or causes.

A materialistic approach to history, for example, assumes that developments are determined by outer events—effects created by material causes. In contrast, Steiner's approach treated outer events only as symptoms. Through his spiritual vision, he was able to point to the hidden causes behind such symptoms. He spoke of this as a "symptomatological" approach to social and historical study.

I would suggest that a similar approach can fruitfully be applied to understanding contemporary life and culture, and we can all aspire to perception of this fuller reality. Causes exist on many levels, and it is not necessary to have clairvoyant vision to make a useful contribution to such symptomatological study. I will speak here of three principle levels of cause and effect:

1. Outer History

On the most basic level, it is critical to strive to see clearly the train of events that occurs on the Earth plane. By this I mean the layer of reality which is recorded in history books. Getting to the truth at this level can be an enormous challenge. In some ways this task is made even more difficult for us today, as in many instances the most influential sectors of the mainstream media offer us a single and often one-sided interpretation of events. In this sense, we are all under a kind of "media siege" today, particularly in times of conflict and war.

As demonstrated in chapter 1.1 in relation to the Gulf War, 24-hour media coverage conveys the impression that we are being given access to more information than our parents and grandparents had, when in reality we are often presented with an illusory version of events. Public relations "spin,"[3] propaganda, hidden agendas, secret policies, and even outright lies—all are things we need to be aware of. (There are many social and political commentators who seek to see beyond the simple "messages" that many of our leaders wish us to swallow undigested, although the analysis in their work is often tinged by a political lean to the left or right.)

This layer of reality is the realm from which conspiracy theory feeds. In recent years the "conspiracy theory" label has been used by some as an effective way of dismissing ideas and dissuading serious investigation into certain matters (see further in chapter 3.2). Certainly, there is a lot of rubbish that comes under this heading, and in many instances conspiracy study is indeed the preserve of paranoids and recluses. But on the other hand, by using the term conspiracy theory as a dismissive tactic, critics are in effect implying that conspiracies do not occur, that people do *not* conspire! This is silly, as history is full of recorded and unrecorded conspiracies. Individuals, groups, companies, agencies, and governments all sometimes conspire to carry out certain deeds and to cover up their tracks afterwards. Striving to see these external events clearly is an essential task.

Keeping in touch with a wide range of sources of news and current events, not relying on a single media outlet, is a good way to begin tackling the problem of biased reporting. Try not to rush to judgments or to take things always at face value. Remember that even a single news event can be seen from many different points of view. A particular source may be influenced by sectarian, party, or national interests. In fact, all single points of view are by definition one-sided. A tree can be viewed from many sides, and can present a completely different picture when looked at from the south than from the north. Therefore, initially at least, reserve judgment and seek to widen your picture of events in order to gain as many perspectives as possible.

It is also important that we do not become sidetracked at this level of reality. It is easy to become all-consumed by outer events, but then the wider perspectives get lost. We should particularly avoid becoming obsessive and losing balance. It is also a danger that one focuses solely on negative aspects of modern life. It is easy to get lost in the darkness, and that is no help to anyone. Apart from forces of evil, there are also unimaginable quantities of goodness and light in the world, and we should consciously focus on these as well.

Finally, while one should strive not to be naïve, it is important not to become cynical and jaded either. As will be shown in the next chapter, outer manifestations of evil occur according to certain laws. Essentially, they are catalysts which are calling us to awake. Our task is not to feel hatred or condemnation, but to be fully alert and comprehend truly what is around us.

2. Occult History

This is the level on which history is influenced by more or less hidden individuals and groups. As it is not possible to provide the usual evidence about the existence of such people, one must often rely on reports by seers and initiates (see further in 3.2). In simplistic terms, the intentions of such individuals and groups can be "good" or "bad"; they seek either consciously to further human evolution or to hinder it. For the most part, these individuals are not detected by conspiracy theorists as their work really is "occult," i.e., hidden from the physical eye. They are "adepts" who have learned to use spiritual forces either for the good of humanity or for their own selfish causes and one-sided interests.

In conspiracy circles, much has been made of the Bilderberg conferences, the Council on Foreign Relations, the Trilateral Commission, and the like. I do not think it is right to relate such overtly political groups with these more occult societies, or "brotherhoods" as they are often referred to. While the work of the mentioned political groupings may further the retrogressive aims of such occult brotherhoods, generally the connection between such groups and true occult societies is one of inspiration rather than direct control.

Secret initiatic groups, built on Masonic principles of secrecy and ritual, are probably far closer to the reality of occult brotherhoods. Such hierarchical groups are structured on levels of initiation, using ceremony and ritual which, in the wrong hands, could allow specific individuals to manipulate members of the lower ranks of the organization. In such a context, certain people with malevolent intent could choose to abuse the spiritual forces of others for their own ends. (I should make it clear that I am *not* suggesting that most people involved in initiatic or Masonic groups have malign intentions. On the contrary, many clearly enter for idealistic reasons.)

3. Spiritual History

On this level, purely metaphysical causes are in operation. Here it is necessary to speak of entities of soul and spirit whose work can be identified in relation to the "symptoms" of history. It goes without saying that true research on this level requires spiritual means of perception. However, based on the study of spiritual literature, it is also possible to gain concepts which bring our perceptions to life, allowing for a fuller cognition of reality.

It is also possible to speak of the spiritual forces of karma or destiny. These relate to the law of cause and effect—sowing what you reap—which can stretch over many lifetimes. The effects of our actions are often immediately perceptible in a superficial sense. However, according to the laws of karma, our actions also have long-term effects which have to be balanced out over time. For example, if somebody commits a murder, he or she will have to repay the "debt" they owe to the person they murdered. The debt cannot of course be repaid in the same lifetime, and so it is carried over to another lifetime.

The laws of reincarnation and karma are extremely complex, and it is beyond the scope of this book to speak about them in any detail. Suffice it to say, however, karma is a metaphysical force which has a determining role to play in the drama of spiritual history. Its forces cannot be ignored if one wishes to build up a fuller picture of reality.

"Moral Breathing" and the Manichean Way

To close this chapter, I would like to mention a particular spiritual discipline called "moral breathing." Although different versions of this esoteric practice exist, the one I am referring to is a meditative exercise. It is based on the expectation that in future times a more developed humanity will literally be able to "inhale" evil and "exhale" goodness. In our time it is possible to make a small start along this path by following the method already described in this book, i.e., by consciously "inhaling" the materialistic conceptions of modern civilization and "exhaling" truly spiritual thoughts and understanding.[4]

This process can be related to the Manichean principle in that it contains within it the mystery of the transformation of evil into good. While it should be emphasized that the most direct meeting with evil and its transformation is a task for the future, today we can already make a small step by approaching contemporary culture with spiritual consciousness.

1.7 Saving the Future: Work in Progress

You have the choice today, either to see reason, to accept what common sense wishes to be realized, or else to advance towards revolutions and cataclysms.

—Rudolf Steiner[1]

The previous chapter led to a conclusion of the argument so far, but it left some questions unanswered. Why transform evil today? What is the purpose of seeking to metamorphose materialism? Why attempt the modern Manichean path? In this chapter, I will address these issues, showing that humanity's destiny depends on our doing this and other spiritual work.

According to modern scientific research, our civilization exists on a kind of precipice. For example, a turn-of-the-millennium report by the United Nations Intergovernmental Panel on Climate Change warned that if the rate of global warming persists, floods, famine, disease epidemics, and other disasters would sweep the world. This would mean glaciers and polar icecaps melting, farmland turning to desert, coral reefs destroyed, entire species—including gorillas, polar bears, penguins, and tigers—dying out, and low-lying land being submerged by rising seas.[2]

The changes would also lead to huge waves of environmental refugees. Enormous numbers of people would be forced to move because they would no longer be able to live on their own land in their own countries due to drought, flood, or famine. This doomsday scenario is corroborated by many other people and organizations, including author Ross Gelbspan who warns of imminent tragedies in Africa due to a forecast decline in food production, and in India due to changes in monsoon patterns.[3]

As terrible as it is to say it, Western humanity has somehow become accustomed to disasters in the so-called "third" and "developing" worlds. What we are not so familiar with, however, are catastrophes on our own doorstep. In particular, those of the Cold War generation, people born after the two great world wars of the last century, and too young to have been called up for Vietnam, know little of major upheaval. Cocooned in the affluence of the West, a false sense of security has been allowed to grow. And indeed, the second half of the last century was a time of unprecedented wealth, peace, and political and economic stability. But signs are now appearing that this situation could, fairly suddenly, change. The events of 9/11 triggered policy shifts which are causing political instability and greater international war and conflict. But apart from this, the Earth itself is now threatening great change to our lives.

Gelbspan warns of the possible effects of climate change in the United States itself, and the "explosive political repercussions" which would follow. Disruptions to the delicate balance of the present climate could lead to a change in the distribution of rainfall, which in turn could mean that, according to Gelbspan, "the continental interiors that produce the grain that feeds much of the world may well experience recurrent and increasingly severe droughts."[4] As recently as the turn of the twentieth century, a prolonged drought caused the movement of sand dunes across the face of Kansas and eastern Colorado. In 1988, a Midwestern drought depressed grain yields by 30 percent, which lowered U.S. crop production below consumption requirements for the first time in 300 years. Sustained changes to the climate could turn the wheat fields of America into a vast desert.

Reading such predictions can lead to pessimism and fear, but I do not intend to encourage such feelings by introducing them here. On the contrary, as I would like to show in the following, there is much light and hope in the midst of this gloom.

The Mystery of Human Potential

From where do humans get the capacity to do good or evil? Modern scientific, sociological, and political theories usually connect behavior with either genetic factors (the idea that we are largely determined by our inherited physical makeup) or environmental influences (that we are products of our social class, cultural background, geographical location). Some people see human nature as a result of these factors combined.

Without denying that these elements are significant, I would like to introduce another factor into the equation. Imagine for a moment that each human is granted a certain amount of spiritual power. This power, intended primarily for the development of our spiritual selves, also gives us the ability to carry out evil actions. To put it another way, the power is essentially neutral and only gives us a certain potential. How we use that potential is up to each one of us. The power can be used positively, for developing the true self, or it can manifest negatively as evil.

Why should this spiritual power be allowed to manifest as evil? One answer is that it is not possible for humans to remain stationary in their development; we tend to progress or regress. The spiritual power that has been given to us cannot remain passive; it must be used one way or another. If that were not the case, human freedom would essentially be a meaningless concept. The possibility to ascend in human evolution must, of necessity, allow for the possibility to descend.

This microcosmic picture, focused as it is on the individual human, is also reflected in the broader development of humanity. The same law can be applied to human evolution in the following sense: Humanity has been given the potential to develop spiritually. But if the available forces for this development are not utilized, those same forces begin to manifest as outer "evil," or perhaps it is better to say "external challenges." By this I mean war, natural disasters, economic collapse, environmental catastrophe, disease, and so on.

This may appear to be harsh, but the law I have referred to contains wisdom. It is an undeniable fact that outer challenges of this kind generally have the effect of shaking us into spiritual wakefulness. Most people can say from personal experience that periods of suffering have coincided for them with moments of spiritual awakening. Such transformation has been forced through outer circumstance. In a broader—national or international—context, catastrophe and disaster also bring metaphysical change on individual and collective levels.

The Two Paths

This leads to the somewhat uncomfortable conclusion that humanity has the choice of following either an archetypal, ideal pattern of development, or else facing the inevitability of development forced upon it through external pressure. To put it bluntly, we can evolve through freedom or through suffering. Both paths allow for forward movement, but the latter is a more tortuous route.

If this idea is entertained seriously it becomes apparent why the present time is so critical. According to many spiritual prophecies and teachings, humanity is faced with a stark choice today. It has to awaken to its spiritual tasks or else it will be faced with a series of crises. Spiritual evolution has reached a pivotal point, and change simply *has* to come at this time. Either we use the forces given to us for their correct purpose, or else these forces will turn on us, manifesting as external challenges.[5]

Two thousand years ago, the Hopi tribe made a prophecy that at exactly this time in history humanity would face a collapse if it did not make radical changes to its materialistic tendencies. This message was repeated in a film called *Koyaanisqatsi*, which means in Hopi: "Dire warning, world out of balance." Many other spiritual teachers have repeated this warning in different ways. The "sleeping prophet" Edgar Cayce prophesied cataclysms toward the millennium. (Although many of these did not come about, his psychic visions are likely to have been pictures of possible events whose timing was not determined.) Nostradamus has been widely interpreted as predicting much unrest and turmoil in present times, and the spiritual teacher Rudolf Steiner spoke unambiguously of the choices facing humanity at the turn of the millennium.

All these considerations lead to the following questions: Can modern society, with all its entrenched materialism and its sleep-inducing comforts and entertainments, make the advance to a spiritual awakening, or must such a shift in consciousness be forced upon it? Can humanity use the forces of spiritual development for their primary function, or must these forces turn on us and act outwardly as evil, as misfortune? (It is often asked why God allows suffering, but from this perspective it is *humanity* that allows evil and suffering to manifest.)

Even a cursory glance at history will suggest that humanity has found itself in similar situations in the past. The two world wars of the last century were surely not part of humanity's ideal plan of development. They were the inevitable consequence of missed opportunities— the inability to awaken to important spiritual and social tasks. At the end of the First World War, for example, rather than rebuilding Germany, the Allies extracted an unintelligent revenge by forcing enormous reparations on its (largely innocent) people. The poverty caused by this, and the general lack of investment and rebuilding of the country, led to the sort of resentment which enabled a pernicious dictator like Hitler to appear, promising to reinstate national pride and "Germany's true place" among the nations.

Looking back at such historical failures can incite feelings of pessimism, but it can also lead to a greater resolution to act and succeed in the present. After all, the concept of the "two paths" is ultimately empowering. The idea that destiny is in our hands liberates humanity from fatalistic interpretations of destiny (or karma) which have ruled for hundreds of years. We see instead that destiny is dynamic, malleable—it changes according to *what we do. We* create the future.

It is interesting to note that this idea is reflected in the near-death experience of Dannion Brinkley, a man whose life was changed after he was struck by lightning. Brinkley describes how, in the spiritual world, he was shown pictures of coming events, among which were images of a terrible third world war. But the entity who is his guide told him: "If you follow what you have been taught and keep living the same way you have lived the last thirty years, all of this will surely be upon you. If you change, you can avoid the coming war."[6]

The significant concept here, which should be repeatedly emphasized, is *choice*. The essential message of these many spiritual communications is that the human race stands at a crossroads in its development, and things can change for better or worse depending on what we do. The divine world responds to our actions. It is not that our spiritual guardians wish to abandon us to an unpleasant fate; but neither will they simply save us from any catastrophe of our own making. We have the freedom to live harmoniously with each other and the Earth, or to face the consequences of our misdeeds. Nothing is determined.

"Freedom and Love" or "Wisdom and Necessity"

The two paths can be labeled "Wisdom and Necessity" and "Freedom and Love." Wisdom and necessity are dominating principles in nature, as can be observed in what we see around us. Nature is infused with wisdom. Think for a moment of the graceful spider that spins its intricate web with such beauty and precision. It does not need to study how to do it; neither is it taught how. It spins its web out of an instinctive knowledge; it is imbued with the ability to carry out such an action.

But it is also apparent that the whole of nature is ruled by the principle of *necessity*, i.e., it has little or no possibility of free will. For example, unlike a human mother, a cat cannot consciously choose to mother its kittens; it does so instinctively. Likewise, a tiger that viciously kills its prey cannot be accused of evil; its viciousness is not a choice, but is part of its nature. In contrast, we can choose whether or not to care for our offspring, whether or not to kill.

Humanity has been given the task of redeeming and metamorphosing outer nature. This long process is brought about through the transformation of the individual's inner nature, through becoming beings of freedom and love. When change is forced through outer adversity, through evil which is permitted to manifest by the divine world, then we fall back on the old principles of wisdom and necessity. In that context, divine wisdom is obliged to enable our continued development through the only available option that respects our free will. However, this then becomes a path of "necessity," as we have little choice but to face the events which confront us. On the other hand, when we take control of our destinies and use the spiritual power we have been given for its true purpose, we follow the principles of freedom and love.

Balancing the Scales

This spiritual law can be pictured as a great cosmic pair of scales. The less spiritual work we do, the more the evil is allowed—or enabled—to manifest. To bring the whole into balance, we need to exert spiritual pressure on our side of the scale, and we do this by individual and collective spiritual development. Such spiritual transformation can take place through many legitimate spiritual paths available to humanity today, including the path described in this book.

The less work we do, the more the scales get out of balance and the more the evil is able to act. In a sense, we give a license for evil to manifest. The more spiritual work we do, the more we begin to transform the destructive elements of our culture, and in turn the scales come into balance. Another useful image is that of a candle. There is much darkness all around, but the more spiritually awake we are, the more each of us becomes like a candle shedding its light and dispelling the darkness.

The more awake we are to the retrogressive aspects of our culture and the more conscious we are of the spiritual realities around us, the less the evil is able to manifest. Knowing, seeing, and perceiving evil, an act of cognition, is the first step to overcoming it. Likewise, being aware of the good strengthens it also. This is a powerful faculty we all have and can use today. It can begin to have an immediate and a phenomenal effect on the spiritual, social, political, economic, and environmental problems we all face.

Is It Too Late?

In relation to the issue of global warming, it may reasonably be asked what, if anything, can be done to stop it? After all, many commentators believe that our exploitation of the world's natural resources and our polluting ways are already irredeemable, so that even if we stop all emissions of green house gasses tomorrow, nothing could change the momentum of global warming. Others argue that the process of global warming is little influenced by our consumption of fossil fuels in any case, but is a natural phenomenon.

One thing we can be sure about is that our great scientists and scholars cannot predict with any certainty the outcome of our present climatic problems. As humans, we cannot foresee all the hidden factors involved, including of course the possibility our spiritual guardians will forestall disaster at the last moment. At present the world's temperature is steadily increasing year after year with the expectation that global crisis will eventually follow. However, scientists also know that tiny perturbations in the behavior of the sun can lead to fantastic effects on Earth. For example, in the seventeenth century, solar activity decreased fractionally and the world went into a miniature ice age. Records show that the Thames River in London froze over, while glaciers expanded and global temperatures dropped. Such a result was due to only a tiny fluctuation of the sun's rays.

This is just one example of how seeming disaster on the physical dimension could potentially be averted. This will not happen according to the whim of a temperamental God, but in direct correlation to our inner spiritual work. To what extent humanity manages to tread the path of freedom and love in our time will, I believe, become apparent from coming world events, adverse or otherwise.

Part 2

Dispatches: Reality and Illusion in an Apocalyptic Culture

2.1 When Rap Was Hijacked by the Gangstas: The Domination of Art by Commerce

Prologue

"We have reached the point where our popular culture threatens to undermine our character as a nation. Those who cultivate moral confusion for profit should understand this: We will name their names and shame them as they deserve to be shamed."

The year was 1995 and the voice was that of Bob Dole, the Republican majority leader of the U.S. Senate. Dole's stated goal was to stop corporate promotion of "degenerate" culture. In his speech he mentioned the films *Natural Born Killers* and *True Romance*, and cited the subgenre of popular music, "gangsta rap." True to his word, Dole went on to target the giant corporation Time Warner, naming a subsidiary music label Interscope (of which Time Warner had a 50 percent share) which distributed the notorious Death Row Records. Under its mogul Suge Knight—who was soon to be indicted for assault and sent to jail—Death Row had built an impressive roster which featured some of rap's most popular artists, including Snoop Doggy Dogg, Dr. Dre, and Tupac Shakur.

"You have sold your souls, but must you debase our nation and threaten our children for the sake of corporate profits?"[1] Dole went on, unflinchingly pointing his finger at the multinational company.

Two weeks earlier William Bennett, the former Secretary of Education, and C. DeLores Tucker, head of the National Political Congress of Black Women, had taken their campaign against violent and explicit lyrics, also focusing on gangsta rap, to the annual Time Warner shareholders' meeting. "At one point in the meeting," *Time* magazine reported, "Tucker rose from the audience and delivered a 17-minute attack on violent and misogynistic lyrics in songs recorded by Time Warner performers. At the end of her speech, about a third of the packed audience burst into applause."[2] Around the same time the Speaker of the House of Representatives, Newt Gingrich, informed *Time* editors that major radio advertisers should band together to boycott stations that played "explicitly vicious" rap.[3]

Some political commentators inferred that Dole's speech was cynically designed to attract support from the Christian Right. Whatever his motivation, his comments, and those of Gingrich, Tucker, and Bennett, were significant. Outrage against youth culture by major public figures may not be a new phenomenon, but such direct targeting of a major corporation is rare if not unprecedented.

Some months after these events, the campaigners got a result: Time Warner announced that it was selling its 50 percent stake in Interscope. It was a victory of sorts, but in reality only a token and temporary one. Today, several years later, little has changed in corporate record company policy. Potential profits from selling gangsta rap are still huge, and the large record companies continue enthusiastically to promote and distribute the product. And, no doubt, the monetary proceeds continue to delight their shareholders.

From the Street to the Boardroom

The following is the story of how an innovative black urban street art form was exploited by profit-hungry corporations and transformed into what many perceive to be a menacing, foul-mouthed, misogynist monster, a product which could be sold lucratively to the mainstream white teenage music market. The most important thing that can be gained from studying this sad tale is insight into how and why this transformation occurred, and how as a consequence certain spiritual archetypes connected with social science were corrupted and put out of balance. My intention in examining this subject is not morbid indulgence, but to gain clarity of these unbalanced economic processes, and how they impact social life as a whole. As a consequence of seeing the negative, a clearer view emerges of the spiritual archetypes themselves.

Through the study, it will become apparent how a contemporary vision of these archetypes can help us build a healthier society. First, though, it is necessary to study the history and development of rap, and in particular the process through which gangsta rap emerged as such a dominating force in modern music.

Since the explosion of rock 'n' roll in the 1950s, popular music has been arguably the most influential medium within youth culture. But despite its obvious power and influence, the lyrical content of the vast majority of recordings has been fairly conservative, concentrating for the most part on the themes of romantic love and sexuality. Admittedly, some artists have attempted to use music to communicate other ideas, often of a social or political nature, and this became evident in the 1960s as the youth culture evolved and metamorphosed. In particular, the "hippie" movement began with great ideals and vision, which later turned sour through drugs and cynicism.

With the advent of "punk rock" on the streets of London in 1976, this trend towards social commentary accelerated. Although some punk groups had unfocused and unclear intentions, basing their appeal on raw energy, anger, and rebellion, others like The Clash and The Jam had unambiguous social and political agendas. When the Sex Pistols' irreverent antimonarchist single "God Save the Queen" reached number one in the UK pop charts during the week of the Royal Silver Jubilee celebrations in 1977, pop music's potential as an anti-Establishment force became apparent.

Despite the embarrassment that the hippies, punks, and other youth movements have caused the Establishment over the years, pop music has been largely ineffective as a catalyst for genuine social change. This can be attributed partly to the fact that the classic three-minute pop song is not the ideal form for the communication and development of complex messages or ideas. But in the mid-1970s this situation was to change.

Seemingly out of nowhere, a new genre within popular music was born which took the name "rap" or "hip hop." With its dynamic, fluid structure, this music was far better suited to an interplay of thoughts between artist and listener. Rap, which emerged from the largely black neighborhoods of the Bronx in New York City, featured an MC (master of ceremonies) who would speak lyrics, rhythmically and in rhyme, over a backbeat produced by a DJ (disc jockey) manipulating two copies of the same record on double turntables. Where previously the pop vocalist's capacity for expression was limited by the form of the medium and the obvious need to sing, this new type of vocal delivery freed the "rapper" to produce free-flowing lyrics at length over the rhythm.

With the release of the first rap record, "Rapper's Delight" by the Sugar Hill Gang in 1979 (it sold more than two million copies), rap was instantly transformed from an underground black urban culture to an international commodity. Lyrically, the content of rap records remained within black street slang and word-battles known as "the dozens" and "signifying."[4] The rapper would speak of his own prowess and bravado, his skills and wealth, and "dis" (show disrespect to) his opponents and competitors. However, with the release of "The Message" (Sugar Hill Records) by Grandmaster Flash and the Furious Five in 1982, a new type of rap emerged. With its strikingly vivid first-person account of the urban ghetto, "The Message" was the first rap record to attempt a social commentary: "I can't take the smell, can't take the noise / Got no money to move out, I guess I got no choice / Rats in the front room, roaches in the back / Junkies in the alley with a baseball bat."

Although a number of hit rap records followed over the next few years, the genre remained something of a novelty to the mainstream market. But then rap group Run-DMC teamed up with American rock giants Aerosmith to cover their song "Walk this Way," and rap finally gained exposure through MTV. In the process it broke through to the white mass market. Meanwhile, the beats and music of rap, which had initially relied on the live "sampling" of old records by a DJ, had become more sophisticated and complex with the aid of studio trickery and sophisticated recording techniques. Record companies were now forced to take note of a phenomenon which many had written off as a gimmick.

While the now-traditional brand of self-aggrandizing rap continued, a new school of rappers inspired by the social concerns of "The Message" gradually emerged. This new school, which included groups like Public Enemy, BDP, and Gangstarr, was concerned with questions of consciousness, identity, and positivity within the black community.[5] The messages and discussion on these new rap records were directed by black artists to their own people, but, as fascination and interest in rap grew amongst white music buyers, a much wider public was listening. Vocalist Chuck D of the group Public Enemy was aware of this, proclaiming on one of his recordings that he could successfully "reach the bourgeois, and rock the boulevard."[6]

Rap now stood at a crossroads in its development. While the market had expanded with the success of the socially aware (so-called "conscious") rappers, the chameleon-like nature of the art form continued to encourage new styles. Simultaneously, two new types of rap developed: the whimsical, off-beat, and intelligent humor of groups like De La Soul and A Tribe Called Quest, and the violent aggression and rage of what came to be called gangsta rap. Aside from the ever-present black rap fans, the former's quirky style gained much favor from the college audience, while the latter, with its macho descriptions of black-on-black gang violence, drinking, drug-dealing, misogynist sexuality, and the clamoring for material wealth, began to entice the now-mainstream rap market of white, middle-class teenagers.

Although the origins of gangsta rap can be traced back to pioneers of the sound such as Schoolly D, the first record to epitomize its extreme nature was *Straight Outta Compton* (Ruthless Records, 1988) by a then-unknown group called N.W.A. (Niggaz with Attitude). *Straight Outta Compton*, which has since sold millions of copies, is a dirty and raw celebration of criminal street life. Littered with expletives, it deliberately mocks the "conscious" and constructive rap which was popular at the time of its release. On "Gangsta Gangsta," for example, vocalist Ice Cube asks: "Do I look like a motherfuckin' role model? / To a kid looking up to me, life ain't nothin' but bitches and money"; while on the title track he boasts: "I got a sawn-off [shotgun] / squeeze the trigger and bodies are hauled off . . . Here's a murder rap to keep you dancin' / With a crime record like Charles Manson / AK-47 is the tool—don't make me act the motherfuckin' fool."

Straight Outta Compton provided inspiration for a forgotten generation of socially deprived black youth, and as a consequence a host of gangsta rappers was born, including the Geto Boys, Spice 1, and Compton's Most Wanted. Encouraged by record companies, who saw that this new product could be effectively marketed, the new breed began what seemed like a competition to make the most outrageous, violent, and shocking records. When the group Cypress Hill released their eponymous debut album (Ruff House Records, 1991) featuring such tracks as "How I Could Just Kill a Man," "Hand on the Pump," and "Hole in the Head," *The Source* magazine praised them for their "sincerity and self-expression," and "unique approach."[7] Many blacks, however, were not so impressed. The frequent use in gangsta rap of the term "nigger," appropriated from racist white supremacists as internally used black street slang, and the numerous references to women as "bitches" and "hos" (whores), were particular irritants.

Gangsta rap has since become a huge source of revenue for the music industry. The debut album by Dr. Dre entitled *The Chronic* (Death Row Records, 1993) which included songs such as "A Nigga Witta Gun" has to date sold well over four million copies. His protégé Snoop Doggy Dogg had pre-release orders of over a million copies for his album *Doggy Style* (Death Row Records, 1993), which swiftly went on to emulate sales of *The Chronic.* Since those early successes, it has become common for gangsta rappers to enjoy platinum sales (over a million copies), and it is not rare for new rap releases to enter the U.S. pop charts at number one. But it took a white rapper, Eminem, finally to break through to superstar status. Elvis Presley was the marketable tool for taking black rock 'n' roll to the masses, and Eminem unwittingly did the same for hip-hop, selling over 10 million copies of his *The Marshall Mathers LP* (Interscope, 2000) in less than a year.

No simple copycat rapper, Grammy award-winning Eminem makes his own unique contribution to the art in a stew of homophobic paranoia, psychological angst, and homicidal fantasy. On his debut *The Slim Shady LP* (Interscope, 2000), he asks the "kids" whether they want to "get fucked-up worse than my life is?" Later, he tells a tale in which he kills his partner and drives her decomposing body out to sea while their small daughter Hallie is in the car. "Oh where's mama. She's taken a little nap in the trunk / Oh that smell (whew!) Da-da must have runned over a skunk." He repeats the whole grisly scenario on his second album on the track "Kim," where he kills her over again ("Bleed, bitch, bleed" is his morbid refrain).

Many have commented on Eminem's dexterity at wordplay, his clever rhyming skills, and his use of irony and self-parody. He may well be a master of his craft, but he is also the logical conclusion of an insidious process of product creation; a process which gradually squeezed race, radicalism, politics, and spirituality out of rap and left it as a soundtrack of misogyny and violence for an impressionable youth audience.

Reflecting "Reality" or Creating It?

As we have seen, rap began as a simple form of street entertainment, which improvised with the minimal tools of turntables and microphones, and was gradually transformed into a multimillion dollar industry. Its lyrical themes moved from harmless street bravado to social commentary and "conscious" black politics, to its current domination by themes of violence.

There is no doubt that gangsta rap is popular today, but is it a valid art form? Various arguments are used to justify its existence by interested parties, but one predominates. This argument states that violence, gang warfare, drugs, alcohol, and casual sex are rife in the ghetto, and therefore speaking about these subjects is a legitimate and straightforward reflection of reality.

This argument was put most succinctly by Ice Cube: "We call ourselves underground street reporters. We just tell it how we see it, nothing more, nothing less."[8] Scarface said of his violent rap: "It should be taken as a story. . . . I'm not trying to scare, I'm trying to explain the reality of these situations. I use profanities because people do."[9] And Jerry Heller, one-time manager of N.W.A., asserted: "I firmly believe that N.W.A. are audio documentarians. They tell a story that happens where they grew up, and is still happening where they grew up and live, that needs to be told. And they tell it in the first person, even though much of it is from a third-person perspective. It just happens to work better musically in the first person."[10]

Are gangsta rappers merely "street reporters," documentarians seeking earnestly to educate us to "the reality of these situations"? Whether the true role of art is simply to reflect everyday reality is questionable; nevertheless, suppose for a moment that the gangstas are reporters. While few would deny that the themes of gangsta rap are everyday realities in the lives of many, its crudely articulated violent pictures represent only one version or perspective of social "reality." Critic Stanley Crouch warned: "You cannot make a powerful Afro-American culture if you're going to base it on what hustlers and pimps think about the world. Those people have a distorted, vulgar vision of life because they live in a criminal atmosphere in which they see people at their very worst."[11]

Black activist C. DeLores Tucker was likewise convinced that the music sends a message to the entire world that black people are sub-human;[12] while Conrad Muhammad, self-styled minister for hip-hop, complained that gangsta rap portrays blacks as "penny-chasing, champagne-drinking, gold-teeth-wearing, modern-day Sambos, pimps and playas."[13] Even pro-rap writer S. H. Fernando, Jr., conceded that "[gangsta] rap may, indeed, reinforce certain ugly stereotypes and celebrate pathological behavior."[14]

The image of "street reporters," who by definition must be impartial and objective, is weakened by the ethos of gangsta rap, which stipulates that the rapper must be authentic, "real" and not "fake." As black filmmaker Spike Lee suggested: "In America, to be a platinum artist now you've gotta be charged with murder—you'll sell five million albums. Because you're 'real.' You're 'down.' You're 'hard-core.' If you're a rapper who ain't killed nobody or raped nobody [people think] 'shit, I ain't buying that record.'"[15] In the context of this macho culture of being "real," it is difficult to experience any dramatic distance or element of storytelling when, for example, rapper Scarface is "screaming for vengeance" on his record, and threatening to "blow out your motherfucking brains."[16]

But suppose for a moment that gangsta rap *is* a legitimate and true reflection of "reality." In reflecting this "reality" does it educate, as suggested previously, or does it have a negative influence on its listeners and contribute to levels of violence in society? MC Eight was forthright in his dismissal of the latter contention: "Ain't no song in this motherfuckin' planet gonna make you go out and kill nobody."[17] Bushwick Bill of the Geto Boys opined: "How the fuck is my album gonna tell you to go out and kill people. It's something that was already within your heart to go out and do, and you just wanted a good excuse."[18] Similarly, Snoop Doggy Dogg reacted negatively to the point: "They bring out that I'm a gangsta rapper promoting violence. How the fuck am I promoting violence when it was goin' on before I was born ?"[19]

No sane person would contend, of course, that gangsta rap or any other art form is the original creator of violence, or is solely responsible for society's ills. Some people, perhaps understandably, see the focus of attack on phenomena like gangsta rap as a diversion from the actual root causes of social problems such as crime, poverty, unemployment, and so on. But it would be wrong to be content with this thought, for the question that should be asked in this context is whether gangsta rap contributes to the general *atmosphere* of violence in society. In this sense, in an indirect way, it might be a pernicious contributory factor to social problems.

Certainly, as psychologist Na'im Akbar, a former president of the Association of Black Psychologists, pointed out: "You can't prove that it [gangsta rap] is causative, but it's certainly correlational."[20] And indeed black-on-black violence has escalated sharply since the late 1980s (when gangsta rap began gaining popularity) while the number of juveniles arrested for murder increased by more than 50 percent from 1988 to 1992, with juvenile arrests for violent crime increasing at almost the same rate.[21]

Ronald Ray Howard, who was sentenced to death in Texas by a jury in July 1993 for the murder of a highway patrolman, attempted in his defense to make a direct link between gangsta rap and his own violent actions. Howard, who was listening to Tupac Shakur's *2PACALYPSE NOW* while driving in his car, is reported to have said: "The music was up as loud as it could go with gunshots and siren noises on it and my heart was pounding hard. I watched him [the patrolman] get out of his car in my side view mirror, and I was so hyped up, I just snapped. I jacked a bullet in the chamber and when he was close enough, I turned around and bam! I shot him."[22]

A lawyer for Time Warner (then part-owners of Interscope Records who released *2PACALYPSE NOW*) stated in his company's defense: "Unfortunately, the focus in the press has not been on the evil conduct of a career criminal, who appears to be a classic sociopath, but on the music he listened to. It was not a song that killed this fine officer but a bullet."[23] Of course that is true—but it does not prove that the violent music did not act as a contributory factor.

Although rap is relatively new to this type of court action, rock music, in particular heavy metal, has been the target of a number of lawsuits. One of the worst cases dates from 1996, when three teenage boys murdered a 15-year-old girl and sexually abused her dead body, allegedly inspired by the necrophilic sacrifices described in the lyrics of the California group Slayer. The girl's parents later sued the group and the companies that distributed their music. The lawsuit stated: "None of the vicious crimes committed against Elyse Marie Pahler would have occurred without the intentional marketing strategy of the death-metal band Slayer."[24]

The Bottom-Line Reality of Gangsta

Despite all the difficulties with the gangsta rap genre, countless rappers turned their backs on constructive and positive forms of rap and jumped on the gangsta bandwagon. Why? C. DeLores Tucker, an antagonist of the "reality" argument, gave an important indication, pointing to economic enticements: "We can't say that they [gangsta rappers] are just speaking of reality. The reality is that they don't hate their own people; they are paid to say that. So many of them have said that it's the money. *The money*."[25] Rapper Dr. Dre, speaking in an issue of *The Source*, was quite open about his interests in this regard: "Bottom line: We ain't doing this shit to send out no messages, fuck all that, we in this shit to get paid."[26] Snoop Doggy Dogg also betrayed this "bottom-line" interest: "I'm trying to sell records. I ain't trying to make nobody happy. I'm trying to sell records."[27]

But why should this type of rap be so popular with music buyers as to offer such great economic incentives to its creators? Snoop Doggy Dogg went some way to answering this question, suggesting why gangsta rap exercises such a strong fascination on the majority white market: "Because it's like a movie to them. It's a situation that they've never been in, but they're interested to know the mystery behind why blacks kill blacks, why there's gang violence, why there's drug peddling going on. It's just like a big movie to them."[28] *Washington Post* feature writer David Mills made the point more directly: "Gangsta rap isn't about the reality of underclass America; it's about shock value. Show business. If these rappers were dedicated to 'reality,' how come they never deal with the results of the gunshots . . . ?"[29]

If gangsta rap is just about show business, about thrilling its audience in the way that a horror film does, then it could be reasonably concluded that the exploitation of it by record companies is cynical. Lynne Cheney, a fellow of the American Enterprise Institute, subscribed to this view, suggesting that in backing gangsta rap, record companies are "polluting the culture" and that they should rather "use their vast talents and resources to put us in touch with our best selves—instead of the worst part of our nature."[30]

But the record companies which promote gangsta rap are keen to counteract this objection by characterizing their critics as opponents of free speech and advocates of censorship. In this vein, Time Warner chairman Gerald Levin wrote in defense of his artist Ice T in the *Wall Street Journal*: "The test of any democratic society lies not in how well it can control expression but in whether it gives freedom of thought and expression the widest possible latitude, however controversial or exasperating the results may sometimes be." In a firm stand he added: "We won't retreat in the face of threats of boycotts or political grandstanding."[31]

This argument can be seen as a diversion. Of course, censorship cannot be a cure for political, social, and spiritual problems—it is only a way of covering them up. But this supposed conviction to free speech is clearly not the reason why record companies have concentrated resources on gangsta rap. So why has it predominated and been promoted over and above other types of rap?

This question is not only a concern of politicians and newspaper critics. Chuck D of Public Enemy—his record *It Takes a Nation of Millions to Hold Us Back* is considered by many critics to be one of the finest rap records of all time—said in an interview: "... the record companies found it [gangsta rap] was a way to sell many, many records. Therefore their A&R [Artist & Repertory] departments pretty much kept the point of view one-sided."[32] This opinion is backed up by gangsta rapper MC Eight, speaking during a debate in which he defended gangsta rap. In a shrewd mimicking of record company executives, he said: "'Ain't no way you gonna stop us makin' money off these niggers.' And that's when you gonna get the president of Epic and Warner Brothers comin' to court."[33] Will I Am, of the rap group Black Eyed

Peas, also blamed the record companies: "I'm not mad that gangsta sells that much. I'm glad hip-hop is selling. But I'm mad at the corporations, the record companies. Those are the people that are limiting hip-hop's diversity with only one kind of music."[34]

In an earlier interview, Chuck D suggested action: "You know, black kids shouldn't be pointing guns at each other; they should be pointing them at the record company presidents. Then you'll see the shit cease. Ain't that a trick! You want to roll up to these record companies and tell 'em to stop getting behind this stuff and exploiting it. Because they feel like, 'Hey! It ain't my community!'" To the retort that the rappers themselves surely were also responsible, Chuck D answered: "But they're young. In this business they're the youth, and they're only doing things to survive. The ones that are on top of them, paying them—they're the ones that are responsible."[35]

How true is this accusation, that record companies have focused on gangsta rap because of its money-making potential? Writer Jim Shelly gave an important indication regarding this question, relating the significance of interest in rap by white people to the rise of gangsta rap. In the ghetto, he pointed out, rap is consumed "through radio, home-made tapes, pirate copies, parties and clubs," whereas whites are much more likely to purchase compact discs and other official record company products. "This has returned some of the collective control over rap to the big white corporations and marketing departments,"[36] he added. A film which parodied rap, *CB4*, has a scene in which a worried record company executive asks his prospective gangsta rapper signings: "Do you defile women and cuss on your records? Do you fondle your genitalia on stage and glorify the use of guns?" When they say yes, he beams and shouts, "Sign here."

It is interesting to note that in Africa, where rap music is burgeoning but is not yet commercialized, lyrics have remained in a positive vein. One young Tanzanian rapper, Sam Stigillydaa, commented: "American rappers talk about crazy things—drinking, drugs, violence against women, American blacks killing blacks. I hope African rap stays African and doesn't turn crazy."[37]

It must be said that such exploitation by record companies, however cynical, is entirely within the bounds and rules of free-market capitalism. According to the economic laws of supply and demand, the record companies are providing products which people freely choose to purchase. That the companies might be seeking deliberately to appeal to "the worst part of our nature" is, in the context of the amoral laws of the free market, irrelevant. Author and professor John Edgar Wideman pointed out this contradiction in modern American social thinking: "Let's deregulate everything; let the marketplace rule. Except when rap music captures a lion's share of the multibillion dollar music market. Then, in the name of decency and family values, we're duty bound to regulate it."[38]

Gangsta rappers and record companies are working (in a somewhat unholy alliance) within the American traditions of free speech and free market capitalism. Given that the marketplace rules, it is understandable that such economics will work to the lowest common denominator, taking advantage of people's base fascinations and desires. As writer Steven Daly concluded at the end of an interview with gangsta rapper Dr. Dre: "He's giving the people what they want: an amped-up mix of profane free speech, guns, and sex. And making millions in the process—what could be more American than that?"[39]

Culture and Economics

This brief survey of rap has shown how basic economic imperatives, when allowed to run their course through the free market, conspire to deliver an increasingly degenerate culture as their "product." Such an outcome is almost inevitable within the modern economic system as better financial returns are achieved from products which appeal to greater numbers of people; and products which appeal to people's lower instincts are often more popular than those which don't. In rap music, a potentially fruitful form was snatched up by corporations which then encouraged its most violent and ugly manifestation in their hunger for profits. The eventual triumph of the subgenre of gangsta rap was a process determined, therefore, by economics.

Bob Dole castigated the record companies for cultivating "moral confusion for profit," while others blamed the gangsta rappers for selling their souls, but both these accusations do not address the core of the problem or its causes. The truth is that the pernicious rise of gangsta rap was due, ultimately, to the present structure of the social system, i.e., the fact that culture (music in this case) is controlled and subjugated by economics (the record companies and their markets).

How can we come to a deeper understanding of this problem, which goes beyond socio-economic-political thought? If we go back in history, more than two thousand years ago, the Greek philosopher Plato developed an influential set of ideas. He spoke of universal, archetypal, spiritual forms which exist in distinction to physical things. Physical forms, he said, are expressions of these spiritual archetypes. Hundreds of years later, the nineteenth-century German scientist and philosopher Goethe observed similar archetypes which related to the physical forms of plants. Behind each individual plant, hidden from view, was the spiritual form of the archetypal plant, he suggested.

It is possible to take Goethe's concept further and, like Plato, imagine that behind each physical manifestation lies an ideal, archetypal form. As argued earlier in chapter 1.4 for example, behind all the many earthly manifestations of the Christian religion lies an ideal, archetypal Christianity which awaits eventual incarnation in a physical form. This is not to say that the manifestations which currently exist are useless, but that they are flawed and await perfection. Such perfection can be aspired to, and eventually reached according to our individual efforts.

The social system itself has a spiritual archetype. "Society," like Christianity, is not an abstract thing, but a living idea whose universal form awaits physical manifestation. Despite the many flawed versions of social systems which have existed in all cultures over the ages, its archetypal form remains uncorrupted. Seen from this perspective, bringing change to a system which, due to its structure, inherently throws up phenomena like gangsta rap, does not involve the promotion of political agitation or the dissemination of a particular ideology.

On the contrary, the first step in transforming the system is to perceive the true archetype and to understand it. Without that clear knowledge, arbitrary change for its own sake is usually only meaningless tinkering.

The archetype of the social system presented here (and which has been developed over the past century[40]) consists of three aspects: economy (business), politics (government), and culture. In modern society the boundaries between these are often blurred. For example, politics and economics commonly get entangled, politics intervene in culture, and so on. From a spiritual perspective, each sector of the social system has individual and contrasting roles to play. These roles should be understood and seen as distinct from each other.

The function of the economy is the distribution of goods and services. In this sphere of life we are all dependent on each other. In contemporary Western societies we use a whole raft of different products and services, each of which is provided as a result of the contributions of countless individuals. Therefore, in order for economic life to function properly, the spiritual ideal of *fraternity*, or fellowship, is required. If proper fraternity does not exist in the economic sector, the result can be varying degrees of economic collapse and deprivation, including worker discontent, strikes, and general chaos.

In contrast, the primary function of politics is to protect individual human rights. As modern people, we all expect and deserve to have basic protections and to be dealt with equitably by the law. In this sense, the spiritual ideal connected with politics is that of *equality*. If people do not have equal rights, social unrest is inevitable. In South Africa, for example, part of the population (whites) enjoyed certain privileges based on the color of their skin. Apartheid meant that blacks did not have certain rights, such as the ability to vote. The result was uprising and the eventual collapse of the regime.

The role of culture (arts, sciences, religion, and spirituality) is to allow us to express ourselves as individuals; to use our creative abilities to their highest potential and according to our will. In this sense, the spiritual ideal of *freedom* is related to culture. Culture needs to be free in order for people to be able to express the inner aspects of their soul. No one person can dictate a culture for a nation, and in cases when this has been attempted (for example in Nazi Germany) it either leads to docility and the paralyzing of true creativity, or tremendous existential pain.

From this perspective, the abstract slogan of the French Revolution, "freedom, equality, and fraternity," finds its true fulfillment. A society whose culture is free, whose economics is based on fraternity, and whose citizens enjoy equal human rights, is approaching the archetypal spiritual ideal.

But just as it is important that each sector of society aspires to its own ideal, so it is critical that each area of life remains independent and distinct. Throughout history, there are many examples of difficulties which have arisen when one of these aspects of social life has predominated over the others. For example, in "fundamentalist" religious states the cultural domain can stifle both economics and politics. So, for example, the Taliban regime in Afghanistan used religion—in this case it was a very extreme interpretation of Islam—to overpower individual human rights and economics. Women's rights were affected by the fact that they had to observe strict laws which did not allow them education or the right to work. They were also not given a choice about their appearance in public, and were forced to wear the *burkha*, which covered their faces and bodies. Likewise, the Taliban (meaning "the religious students") controlled the production and distribution of goods by banning items they did not like such as musical recordings, non-Muslim books, and so on.

The former USSR was an example of what occurs when the political domain predominates over culture and economics. Under Stalin in particular, the state became supreme over economics; all business was nationalized and farms collectivized and owned by the state. The result was starvation and a shortage of many consumer goods. Also, culture was controlled with an iron grip, with free speech and literature suppressed. Essentially, politics stifled all other aspects of society.

Many other examples could be given from world history of the turmoil and misery caused by such imbalances in the social structuring of society. However, we are not perhaps always so awake to the imbalances which exist in Western capitalist societies. Since the collapse of the Eastern Soviet block in 1989 and the subsequent ideological "victory" of free-market capitalism over Marxist Communism, Western societies have been in no mood for self-examination. On the contrary, the present structure of Western society has been hailed as the ideal model for the rest of the world to follow.

In his 1992 book *The End of History and the Last Man,* Francis Fukuyama argues vigorously for this notion, claiming the liberal democracies of the West to be the blueprint for a successful society. Since the 1980s, the Western capitalist model has also been encouraged through agencies like the World Bank, where political ideology is implemented as a condition for economic aid.

Examples have been given of what has transpired in history when the cultural and political domains, respectively, have dominated the others. In the West, however, increasingly it is economics which rules politics and culture. This is evident in the realm of art, which constitutes part of the cultural sphere. Of course, economics does not dominate art in an absolute sense and there are many examples of "free" artistic expression in Western cultures. However, if art is considered in its manifestations in "mass" or "popular" culture, which is how it is experienced by the vast majority of the population, then it is clear that it is ruled by economics. Think of film and popular music, the main expressions of art in pop culture.

The very phrase used to refer to these types of media collectively, "the entertainment industry," points to the problem. In pop culture the role of art is reduced to mere "entertainment" or amusement. And the word "industry" (defined in the *Oxford Dictionary* as "a branch of trade or manufacture") which is appended to this, makes it clear that entertainment is created as a product in common with the methods of any other industrial manufacturing system. Thus, the phrase "entertainment industry" itself explicitly points to the fact that art has been hijacked and bound by its economic counterpart.

It is apparent that with gangsta rap the economic imperative predominated over the art form to disastrous effect. Here is a perfect example of what happens when culture is dominated and driven by the bottom line of economics. Instead of being enslaved by economics, culture according to the ideas set out so far should encompass the quality of freedom. Rather than being dictated to by record companies searching for the most lucrative product, artists would ideally enjoy genuine freedom of expression.

It is not appropriate here to enter into practicalities of how this could manifest. Others have worked on this in detail.[41] The goal of this chapter has been to describe the process by which gangsta rap rose to prominence, and to point to the underlying social structure which caused and encouraged it.

Epilogue

While gangsta rap continued to provide fantasy violence for its mainstream white audience, an ominous turn of events caused it to become frighteningly real to its artists. In 1996-97 two of its best-selling recording stars, Tupac and Notorious B.I.G., were shot and killed on American streets. With the deaths of these two young men, violent "entertainment" broke through the gloss of packaging and became bloody reality.

Before they signed to competing record companies the two rappers were the best of friends. But as each artist developed his own gangsta persona for his recordings, a bitter feud broke out between them and their cliques. In an interview in the March 1996 issue of rap magazine *The Source*, Tupac hurled insults at Notorious B.I.G. and boasted of sleeping with his wife. Significantly, he accused him of being a fraudulent gangster ("He touched my style, I touched his wife. . . . Imagine that gangster shit he's talking, how plastic that shit is"). This was followed in the summer by a single entitled "Hit 'em Up" in which a torrent of abuse was leveled at his rival and his record company Bad Boy Entertainment.

In the September issue of *The Source*, the president of Tupac's recording company, Death Row Records, joined in the conflict, calling Sean Combes—the head of Bad Boy Entertainment—a "phony nigger."

Days after the publication of the interview, Tupac was shot four times in Las Vegas. He died on 13 September, at the age of 25, from wounds sustained from the shooting. Six months later, on 8 March 1997, Notorious B.I.G. was to suffer the same fate—gunned down on the street in Los Angeles. He was 24 years old.

Both rappers seemed to be obsessed with death and violence. Tupac's 1995 album *Me Against the World* (Interscope) includes the tracks "If I Die Tonight" and "Death Around the Corner." Notorious B.I.G.'s debut album was entitled *Ready to Die*, while his second album—he finished recording it shortly before his death—was entitled, ironically, *Life After Death* (Puff Daddy Records). It features the tracks "Somebody's Gotta Die," "My Downfall," and "You're Nobody 'til Somebody Kills You." The cover artwork, completed before his death, shows the rapper standing beside a hearse.

While it cannot be said that the phenomenon of gangsta rap was directly responsible for their deaths, it is certain that the public image which the music encouraged Tupac and Notorious B.I.G. to develop led to an *environment* of violence within which they became victims. From the point of view of their record companies, it was necessary that the music these artists produced become increasingly explicit and aggressive in order to provide sufficient titillation to their amusement-seeking audience. In turn, for their own self-respect in the rap world, in order not to appear as "fake gangsters," the rappers were expected to act out the personas represented on their records in real life.

The irony here is that the economic principle, referred to earlier in relation to the social system, has only strengthened itself through these events. While the lives of two humans have been destroyed, the record companies have not suffered at all. On the contrary, *Life After Death* was released two weeks after Notorious B.I.G.'s murder, and entered the pop chart at number one. Meanwhile, Tupac left behind several albums' worth of unreleased recordings, the first of which was released shortly after his death (under the pseudonym Makaveli) and sold several million copies. To date, a handful of full-length recordings under Tupac's name have been released, to good profit.

Earlier, the domination by economics of art (culture) and the subsequent stifling of its true tasks was spoken of. In this situation, it seems, the scenario becomes more extreme: Art is not only crushed by economics, which reduces everything to the lowest common denominator (i.e., whatever will sell to the greatest numbers of people), but economic factors indirectly—though literally—*kill* the artist. Tupac and Notorious B.I.G. were sacrificed on the altar of business. Will we, as a consequence, take account of the imbalances in the social structure of our society? The loss of these two young lives seems to be calling for an awakening: How much longer can we afford to allow economics to rule our culture?

A Note on Method

At the end of this chapter, the reader may have some questions about my approach to this theme and how it relates to the method outlined in part 1. Why have I asked you to join me in surveying a phenomenon which many might conclude to be distasteful and even degenerate? I should first reiterate that the subject matter of the chapters in part 2 is based on phenomena which I personally have been drawn to or even simply been fascinated by. In line with the central theme of this book, I have tried to penetrate these phenomena through thought and observation, and to relate spiritual ideas and concepts which, at least to some extent, illumine what is working in the background. Through this process of immersion in a particular theme I hope to bring some light to what are often troubling and dark areas of modern culture. This is in line with the Manichean approach described earlier, which seeks to transform evils of our time through perception and understanding.

These essays are meant as nothing more than examples of this approach, based on my own interests. They are in many ways tentative first steps. This is a method which will need constant development, deepening, and broadening. It involves forming a view of life which takes spiritual realities into account. Given that most of our culture ignores this dimension, or sees it as belonging only in a place of worship, this is by its very nature a largely untrodden path.

In particular relation to this chapter, I have shown how gangsta rap is a product of the disorder of social processes, and that ultimately this is due to a distortion of the order to be found in spiritual archetypes. These spiritual archetypes need to recognized and respected, and ideally reflected in the way we choose to organize our society.

2.2 The Lost Boys: The Panchen Lama of Tibet and Kaspar Hauser

In December 1995 a remarkable event took place in Beijing, China. The country's ruling Communist Party, purportedly atheist and opposed to any form of religion, organized a selection process to ascertain the "true" reincarnation of a Tibetan Buddhist spiritual leader, the Panchen Lama. In May of that year, the Dalai Lama, the Tibetan head of state in exile, had made a public announcement concerning his personal recognition of his reincarnated colleague. Regarding the Dalai Lama's declaration, the Chinese Foreign Ministry's spokesman had stated the following: "Our work to select the reincarnated soul boy is still under way. The Dalai Lama's arbitrary selection of a soul boy as the reincarnation of the Panchen Lama is null and void."[1]

The Dalai Lama and Panchen Lama are perceived by Tibetan Buddhists to be the highest spiritual authorities and guides of their religion. The Dalai Lama, or "Ocean Teacher," is the honorific title given to the abbot of the Geluk Order who, it is believed, has been in incarnation for several hundred years. Since the seventeenth century he has been the temporal and spiritual ruler of Tibet. The Panchen Lama, on the other hand, is the reincarnate abbot of the Tashi Lhunpo monastery, and the second most important religious figure for Tibetan Buddhists.

According to Tibetan tradition, when a Dalai Lama or Panchen Lama dies, it is the task of the surviving Lama to identify the boy who constitutes the new vehicle for the reincarnating soul of the dead Lama. In Tibetan Buddhist teaching it is said that the soul of the dead Lama reincarnates almost immediately, usually within a space of not more than a few months.

Until the death of the last Panchen Lama in 1989 (and since the Chinese armies of Mao Tse-Tung invaded Tibet in 1950), the necessity for an identification of a reincarnated Lama had not arisen. Given the fact that the two Lamas have lived on opposite sides of a political divide for some 36 years, the matter was certain to have political overtones, particularly for the Chinese. Following the revolt against Chinese rule by Tibetans in 1959, the Dalai Lama and thousands of his fellow compatriots fled into exile. The Panchen Lama remained in Tibet, bravely fighting the many attempts by the Chinese to control and indoctrinate him over the years. In 1989, shortly before his death, the Panchen Lama declared: "Take away my chair [in the Congress], it doesn't matter. My real position has nothing to do with you. It is not yours to take or give." Such strident comments against the Chinese raised speculation that he may have been poisoned by supporters of the Beijing government.

The legacy of recent Chinese involvement in Tibet is well documented. Before 1950 there were around 6,000 Buddhist monasteries. By 1976, following wide-scale sacking and desecration of Tibetan religious sites, the Chinese government had reduced that number to only eight. These remaining monasteries remain to this day under strict control of the Chinese Communist Party, which through its Bureau of Religious Affairs directs every aspect of life within them. The Chinese relationship with the exiled Dalai Lama, whose gracious statesmanship has gained him and the Tibetan cause substantial support in the West, has always been tense. The Chinese perceive control over Tibetan Buddhism as a key to controlling Tibet and its people. The Tibetan people, on the other hand, appear doggedly to support their exiled spiritual leader.

Following the death of the Panchen Lama in January 1989, the struggle to control Tibetan Buddhism took on a new urgency. The Chinese were aware that the Dalai Lama would consider it his spiritual duty to recognize his reincarnated colleague. The Chinese authorities, however, were equally determined to impose control over the religious situation, and assigned Chadrel Rinpoche, the abbot of Tashi Lhunpo Monastery in Tibet (the seat of the Panchen Lamas), the task of finding the boy. The exiled Dalai Lama, with the aid of loyal Tibetans, began his own search.

Tibetans recognize three stages in the official procedure for locating and authenticating a high lama, involving the use of mystical signs to identify a number of child candidates; tests with objects belonging to the previous incumbent to narrow the choice down to the most likely candidates; and finally oracles and divination to confirm the identity of the chosen child. The surviving Lama is usually consulted at the third stage and has the duty of confirming the final choice. The Chinese government altered these rules somewhat, using a lottery system (to be drawn by its own government official!) to pick the final candidate, and reserving the right to sanction the ultimate decision.

Given the complex and delicate political situation, and following a great inner struggle to come to the best strategy, the Dalai Lama finally decided to make his personal selection public. Having made use of the usual religious methods to ascertain his choice, he declared in a public statement: "I am fully convinced of the unanimous outcome of all these recognition procedures performed strictly in accordance with our religious tradition." The reincarnation of the Panchen Lama, he stated, was Gedhun Choekyi Nyima, born on 25 April 1989, three months after the end of his supposed previous incarnation.

Following the Dalai Lama's announcement, the six-year-old boy and his parents were detained—abducted—in May 1995, and reportedly flown to Peking. Chinese anger was fueled by the fact that the appointed head of their officially nominated committee, Chadrel Rinpoche, had agreed with the Dalai Lama's choice. As a result, he and several dozen monks were also arrested and detained.

Nobody knew what had happened to the Dalai Lama's chosen boy.

The exiled leader was concerned that the boy may have been "killed, drugged, or put in some sort of asylum where he will be rendered useless." Meanwhile, following their own newly devised selection procedures, the Chinese enthroned another six-year-old boy, Gyaltsen Norbu, as the new Panchen Lama. Although the young Panchen Lama is traditionally raised and instructed in the Tashi Lhunpo monastery, this boy was taken to Beijing to be educated.

At time of writing, the whereabouts of the young Panchen Lama and his family are unknown to all but the elite within the Chinese state. Despite numerous requests to visit him by interested parties, including officials from the United Nations, Amnesty International, Human Rights Watch, and various governments, the Chinese government has consistently refused any contact between him and the outside world.

Not surprisingly, human rights activists labeled Gedhun Choekyi Nyima the world's youngest political prisoner. And indeed, this did— and still does—appear to be a struggle for political power: the Chinese Communist Party's desire to control the Tibetan people through domination of their cultural and religious affairs. After all, if the motivation behind the Chinese government's actions was not political, how else could its interest in Tibetan Buddhism be explained, given that all religious teaching contradicts its own, avowedly atheistic, official stance?

A true dialectical materialist could have no faith in religion, what Marx and Engels once derided as the "opiate of the masses." That famous duo of political theorists would no doubt have regarded the mystical selection of a spiritual teacher as a religious charade. And yet, bizarrely, the Chinese state has repeatedly attacked the Dalai Lama with great fury on specifically *religious* questions. In one politically controlled Tibetan daily newspaper he was accused of "wildly attempting to use godly strength to poison and bewitch the masses . . . a blasphemy of Buddhism!"

But the whole affair has a more puzzling aspect. If the Chinese were only interested in the political aspects of the Lama selection, why did they not simply accept the decision of the Dalai Lama (which, after all, coincided with the decision of their own representative), proclaim the chosen boy as the true Panchen Lama, and then keep him under their control to educate, indoctrinate, and eventually control as their political puppet? Presuming that their actions were directed by a straightforward wish for political control, surely this would have been the most pragmatic option. The strange behavior of the Chinese authorities suggests a different concern: that its ruling elite has entertained seriously the possibility that there might, after all, be a spiritual significance in the Dalai Lama's choice of the reincarnated Panchen Lama.

This conclusion leads to a question: If the Chinese are fearful of the young Panchen Lama because of who he is, then *who actually is he?* From a spiritual point of view, such a question cannot simply refer to his present biography, but needs to encompass his essential nature as an individual, eternal soul. Is he, in fact—as claimed by the Tibetan Buddhists—the reincarnated consciousness (soul) of the previous Panchen Lama, who died only three months before his birth? Could the traditions and reincarnation teachings of Buddhism, which are ancient, hold good for the modern age as they have for past centuries? These questions lead to other related issues, such as whether certain individuals are indeed given the *same* responsibility and position in each incarnation, or do people need to grow and develop amidst different cultural backgrounds, according to their developmental needs and tasks?

These are questions which cannot be resolved here. They require concentrated thought and meditation, and ultimately the ability to spiritually research the facts. Certainly, the possibility that the young boy Gedhun Choekyi Nyima is a reincarnation of the recently deceased Panchen Lama cannot be ruled out. Another possibility, however, is that the ancient methods used to recognize the reincarnated lamas (oracles, divination, etc.) are, within the context of Tibetan Buddhism today, a legitimate means of identifying certain special individualities in whose destiny it lies to spiritually lead the people of Tibet. Following this line of thought, the individuals concerned would be significant, but they might not necessarily be the identical soul. A study of the available evidence certainly does not contradict this theory. The Dalai Lama is clearly a man of great spiritual stature who represents his religion and people with great fortitude, and the recently deceased Panchen Lama fought for his religion with great courage and determination in the most appalling circumstances of political repression.

Presuming that there is some substance to this speculation, the enigmatic behavior of the Chinese becomes more comprehensible. If the boy that the Dalai Lama chose is the vehicle for an individuality of some spiritual consequence—and by definition he will be opposed to Marxist materialism—his abduction is understandable. The Chinese could not take the risk of attempting to indoctrinate and control such a specially prepared soul; to replace him with another boy would be a far safer option.

Once this child, this "false Panchen Lama," is grown to be a man (by which time the present Dalai Lama would probably have died), the Chinese authorities would be in full control, through him as their puppet, of the selection of the next Dalai Lama, thereby maintaining the possibility once again of passing over an individuality who may have a special destiny in leading the Tibetan people. In practice, this train of events would effectively kill off Tibetan Buddhism, at least for the foreseeable future, and may well break the spirit of the long-suffering Tibetan people.

Such a hypothesis involving conscious spiritual knowledge on the part of the Chinese might seem somewhat fantastic and conspiratorial, but gains credence if we consider an historical precedent which bears remarkable parallels to the modern case of the Panchen Lama.

The Mystery of Kaspar Hauser

In May of 1828, a 15-year-old boy, barely able to walk and only able to speak a few words, was discovered on the streets of Nuremberg, Germany. In his hand he clutched a letter, which directed him to some local stables. There he was offered food and beer, but would only accept bread and water. Nobody could communicate with him or understand the few words which he repeated clumsily. When given a piece of paper, he could write only two words: Kaspar Hauser.

Because nobody could help him, he spent that night in a prison cell, but was soon liberated and began to be cared for by a number of well-wishers who were struck by his innocence, naïveté, and gentle, childlike nature. For a long time the boy could only tolerate bread and water as a diet, and was highly sensitive to light. Two examinations by doctors led to the conclusion that he had been taken out of human society during earliest childhood and reared in a secret place into which daylight could not penetrate.[2] What was particularly striking in the doctors' reports was the fact that anatomical evidence indicated the boy's joints and limbs were not properly developed, pointing to the conclusion that he had been kept in a confined space.

From his own later account and from all available evidence, it transpired that Kaspar Hauser had, since early childhood, been imprisoned in a darkened space, within which he had not been able to stand or walk. He never saw the sky, sun, stars, or moon. During this time his only human contact had been with, in his own words, "the man with whom I have always been" who would pass him food through a hole in his cage and clean and change him when the boy was in a drugged state. Kaspar Hauser's only solace were two wooden toy horses he had been given.

Despite these incredible handicaps, after his liberation Kaspar Hauser was able to develop and mature with the friendly and kind guidance of a number of individuals. He began to display extraordinary qualities, such as a stunning memory. The mystery surrounding his past became a national preoccupation, and soon Kaspar Hauser's story was known throughout Europe. This widespread publicity and interest was evidently a threat to some interested parties, presumably those who had orchestrated the crime against him. It also became known that the young boy was planning to write his autobiography. This last fact proved to be too much for his enemies, who perhaps feared being exposed. In October 1829, barely a year and a half after he was first discovered, an attempt was made to assassinate him in his guardian's house by a man in a black mask. Kaspar Hauser survived this assault, but was stabbed to death shortly after his 21st birthday in December 1833.

During his life and after his death, repeated attempts were made to discredit him, most conspicuously by a supposed friend, the English Lord Stanhope.[3] It was claimed that Kaspar Hauser was a trickster, a cheap swindler, or a fantasist who made up his story for his own purposes. When attempts were first made to kill him, those with malign intentions claimed that he had inflicted the wound on himself. Later, when he was murdered, they claimed he had committed suicide. But the aforementioned anatomical and medical evidence, as well as the personal testimony and conviction of the handful of highly educated and intelligent men who sought to care for him, point to the fact that he was a genuine, if tragic, victim.

For his own part, despite these persecutions, Kaspar Hauser maintained a state of childlike innocence. As his friend Professor Daumer wrote: "Truly this poor person had been afflicted with an atrocious amount of evil, even by those with whom he lived and into whose care he had been given; and yet he said out of his sheer goodness of heart: 'no one did me any harm.' He died with a lie—*but it was an angelic lie*."[4]

So who was Kaspar Hauser, and why did he have such vicious enemies? One of the main attempts to explain the mystery surrounding him has centered on the idea that he was the victim of a dynastic crime. According to this theory, Kaspar Hauser was of princely descent from the House of Baden, and heir to the throne of the Zahringen dynasty, son of the reigning Grand Duke Karl and his wife Stephanie de Beauharnais (the adopted daughter of Napoleon). Although Stephanie gave birth to five children, the two boys died suddenly as infants (despite good health reports by doctors) and the other children died under peculiar circumstances. As a result, the Zahringen dynasty died out, and the son of the Grand Duchess von Hochberg became the Grand Duke of Baden instead.

The contention of researchers is that the healthy infant—the true heir, later known as Kaspar Hauser—was exchanged with a sick child, who later died. (Although this may sound fantastic, it is actually backed up by an extraordinary amount of research and documentation.[5]) The healthy child was then taken away and allowed to develop normally until around his third year, then placed in the darkened prison mentioned above, where he would be kept until the age of 15.

Presuming that this train of events is true, investigators into the crime are still left with the problem of finding a motive for the imprisonment. In fact this is a difficulty that all researchers into the Kaspar Hauser mystery are faced with. What could possibly be the motivation for imprisoning a small child, in such terrible conditions and with such cruelty, for so many years? If it were a simple dynastic crime, why was the child not killed immediately? It would appear that there must have been an additional motive.

To discover the reason, it is necessary to look at the mystery from a viewpoint which allows for hidden, or occult, forces in human history; in other words, it cannot be understood by using simple, materialistically based logic. The puzzle takes on a new dimension if one considers the possibility that, apart from being of a princely line of descent, Kaspar Hauser was a soul endowed with special forces and a unique mission. Therefore, his spiritual, individual nature was highly evolved, like Buddha, Christian Rosenkreutz, and other special souls who incarnate on Earth with tasks on behalf of humanity.

As part of the above scenario, it is also necessary to picture the presence of forces which oppose human development for their own selfish and one-sided reasons. Such evil forces manifest in individuals and groups who work to their own retrogressive agendas. And just as there are seers and initiates with noble and good intentions on behalf of humanity, the forces which oppose human development are also represented on Earth by people who have access to extrasensory perceptions and abilities.

As researchers in this field have indicated,[6] such individuals knew from clairvoyant perception that Kaspar Hauser was a special soul with a divine mission, which they sought to block. But from their occult knowledge, they also knew that simply murdering the body into which this great individuality had incarnated would not, from their point of view, solve the "problem." For, according to spiritual laws, if such a person is murdered in childhood, it is possible for their soul to reincarnate in another suitable body at the earliest opportunity.

From this perspective, the crime against Kaspar Hauser takes on terrifyingly profound dimensions. The veil is lifted and a cold, inhuman logic and will are revealed:

- The child was not killed at birth because it was known that the soul could quickly reincarnate.

- The child was allowed to develop normally until around the third year because the perpetrators knew that imprisoning a baby who was not able to walk or talk, i.e., before the forces of individual consciousness, as indicated by the ability to remember, are able to take hold, would lead to its certain death.

- By imprisoning the child and impeding its normal development, its soul was trapped in a netherworld between birth and death, unable to be effective on Earth.

- At the point at which the perpetrators believed that the boy's special forces were nullified and he had become an idiot, they ejected him into society, thinking that he would work as a stable boy and fade away.

- When they discovered that, despite his terrible handicaps, his noble qualities were beginning to shine through, he was put to death to halt his mission.

Kaspar Hauser and the Panchen Lama

Do the people responsible for holding the young Panchen Lama of Tibet have similar occult knowledge and intentions to those who conspired against Kaspar Hauser? Whether or not they have access to specific initiate knowledge, it is evident that, as discussed above, their considerations in detaining the boy are not just political. Otherwise they would have brainwashed him. Their treatment of him indicates, rather, a fear that the young Panchen Lama has a special mission on behalf of the Tibetan people and for humanity.[7]As stated, the current whereabouts of the Panchen Lama are unknown. Some claim he is still imprisoned, others that he is being tortured or has been put to death. Rumors purportedly put about by the Chinese suggest that he is leading a "normal" life in an undisclosed location.

The widespread destruction and desecration of Buddhist religious sites, and the rigid control of the few remaining monasteries, suggests that the Chinese state is threatened by the power of spirituality, seeing it as a danger to its own atheistic, Marxist ideology. Will its attempt to control and suppress Tibetan Buddhism ultimately be successful? The question bears a relation to the tragic destiny of Kaspar Hauser, and whether the malevolent forces that conspired against him were successful in their diabolical experiment to hinder his incarnation through imprisonment, confinement, and the deprivation of normal childhood.

In the case of Kaspar Hauser, it appears that attempts to suppress him were thwarted. Through his great sacrifice and the triumph of his inner goodness, he was able to shine like a spiritual beacon. It is quite possible that his mission was able to succeed in an unexpected way. Whether or not the Chinese will be effective in defeating Tibetan Buddhism will likely depend on the world's wakefulness in reacting to this act of malice and sabotage. For their own part, it is unlikely that the Tibetan people will be defeated. Hundreds of years of Buddhism have left their mark on this quietly suffering nation, which does not appear to be bowed by the political-religious meddling of its Chinese colonial master.

2.3 Thinking Machines and Mechanized Humans: The Challenge of Technology

Digital Technology and Consciousness of the Self

On a frequent basis, polls show that increasing numbers of people have access to the Internet or possess a mobile phone. While in the U.S. and some European countries mobile phone ownership creeps towards 70 percent of the adult population, access to the Internet is some way behind, but looks to emulate its technological partner's achievement.[1] There is no doubt that much of the Western world and parts of Asia are embracing the spread of new technology, but many questions regarding its use remain unanswered. Apart from the obvious concerns about health and safety, a key area for discussion is whether new technologies *are* truly emancipating us from the drudgery of life, and in the process allowing for newfound freedoms.

One thing is clear: The dramatic spread of technology such as the Internet and mobile phones has brought increasing stress. Time seems to have sped up. Mobile phones and e-mail may be fun in certain contexts, but for many in office environments the new technology adds extra pressure. Whereas traditional written communication by mail allows the recipient time to think before replying, an e-mail demands an instant answer, and the reply to the answer is likely to come whizzing straight back. This may encourage quick decision-making, but it does not encourage considered thinking. It can also mean hundreds of e-mails piling up in the electronic in-tray, demanding instant replies.

In addition to the Internet, digital mobile technology, in the form of phones and laptop computers has extended the remit of the office. Times which were previously reserved for relaxation have begun to be compromised, with the mobile office becoming an everyday reality.

So what has happened to the dream of the "brave new world," where people would enjoy more leisure while machines and computers took the strain? It is still very much that: a distant dream. Western homes may be bulging with technological toys—DVDs, mini-discs, TVs, CDs, PCs—but working hours have in many cases increased rather than decreased. And rather than shrinking, the total workforce has grown in past decades (with a majority of women now going out to work). Two paychecks are usually needed to pay for all this prosperity.

Recent studies appear to indicate that in other ways new technologies are not providing the liberation people once predicted. The Stanford University Institute for the Quantitative Study of Society, for instance, stated that the Internet was creating a culture where many people stayed home, "alone, anonymous." The World Wide Web was responsible for "a brand-new wave of social isolation in the U.S., raising the specter of an atomized world."[2]

Due to the growing reliance on computers at work, many people face increasing hours of staring at computer screens, leading to a greater sense of isolation. But in their leisure periods as well, many are choosing to spend further time alone with their computer, enjoying the "virtual" sense of social interaction provided by the Internet: surfing weird and wonderful websites, viewing online pornography, or "talking" to others in chat rooms.

The chat room, which allows two or more people to have live conversations via the Internet, is a sign of the times. Although relating to another person via such a medium is a solitary affair, staring at the digital characters and images through the radiating electronic glow of a computer screen, many people report, remarkably, that it creates an unprecedented sense of intimacy. According to a researcher from Nottingham University: "There's a feeling of connectedness online that's not just, 'Oh, I'm getting on well with this person.' There's a deeper level, a moment of real intensity. I call it a mind meld."[3] A 40-year-old man, a call-center operator, reported that: "Even when it's not overtly sexual or dramatic, there's something so intimate about it that is somehow deeper, richer, and more meaningful than any intimacy I've known."[4]

This intimacy-at-a-distance sometimes leads to "chat room sex," where the individuals use their imagination and describe via their keyboards what they are doing sexually—or would like to do—to the one they are communicating with. Such "virtual" online sex can lead to real-life meetings and affairs; more commonly, however, people hide behind their false identities and fatuous monikers.

But why should anonymous communication via a computer lead to feelings of intimacy in any case? As stated in the Stanford University study, the Internet has the potential of creating an "atomized world," with people becoming isolated units. Despite creating more communication between people, more messages and calls, these technologies can contribute to feelings of isolation. Taken to its extreme, it is easy to imagine a dark future of human beings as individualized technological components of a science-fiction superstate, only communicating with each other via sophisticated technology. A similar nightmare scenario was vividly put forward in the popular film *The Matrix*.

On the other hand, it goes without saying that these technologies can be and are used for the good. Responding to the world as a modern technological Luddite is no answer to the present challenges we face. Technology, after all, is a catalyst at the mercy of human intentions. In itself it is not "bad" or at fault. It is our application and usage of it, according to free will, that can be problematic.

From this wider perspective, this new technology is only reflecting back to us what we are already experiencing in any case: an increasing sense of individualization, of isolation, a feeling of being enclosed within one's own ego—an outcome of evolving human consciousness over past millennia. The human soul has become more awake and aware of itself at the cost of feeling naturally close and at one with a wider community, and new technologies are a metaphor for that experience. They offer a sense of protection within that lonely feeling. It is well known, for example, that people act differently when communicating through the more anonymous medium of e-mail than in a face-to-face conversation. "Flaming" is the term given when a person expresses their uncontrolled wrath via an unpleasant e-mail. Likewise, feelings of intimacy, such as in chat-room sex, are also easily generated because the technology enables us to hide our true selves. We do not need to face the person in the real world, burdened as we sometimes are with the negative aspects of self-consciousness which can be experienced through inhabiting a body.

In this sense, computer technology provides a picture of our increased sense of separateness. It reflects a general human "dark night of the soul": a crisis of experiencing the imprisonment of the self, of having to relate from and through it.

It could be argued that the real solution to these increasingly general feelings of isolation—or even the purpose of them—is to come to an increased and intensified search for genuine community. Today, given that the process of individualization has begun to break the natural links of family, tribe, nation, and race, the new community can be built up in a free way, no longer restricted by instinctive connections of blood. The experience of being an island of consciousness and the pain of separateness can give fresh impetus for something new to be born.

The danger posed by the new technologies is that we become complacent within their protection, increasingly hiding behind the shell of a digital world, where it will no longer be necessary to face and physically interact with other people in order to go shopping, to socialize, or even to have sex!

Bill Joy and the Dangers of "Technotopia"

Of all the people expressing concern about the potential dangers of digital technology in recent years, it is surprising to find among them one of the leading computer gurus of our time. Bill Joy, chief scientist and cofounder of Sun Microsystems, one of America's leading computer firms, and also cochairman of Bill Clinton's Presidential Information Technology Advisory Committee, became a computer heretic when he wrote a dramatic article in *Wired* magazine in 2001. In it, he said of computer technology: "Its potential to destroy humanity, even to supplant us as the planet's dominant species, is far greater than that of nuclear weapons; yet we are blindly moving towards a world in which such a possibility becomes a reality. . . . I think it is no exaggeration to say that we are on the cusp on an extreme evil."[5]

In an interview with *The Ecologist* magazine, Joy said: "I may be working to create tools which will enable the construction of the technology that may replace our species. How do I feel about this? Very uncomfortable." The dangers he refers to are the twenty-first-century technologies of robotics, genetic engineering, and nanotechnology, all of which have the potential to self-replicate and "quickly get out of control."

Joy's predictions already appear to be coming true. Shortly after he spoke those words, *Nature* magazine published the most recent developments in robotics. It reported that computers can now design and build their own robots with no intervention from humans. At Brandeis University, a computer was able to produce designs for robots which it "evolved" by introducing random mutations until the required result was achieved. Once the computer had perfected the design, a machine capable of building a robot was instructed by the computer to proceed with production. In a separate development, three computer scientists from the University of Lausanne, Switzerland, reported success in teaching "swarms" of small robots to interact with each other and work "in a self-organized manner, similar to workers in an ant colony."[6]

These experiments point to the possibility of finding something of a Holy Grail for computer scientists: the much-vaunted "artificial intelligence." Ever since computer technology has been developed, there has been talk of creating intelligent machines which have the ability, seemingly, to "think." Science fiction has always fantasized about such technology, for example in the film *2001: A Space Odyssey*, where an intelligent computer in a spacecraft guides the heroes to the outer boundaries of space. As far as it is known, however, no scientist has yet realized the goal of making a machine with real consciousness.

At best, a computer can be made to mimic human intelligence, as in the example of the computer programmed to introduce "mutations" into its designs. Ultimately, all computers and other similar technology are dependent on human intelligence. It is humans who write the programs and provide the original design for such machines. Anything which is in turn produced by such technology, therefore, such as our robot-designing computer, stems directly from human ingenuity.

Only humans, and to a lesser extent animals, are blessed with waking consciousness. Computers, robots, even "nanobots" and the like, are all, ultimately, sophisticated counting machines. And what's more, they are likely to remain so, however powerful the technology becomes. It is predicted that by 2030 humans will be able to build machines which are a *million* times as powerful as the personal computers of today. No doubt the ability to copy external aspects of human thinking and intelligence will also be ever more impressive, and robots may gradually appear to embody human characteristics.

But ultimately consciousness, the ability genuinely to think, feel, and act, is dependent on *life*, and life in turn is dependent on *soul* and *spirit*. Unless our intrepid scientists are able to manipulate nonphysical, supersensible forces and incarnate them into machines, creating something of a real-life Frankenstein's monster, then their goal of creating machines which can think will never be achieved.

Thinking Machines or Mechanized Humans?

As machines gradually take on the guise of having human characteristics, the opposite also becomes increasingly plausible: the danger that humans develop machinelike characteristics. The more we allow modes of thought based on computerized thinking, characterized by cold, deductive calculation, and the more we allow computers to dominate our human relationships, the more we become mechanized products ourselves.

I have already referred to the feelings of isolation that many people experience today as a symptom of the evolving individualized state of human consciousness. I have also shown how technology appears to offer solutions to this problem by substituting real human interaction with chat rooms, interactive websites, and the proliferation of mobile means of communication—in other words, a counterfeit intimacy. But there is also another way in which modern technology gives a material counterpicture or image of processes which are a consequence of evolving human consciousness.

Many people today are beginning to have personal experiences of the potential expansion of the human mind. Through the various philosophies, teachings, and spiritual-developmental paths available in the modern spiritual arena there are countless means available to achieve such experience: meditation, channeling, remote viewing, astral projection, and so on. While many of the methods may be dubious and their results questionable, they all point to a conclusion which increasing numbers of people are accepting as a truth: Humans have the ability to grow and expand beyond the physical intellect and bring to birth faculties which enable us to reach into other times, places, and states of being.

Using differing means, human pioneers of spiritual modes of consciousness have for centuries been paving the way for humanity to advance beyond its present brain-bound awareness. And just at the time when such experience is beginning to be widespread, new technology is itself beginning to *mimic* higher states of consciousness. As with computers appearing to imitate thinking, so the Internet appears to mimic these advanced states of human experience. E-mail, for example, allows us to send thoughts, messages, images, and pictures in a way that seems to transcend time and space. Through the web we can visit millions of sites set up by individuals or organizations based anywhere in the world. This information appears to hang in thin air.

Similarly, we can send information back to the people we communicate with, anywhere, instantly. These qualities are like a parody or caricature of the higher abilities which are being born in many people today: the ability to transcend the physical boundaries of the brain and enter a stream of being unrestricted by human physical concepts of time and space.

The Internet is known, of course, as the World Wide Web. It is indeed a world-spanning web of technology, a material web dependent on machines and electronics. But it is a web which, wholly dependent on matter, ultimately binds people to matter. Our challenge today is to use this web but not to become enmeshed in it.

Despite its enslaving capacities, seen from a broader perspective modern technology is something of a blessing. Apart from its obvious uses which we cannot ignore, it provides us with a reminder of our true task. It shows us the antithesis of our true selves, the hardened, electrified, but in the final analysis *dead* world of matter. Notwithstanding its illusions and tricks, and even its ability to dominate us if we allow it to (through the creation of self-replicating robots or high-powered nanocomputers), it is a world entirely dependent on the material realm.

Meditating on that picture—a web of energy-powered technology bound to matter—provides a constant reminder of what we are not. At the same time it shows us what we are to achieve: the ability to be uniquely *human*, to be able to extend beyond the far reaches of the cosmos, to create a new way of knowledge which can free human beings from Earth-bound consciousness into dimensions which the human mind has forgotten.

If we don't respond positively to the challenge, maybe we will deserve a world populated by "thinking" machines and mechanized humans.

2.4 From Violent Reality to Sci-Fi Fantasy: Materialism at the Movies

The film industry in Hollywood holds a unique position in world culture. Although some other countries produce substantial numbers of films—for example, the Indian but Western-style "Bollywood"—no one surpasses Hollywood for sheer distribution muscle and promotion. Films made in the USA are dubbed, subtitled, or shown in the original English all around the world, reaching many, many millions, if not billions, of viewers via cinema, TV, and DVD/video. The extent of its influence is incalculable. What we know for sure is that Hollywood provides an image of affluence and glamour which acts as a glittering enticement to economic refugees the world over who increasingly want to join the Western consumerist party. But its other effects are less certain and not always apparent.

Hollywood was once called the "dream machine" and was famous for its escapist fantasies, for romantic comedies and musicals which provided a distraction from the mundane aspects of everyday life. Today its scope is wider, taking in comedy, history, drama, horror, and romance, although some would say that, regardless of the subject, Hollywood still essentially deals in dreams and fantasy.

In this chapter I will look at two very different but recurrent themes which have featured in the movie industry over the past few decades. In the first section, I will consider the question of violence in film. Echoing some aspects of chapter 2.1 on gangsta rap, I will ponder the main argument used by filmmakers to justify the graphic, soulless violence they portray. As with gangsta rap's practitioners, they often argue that the content of their art "reflects reality." But what is the nature of this so-called "reality," and for that matter what is "reality" anyway? Whose reality is being reflected in these films?

In the second section of the essay, I will focus on the genre of science fiction, in particular the concept of "aliens" as they appear in Hollywood films, as well as the idea of time travel. I will discuss ways that these themes appear to reflect spiritual realities, although usually in a densified, material form. Finally, I will draw the two aspects of the essay together and consider a possible response through which filmmakers might be able to redeem some of the more negative aspects of corporate cinema.

I. "Real" Violence

In recent years one of Hollywood's most successful genres has been the action movie. At the crudest end of the spectrum are films like the shoot-'em-up *Rambo* and *Lethal Weapon* series, while at the other end are the cool-as-hell gangster films, classics like *The Godfather* and *Scarface* to the more recent *The Usual Suspects*. One of the most influential films of this ilk in recent times has been *Reservoir Dogs*, the directorial debut of a fresh-faced 29-year-old—one Quentin Tarantino.

Made on a low budget, with most of the action taking place in an empty warehouse, *Reservoir Dogs* depicts the struggles and recriminations among a gang of criminals in the aftermath of a failed armed robbery. One notorious scene shows the beating, disfiguring, and dousing in gasoline of a captured policeman by one of the criminal gang. In the film's climactic moment, the psychopathic ex-convict, knife in hand, slices off the ear of his bound and gagged prisoner. Tarantino's clever touch is to accompany the chilling scene with the mellow strains of a 1970s pop song, to which his maniacal character dances and jiggles as he anticipates carrying out the macabre act.

This bizarre juxtaposition of mellifluous music and extreme violence led, at the peak of the film's torture scene, to people walking out of cinemas in revulsion. Tarantino's response to the disgust of some of his audience showed he was unmoved: "It never bothered me when people walked out. It just meant that scene worked. . . . I'm not interested in making a cartoon. I'm interested in making the violence real."[1] Indeed, Stuart Gordon, the director of *Re-Animator* (a classic horror movie), reportedly told Tarantino after witnessing *Reservoir Dogs*: "Quentin, I walked out of your movie, but I want you to take it as a compliment. See, we all deal in fantasy. There's no such thing as werewolves or vampires. You're dealing with real-life violence, and I can't deal with it."[2]

A couple of years later, Tarantino's follow-up film *Pulp Fiction* was shown at the Cannes Film Festival where it won the Palme d'Or. While *Pulp Fiction* was a more commercial and accessible film than its predecessor, Tarantino had no intention of compromising on the violent content: the film featured shootings, stabbings, sadomasochism, homosexual rape, as well as heroin injection and a drug overdose. Defending his film from accusations of gratuitous violence, Tarantino declared: "Gratuitous violence [in films] is when they do it bad . . . and it's lame. I don't know what gratuitous violence is."[3]

On this point fellow director Oliver Stone agreed with him. His film *Natural Born Killers*, which tells of the murderous jaunt across America of a young couple who kill 52 people before being arrested, was refused a certificate for three months by the British Board of Film Classification while it investigated allegations that the film had inspired ten murders. The veteran and well-respected filmmaker Stone stated: "I don't believe in avoiding violence because it's part of life." Echoing Tarantino, he added: "If you're going to show an act of violence, it should really be authentic and real and scary. You aim a gun, blood spurts everywhere."[4]

In terms of explicit violence in modern cinema, none of these films rivals the excesses of "splatter" horror movies such as *Friday the 13th*, *Nightmare on Elm Street*, or numerous others in that vein. However, while for the most part the populist horror genre is not taken too seriously by critics—it's viewed as a sort of "fast food" of the film industry—

Tarantino's films are respected as serious works. One London critic described *Pulp Fiction* as "a piece of genuine brilliance ... with an unerring mastery over every aspect of the filmmaker's craft."[5] This was a typical response to what was to prove to be a remarkably popular film.

Although Tarantino was to disappoint fans with his follow-up *Jackie Brown*, *Pulp Fiction* demonstrated a special talent for directing and scriptwriting. The film masterfully weaves together the threads of three narratives, moving forwards and backwards in time, with certain scenes repeated to allow the audience to see events from different points of view. But it also features scenes of ruthless murder, which have proved to be by far the most popular aspect of the film to young viewers. In one instance the two lead gangsters, Jules and Vincent, are sent to execute members of a rival drug ring. After terrifying his unarmed victims with pointed questions, Jules, with an air of self-righteous indignation, booms out Old Testament lines before he and his accomplice pump dozens of bullets into the bodies of their victims. What gives the scene such an uncanny edge is that minutes before carrying out the execution the affable Jules and Vincent, in languid mood, had been discussing what a Big Mac is called in France, and the fact that the Dutch put mayonnaise on their French fries. Apart from the Old Testament mock-dramatics, the murders are carried out with seeming indifference, as one might set about any slightly tiresome job.

This, in fact, is where *Pulp Fiction* is so "successful." Murder is integrated into its script as an almost casual occurrence—an unfortunate but not uncommon part of life—to the point that it appears to be comic. In one scene the gangsters are driving along in their car when Vincent, who is loosely holding his .45 pistol, accidentally pulls the trigger. His side-kick Marvin happens to be in the way of the bullet and is promptly killed. This is intended as a piece of dark comedy, and the audience duly laughs.

Reflecting Reality?

Are such depictions of violence valid in film? Does the work of Tarantino, Stone, and others warrant serious consideration as "art," or are these films merely products to cause amusement and sensation to their distraction-seeking audiences and, in turn, to make big profits for their makers and backers? Do these films stand up to deeper criticism, or are they mere entertainment for the masses (rather like the circuses which the Romans created to placate the hordes of common people). If they are the former, which the pretensions of their makers suggest, then their use of violence as a device should be justified.

When challenged on the violent content of their films, the stock defense by many filmmakers is that somehow their task is simply to "reflect reality." Following this argument the modern filmmaker is thereby justified in portraying the most sickening violence. Thus Tarantino said of *Reservoir Dogs*: "I think one of the strengths of the film is that it is realistic."[6] Or Oliver Stone, explaining the violence in *Natural Born Killers*, stated: "The world is violent, and we're swamped in it in this century. So I mirror that."[7] In another interview, Stone, when challenged on the point of whether his film merely adds to a culture of violence, responded: "So what if it's part of the problem? You don't have to have a solution in a work of art."[8]

Few people would expect artists to offer solutions to society's problems. As Stone so rightly says, it is not their task to provide answers to complex social and political problems. But most people would not expect art to be "part of the problem" either, in the sense that it might contribute to a culture of violence.

Historically, fiction, whether written or performed on stage or screen, has been an important catalyst in helping people come to terms with the many issues and problems of life. Rather than providing simple solutions and political slogans, the best literary works play out aspects of the human psyche, enabling us to better understand ourselves. The greatest art delves deep into the human condition, facilitating catharsis and metamorphosis. It helps us move on, develop, grow. Reading a well-written and thoughtful work on war—for example, any of Earnest Hemingway's classic books—will not make us want to commit an act of violence. On the contrary, through a deeper comprehension of human motivation, we come to understand the characters, and begin to sympathize with them and their shortcomings. Intuitive knowledge is awoken, and life appears richer, more profound, and more manageable.

When a writer is inspired to portray the human condition, art can legitimately incorporate all aspects of life, including violence. In fact, much classic literature includes violence in many forms. To use the most obvious example, Shakespeare's historical dramas and tragedies are littered with premeditated and often brutal murders. Many key characters exhibit evil intent and conspire to bring about the deaths of others. Two of Shakespeare's most famous characters—Macbeth and Hamlet—are cold-blooded murderers. But what distinguishes them from Oliver Stone's "natural born killers" is Shakespeare's complex and elaborate character portrayals, often penetrating to depths of soul and spirit. Shakespeare helps and encourages us to conceive the intricacies of human life and destiny. In his best work, he presents archetypes which represent stages of our evolving humanity. Through such wider perspectives, we are able to assimilate the tragic and violent aspects of the drama.

In contrast, Tarantino does not allow us to penetrate the psyches of his characters. They are given little background, motive, context, or spiritual depth. As critic James Wood observes: "He [Tarantino] represents the final triumph of post-modernism, which is to empty the artwork of all content, thus voiding its capacity to do anything except helplessly *represent* our agonies. . . . Only in this age could a writer as talented as Tarantino produce artworks so entirely vacuous, so stripped of any politics, metaphysics, or moral interest."[9]

What we are left with is the shell of the human being. We see colorful pictures on the screen, the actions and deeds of the characters, but are left devoid of insight or understanding. In such a context—or lack of context—portrayals of violence can easily take on a glamorous aspect. The aforementioned execution scene in *Pulp Fiction*, for example, has no background or aftermath. We don't understand what motivates the characters, and neither do we witness the consequences of killing, only the fantastically brutal way it is carried out.

By scratching below the surface of this so-called "reality," it soon becomes clear that it hides a very materialistic supposition. Many spiritual teachings talk of the physical realm as one of "maya," or illusion. According to this notion, what we relate to around us is "real" and tangible, but does not constitute the totality of our existence. By stating that physical life, or its reflection in film, represents "reality," an assumption is being made that other dimensions are not significant, or simply do not exist. Visionaries and seers contradict this by asserting that everyday "reality" is actually far less *real* than the vivid worlds of soul and spirit which interpenetrate the material dimension. It is the dazzling illusion of the sense-perceptible world that hides the thin veil which separates everyday experience from the extraordinary spiritual reality on which human life is based.

No doubt Tarantino might shrug off such criticism by pointing to the very title of his film, and to the dictionary definition printed at the beginning of the published screenplay, which states that pulp fiction is: ". . . a magazine or book containing lurid subject matter." Perhaps his intention, as intimated by the title of his film, is merely to create a tacky, racy series of pictures, without seeking to penetrate below the surface of events. But if that is the case, then the "reality" argument is seriously called into question.

An "Unreal" Training

So what is the nature of the "reality" that is reflected in films such as *Pulp Fiction* and *Reservoir Dogs*? It is interesting to note that Tarantino—he has had no formal training in drama or film-making— represents an unprecedented generation of filmmakers that has been "schooled" by the medium which it seeks to create: a so-called "out-of-the-video-stores-and-onto-the-screens" movement. As Tarantino's friend Roger Avary put it: "There's a fresh generation of filmmakers, and they're coming out of the video stores. All of us have the advantage of a data base of thousands of movies."[10]

Already as a youth Tarantino spent hours at the cinema. "Basically, I spent my life at the movies,"[11] he said candidly when interviewed. Later he became an usher in a pornographic film theatre, and then, finally, got a job working in a Los Angeles video shop. "I basically lived there for years. We'd get off work, close up store, then sit around and watch movies all night."[12] On Fridays he and his friends would "plot things out so we could see all four new movies we were interested in."[13] This obsession with film was set to continue. Around the time when *Pulp Fiction* was released, he was asked what his typical day consisted of. He replied: "I go to movies, sometimes more than once a day, and I watch TV with friends. Occasionally, I go to coffee shops. That and work. That's what I do."[14]

What can be the result of this self-perpetuating "school" of modern cinema? Through such internal education and training, does it not begin to create its own "reality"? It has already been observed by critics that many of the lines, situations, and even camera angles in *Pulp Fiction* are borrowed wholesale from other films. In a sense, the whole film is made up of references. Even the stage directions for the opening scene run: "Their dialogue is to be said in a rapid-pace *His Girl Friday* fashion."[15]

Creating Reality?

Given this derivative and self-referential vortex in which art begins to create its own illusory reality, it is legitimate to question whether film in turn contributes to creating the "reality" of modern culture. To put it another way, does violence in films create or contribute to violence in real life?

This complex question has sparked a debate which has raged, and will continue to rage, for many years and cannot properly be resolved here. Although various scientific studies have been made, direct proof of a link between screen violence and violence in society is difficult to draw, although indications of such a link are beginning to emerge. When the toddler Jamie Bulger was killed by two young boys in England in 1993, the trial judge opined that the children's exposure to violent videos like *Child's Play 3* could have played a part in the two-year-old's death.

Eight years later, in January 2001, a report from the U.S. surgeon general's office appeared to confirm this suspicion. A six-month study, which tested groups of eight-year-olds, identified a "scientific link between graphically violent television programming and increased aggression in children." It discovered that those who watched less violence were involved in fewer acts of taunting and teasing in the playground. The paper, commissioned by the White House after the Columbine school shootings, reported: "Research to date justifies sustained efforts to curb the adverse effects of media violence on youths. Although our knowledge is incomplete, it is sufficient to develop a coherent public health approach to violence prevention that builds upon what is known, even as more research is underway."[16]

A few months later, a second study, this time from Wake Forest University in North Carolina, found that teenagers who watch television wrestling are more likely to be violent and antisocial. They commit more drunk-driving offenses, use drugs more often, and are more likely to carry weapons. The findings mirrored another study by the Independent Television and Broadcasting Standards Commission, which also found that TV wrestling encouraged children to be violent. It claimed that youngsters as young as six were copying television shows and using objects such as tables as weapons.[17]

Of course, many will continue to question the results of such research. But we can each draw our own conclusions as to what effect the depiction of an act of violence has when it is stripped of any real background or motive, and when it is divorced from its consequences of suffering, grief, and pain. It is hardly surprising that such scenes are superficially attractive and fascinating—particularly, of course, to children, who have less ability to discriminate than adults. In a special report on violence in films and music, *Time* magazine reported the words of a 15-year-old boy picked at random in a fast-food restaurant: "I liked the part in *Pulp Fiction* where the guy points a gun and says a prayer from the Bible and then kills everybody. You hear the gun go *brrr*. It's cool."[18]

Psychological "Reality"

While Tarantino is content to create a lurid series of pictures reflecting a particular perception of reality, Oliver Stone has greater pretensions in his *Natural Born Killers*. In a bid to mirror what he calls the "collective unconscious for the century,"[19] Stone creates something of a subliminal method which subdues our ability to counteract what we see on the screen. The film comprises a swirling kaleidoscope of images which utilizes black-and-white, color, Super 8 and standard film, animation, back projections, and fast editing—all pieced together over a loud rock-music soundtrack.

With this technique, Stone seeks to serve two purposes, which he clarified in an interview: "It reflects the junkyard culture of the time, it has a TV sensibility where everything is changing, channel-surfing, coming at you. But stylistically, we also wanted to enter into the heads of the two killers, make it subjective, hallucinatory. They've watched a lot of TV. They're desensitized to it."[20] Elsewhere he stated: "We wanted to put the audience right in the driver's seat—make them the killers. Virtual reality goggles, so to speak, where you would participate, you would enjoy the ride."[21]

So what is Stone's intention in reflecting "junkyard culture"? Is he not merely adding to it by lulling his audience's consciousness to the pictures being projected on the screen? When asked in an interview if *Natural Born Killers* is an amoral film, Stone retorted: "No, the film is moral in that it posits the notion that killing is inevitable in the environment that has grown up. . . . The reasons for violence are social: poverty, neglect, lack of family, huge arms sales abroad and at home."[22]

True to his analysis, amongst the jumble of images in his film Stone interjects his own attempts to *explain* social problems. But his particular tool for comprehending the mayhem of mass-murder appears to be a brand of rather basic pop psychology. To elucidate the reasons for the viciousness of his murderous female heroine Mallory, he shows scenes from her abused childhood; but even here the message is confused by the presentation. No doubt seeking further to reflect "junkyard culture," Stone shows images of her family background in the style of a good-old American sitcom, complete with prerecorded laughter.

Before the viewer is able fully to comprehend this psychological interpretation, the film abruptly turns into a satire of the media and its presentation of violence. In contrast to the cynical and manipulative media, the killers Mickey and Mallory—now imprisoned—see themselves as innocents. Mickey explains in his own words why he is a mass-murderer. In relation to the decadent world around him an act of murder, he says, is "pure." What's more, he has realized his "true calling in life": "I'm a natural born killer," he drawls contentedly.

No doubt, Stone has the best of intentions. But what is the actual effect of his film? His images of extreme violence, together with rather weak attempts at analysis, are set in a confused blur of "meaningful" pictures, against which the viewer has to battle to retain waking consciousness. Arguably, in the final analysis this is more dangerous than the relatively honest "living reality" of Tarantino.

II. Fantasy and Sci-Fi

At the other end of the Hollywood spectrum, far from the gangsters and "real" extreme violence, is the perennially popular genre of science fiction. One of the biggest successes of recent times has been the alien fantasy film *Independence Day*. In the first two weeks following its opening, the film took over 160 million dollars in ticket sales, the most successful opening ever at the time in July 1996.

But despite its populist and financial achievement, its spectacular special effects and impressively gruesome aliens, *Independence Day* was hardly an artistic triumph. Almost unanimously, critics concluded that its script was embarrassingly awful, its characters wooden, and the plot somewhat ridiculous and far-fetched. (It has been called the biggest "B-movie" ever created.) Nevertheless, its themes gripped the imagination of audiences around the world.

In the scenario of the film, alien beings from another part of the cosmos arrive in huge, fifteen-mile wide space ships with the goal of extinguishing mankind and occupying the Earth for their own ends. Eventually one of the alien creatures is captured and, thought to be dead, operated on. Dramatically, it comes to life and kills a human with its long, lashing tentacles. The President of the United States, who witnesses the attack, asks the creature what it wants from humanity. The alien responds using telepathy, communicating that it wishes human beings "to die." Finally, through various fantastic means, and in a blaze of international anti-alien fervor, the occupying ships are destroyed and the aliens beaten.

Despite its tremendous success, there was not much that was new in *Independence Day*. Hollywood has long been fascinated with aliens, be they of the more friendly variety as in *ET* or *Close Encounters of the Third Kind*, or the more belligerent kind in the *Alien* series. This interest in aliens is, within the field of science fiction, paralleled only by a preoccupation with the concept of "time-travel," as epitomized by the film version of H. G. Wells's classic *The Time Machine*. From the British *Dr. Who* through to the popular series *Back to the Future*, many films have followed in the steps of Wells's pioneering work.

One of the most sophisticated of such time-travel films was *12 Monkeys* (ensured commercial success through the inclusion of star actors, despite its complex and rather convoluted story line). *12 Monkeys* is set initially in 2035, a period of history which is ravaged by a strange viral disease. A prisoner is given the job of traveling back in time to 1996 to change the course of history by stopping a terrorist group from releasing a virus which is to destroy much of humanity and make the surface of the Earth uninhabitable.

This idea—that the present can be changed by a person returning to the past to rearrange events—is fundamental to the concept of time travel. As the lead actor, Bruce Willis, says of *12 Monkeys*: "One of the most fascinating ideas in the picture for me was the concept of this nine-year-old boy going to witness his own death, but surviving to go on and continue the cycle."[23]

Extraterrestrial Entities?

Over the years, the themes of aliens and time-travel have been consistently successful in drawing audiences to films. Why are they so enduring?

The question of whether or not alien beings exist in the cosmos is, for most people, an intriguing one. From an objective scientific standpoint, the potential for such beings to exist somewhere in physical form cannot be ruled out, and the second half of the last century appears to have provided some evidence supporting this possibility. There has been an explosion of interest in UFOs, with many people claiming to have sighted extraterrestrial entities, and many thousands believing that they have even been abducted by them. Regardless of how genuine these experiences are, they are clearly real to many people, and there are also millions of others who want to believe them.

I suggest that the best way of comprehending this phenomenon is to view it as a symptom of something else, the underlying existential question which lies in the soul of humanity. This question can be expressed as follows: "Are we the only conscious beings in the universe?"

This question originates from the distant past, from the time when humans began to be separated from, and as a consequence, began to forget, their spiritual origins. The concept of aliens—by this I mean physical beings who inhabit some distant planet or star somewhere "out there"—offers some kind of answer to this question. In *Independence Day* the President of the United States declares in a public announcement: "The question as to whether or not we are alone in the universe has been answered." But the answer in the film comes in the form of base, *physical* life. The primal *spiritual* question is left unanswered.

Over the past century, a strong message has been conveyed repeatedly from multiple sources to humanity. The style and method of presentation has varied according to the source, but in essence the message remains the same. It tells us that now is a critical point in human evolution. In order for our development to continue in a harmonious way, we must rediscover our spiritual nature and knowledge of our place in the cosmos in relation to the hierarchies of spiritual beings. Our primary task today, it could be said, is to build a living relationship, while on Earth, with *spiritual* beings, from the lowest elemental entities through to the angels, and to the highest spiritual consciousness which we refer to as God. If these beings and their relationships to us are indeed real, then it could be expected that a subconscious yearning for knowledge of them would exist in each person alive today.

Films like *Independence Day* go some way toward meeting this thirst for knowledge. But what they offer is only a materialistic substitute. We are not alone in the universe, they tell us. However, although they may look a bit different, the beings we share creation with are in essence just like us. They are material and have material needs, and may even have a more evolved civilization than we have. The essential difference between us is that they happen to live in another part of the cosmos. The effect of such messages is that they lock us into a spatial, material conception of other worlds and beings. The idea of purely spiritual dimensions is buried under the weight of this materialistic view.

Another tendency of such films—with the exception of kiddie alien flicks like *ET*—is to encourage fear of what is "out there." (The television series *The X-Files*, in particular, contributed massively to this feeling by suggesting that most "paranormal" phenomena were in some way sinister.) The idea of the Earth being attacked was, of course, initially introduced by H. G. Wells's *War of the Worlds*. So effective was the famous first radio transmission of the drama, that people thought an actual attack by Martians was going on. The message of *Independence Day* is likewise that humanity should be awake to the possibility of physical attack from alien beings. Whatever is out there in space is dangerous! The consequence of such thoughts is to encourage a feeling that what is unknown is destructive or frightening. Such an attitude—subliminal or not—is not conducive to developing a positive relationship with hidden, spiritual dimensions.

But what if the concept of alien attack was effectively cloaking another, and perhaps more real, assault—an invasion from truly "cosmic" beings? In other words, what if the attack by "extraterrestrial" beings is *spiritual* in nature, not physical, and is actually already taking place, unknown to most of us? Again, according to many testimonies, attacks by demonic spiritual entities, beings given the task of acting as our adversaries, are taking place right now. The goals of these beings are varied, but their main aim in our time is to draw us more deeply into matter, to the extent that we become deluded and deny, in effect, the spiritual reality which is the foundation of our lives. From this point of view, encouraging humanity to stare at the skies in fear of alien attack is a fine diversionary tactic from this other, spiritual, attack!

Traveling in Time

In the case of time travel and the film *12 Monkeys*, the relationship to spiritual reality is more complex. In the last century, the idea of reincarnation was widely introduced to Western humanity. Increasingly it has become a reality to many people, particularly through new age teachings. The doctrine of reincarnation tells us that we have all lived on Earth before, are presently working through our destiny (karma) from the past, and creating new situations for the future through our present deeds and actions. If there is some truth to this teaching, then one would expect that its reality would be hidden somewhere in our subconscious, awaiting knowledge and realization. What's more, we would have a subliminal thirst for clear concepts of such ideas, in order to help bring the truth to our awakened consciousness. The concept of time-travel partially satisfies our need for this, although again it is represented in a material form. We are told that through the medium of a machine, time warp, or whatever, we can live in the past or future. But rather than our soul or spirit making this migration from life to life, we take our *physical* form to these periods of history. Again, this is a materialization of a spiritual idea.

The other significant aspect of time-travel in this context is the notion that it is possible to alter the present by changing the past, that history can be changed by humans traveling into the past and tampering with events which have already taken place (as in *12 Monkeys*). This idea infringes on the freedom inherent in the spiritual concept of "destiny," i.e., you sow what you reap. The teaching of destiny (or, to use the Eastern term, karma) tells us that our past deeds and actions determine our present conditions, and that it is through our current deeds and actions that we determine the future. There can, in reality, be no "quick fixes" through zipping back into the past. Our task is to learn from the past, but to act in the present and future. The concept of time-travel sponsors the illusion that the past can be tampered with and made good through clever, technological manipulation.

Finally, another important spiritual truth can be detected in a distorted form in the idea of time-travel. Through "remote viewing" (a term coined by the U.S. military to label its efforts to exploit psychic capacities to gather intelligence information), the possibility of traveling out of the body to another "location" in time and space has been popularized. Remote viewing is comparable to astral projection—another means of out-of-body experience. In esoteric training, a more exact method of researching past periods of human history is known as reading the Akashic Record.

Through diligent self-training and practice, an individual can develop clairvoyant capacities which enable him to perceive the spiritual records of all human deeds and events.[24] This, we could say, is a spiritual "time-travel"—but it does not affect human freedom as its only ability to influence the present is through offering spiritual knowledge to humanity (and whether or not we take heed of that knowledge is up to us). Unlike this subtle spiritual reading of the past (and to some extent also the future), the time-travel of science fiction is crude and materialistic. Yet, as a concept, time-travel apes this faculty to research spiritually, and presents it as a pseudo-scientific goal to be achieved through machines and technology.

Redeeming Materialism

As stated, the elementary appeal of films which feature aliens and time-travel is that they encapsulate an underlying spiritual truth. But their very method, whether deliberate or not, involves taking such objective truths and offering them back in a distorted and most significantly in a materialized form, which in turn appeals and is comprehensible to everyday, twenty-first-century consciousness. The net result is that these films tend to reinforce and strengthen materialistic thought-forms; they have a hardening, materializing influence, and hence make it more difficult for spiritual thinking to exist.

Considering such a process, can these films and their effects be redeemed in any way? As already outlined in the first part of this book, redemption of materialism can come about through the development in individuals of a living spiritual practice based on knowledge and cognition. But could the film makers themselves do anything to redeem the worst aspects of materialism in their films?

The very fact that, through the medium of film, a concept such as aliens is so phenomenally popular today begs the question as to why *spiritual reality* is not being portrayed in films so that it might be more accessible to greater numbers of people. The potential to do this is absolutely huge, because the silver screen offers so many opportunities to be creative and imaginative. Admittedly, the challenges involved in doing it are equally vast. How do you present spiritual ideas on screen? How can you depict spiritual beings such as angels or demons, or the realms that the spirit enters after death, and so on?

There are no easy answers, but a typical Hollywood megabudget would help push research along a little. In recent years there has been some delving into this territory, for example in Jerry Zucker's *Ghost* and Vincent Ward's *What Dreams May Come* (which tackle life after death) or Wim Wenders's *Wings of Desire* (about angels). But there is still some way to go for the medium of film to fully explore the conveying of spiritual ideas to a wide public. Perhaps such spiritual films could go some way towards redeeming some of the more materialistic science fiction spoken of above.

What of the "real" violence of Tarantino and the speculative psychology of Stone? How can the ultraviolence of such films and their inadequate attempts at analysis be redeemed? In recent times a number of films have been made which successfully portray something of the intricate complexities of the destinies of individuals and their relationships. There are many such examples of this, for example Atom Egoyan's *Exotica*, Krzysztof Kieslowski's *Three Colors* series, or Robert Altman's *Short Cuts*.

Individually, these films offer useful insights into the human condition, and delve into the ways people relate to one another. Building on such a basis, it would be possible to develop an art of film which not only studies human relationships, but begins to depict the hidden spiritual forces of destiny at work in the background. Many mysteries could be usefully explored: Why do some people have such strong sympathies or antipathies toward each other in this lifetime? Is something working from the past, and if so, how do these forces work into the present and future?

As stated at the beginning of this chapter, film, and Hollywood in particular, has a huge influence on world culture. With its suggestive images and subliminally active themes, its impact on human thought is already significant. But its potential for positive change is also huge. Careful commissioning, insightful writing, and inspired film-making could begin to present other interpretations of life than the purely materialistic one. The medium in itself is not the problem—but the message needs some attention.

2.5 The Cartoons Bite Back: Beavis and Butt-head and the Risks of Individuation

Once upon a time, cartoons were the preserve of children's entertainment. Under the guiding hand of Walt Disney, classic fairy tales and popular stories were transformed one by one into popular animations for the big screen. Disney also created cute comedy for the pre-teens: cartoon mice, dogs, and ducks, in bright colors and with funny voices. It was a Saturday afternoon treat at the cinema, or tea-time viewing on the television. Adults may have watched from the corners of their eyes, but it was not really for them.

But then in 1987, that crazy, dysfunctional all-American family "The Simpsons," came along and suddenly cartoons were no longer strictly for the kids. Ingeniously, "The Simpsons" presented a format which would appeal to children, but with a subtext full of witticisms, jokes, and humor aimed squarely at older generations. The smart, quick-witted, and naughty character Bart Simpson swiftly became a young people's favorite, adorning tee-shirts, baseball caps, and all sorts of other merchandise. Bart had attitude. Bart was cool.

"The Simpsons" is a clever, satirical show, with fine social observation, good humor, and well-written narratives. Its success predictably launched a host of copycat imitations. With the appeal of the cartoon medium no longer restricted to the very young, teenagers and people in their twenties and older watched such programs. Significantly, these were people with disposable income.

Perhaps it was the latter fact that turned the music television channel MTV on to the idea of introducing a cartoon act onto their schedules. MTV—a brand and institution which is now as established a part of international American culture as Coca-Cola—has since its inception been devoted to screening popular music. It first enjoyed success in the 1980s by utilizing music videos which had been invented by record companies as a means of promotion to a predominantly young audience. As modern pop music entered its fourth decade in the 1980s, it faced an increasingly apathetic youth audience—more thrilled by computer games than music—and the video became a crucial means of marketing "product" to the new generation.

Recorded music is already one step from the reality of live music. The music video, with its mini narratives and abstract images, increases that reality gap. But the new animated attraction, "Beavis and Butt-head," which MTV introduced in the early 1990s, took this peculiarly modern experience one step further. As viewers of the program, we were shown clips of the "heroes," two crudely drawn teenage boys, watching music videos. But we also saw the videos as if we were watching them along with Beavis and Butt-head, and in addition heard the characters' voices imposed over the music, giving a commentary to the sounds and visuals. From time to time images of Beavis and Butt-head flashed back on the screen; we saw them sitting on their tattered armchair, in all their animated glory, watching television.

In the scenario of the show it was Beavis and Butt-head who controlled what was being seen on the screen, for they had the remote-control box to flick channels when they got bored. And they often got bored or did not approve of what was shown. Through this format, the viewer of the program was given an incessant subjective commentary on the music. But as you might expect, Beavis and Butt-head's criticism was crude, and their vocabulary strikingly limited. The videos were deemed to be either "cool" or they "sucked." As music critics, these two were ruthlessly selective in their tastes: for the most part they favored only the loudest and fastest guitar-based rock music ("thrash," "death-metal," or "hardcore") and the most bellicose rap. Standard pop music, naturally, was reviled.

Spliced within all this music-video viewing were the remarkable adventures and antics of the two teenage cartoon characters. Two different narratives were shown every week, each about 15 minutes long. One week the characters were asked to prune the branches of a neighboring old man's tree in return for payment. Taking a chainsaw they sawed through the trunk of the enormous tree which promptly fell on the old man's house. Their response to the calamity, amidst fits of giggles, was: "I'm afraid we're going to have to charge you extra, sir, for demolishing your house."

In another episode they decided to "couch-fish," sitting back on their armchair with a fishing-line cast out of the window. After pulling in a live raccoon, followed by a school acquaintance with the fishing-hook caught through his thumb, they dragged in an old woman who had been tempted by the "bait" of a prune box. In another adventure, "Car Wash," they were given the task of washing a 1959 Corvette, the prize possession of a neighbor. Finding the keys they drove the car away and caused a serious road accident. Sitting in the wrecked Corvette, with flames erupting around them, their inane response was: "Whoa—that was cool."

All the time, from the opening theme music, through the video-watching and the narratives, the nervous, staccato snickering of the two characters is heard: "Huh huh huh—heh-heh m heh-heh—huh huh huh—heh-heh m heh-heh . . ."

An officially sanctioned book, *Beavis and Butt-head, This Book Sucks*,[1] gave an insight into the sensitive formative years of our fun-loving characters. The book pictures Beavis as a five-year-old boy pouring lighter-fluid on his birthday cake in order to make his "wish come true." At nine he is depicted holding a baseball bat with a squashed frog stuck to the bottom. Elsewhere cruelty to insects is justified by an "Insect Court" chart which shows a picture of the insect (e.g., "Daddy Longlegs from backyard") and the "crime" ("loitering"), the "verdict" ("guilty"), and the "punishment" ("de-legged; death by magnifying glass"). Violence is never far from view in the book: one image shows the two smashing a private mailbox with baseball bats.

The volume, packaged in gaudy colors to attract a youth readership, also includes some of Beavis's and Butt-head's poetic efforts to compose verse in the traditional Japanese Haiku style. One sample runs: "It's cool not to suck / 'Cause I don't like stuff that sucks / I like stuff that's cool." Also featured are philosophical thoughts in an essay on the subject "Freedom and what have I done to deserve it": "Kicking Beavis's ass, blowing up stuff, watching TV, hanging out at the convenience store, or the park. That is what freedom means to me."

Beavis and Butt-head are of course cartoon characters that do not exist. MTV soon became keen to emphasize this fact in response to mounting criticism of the program. Thus each episode began with a disclaimer, stating that Beavis and Butt-head are not "role models." This is reiterated in the book, which elaborates: "[T]hey're not even human. They're cartoons. Some of the things they do would cause a real person to get hurt, expelled, arrested, possibly deported. To put it another way: Don't try this at home." MTV had good reason to be concerned. *Time* magazine reported that an Ohio mother had charged that certain episodes of the program—they showed the two characters gleefully planning fire pranks—incited her five-year-old son to set their home ablaze, killing his two-year-old sister.[2] As a result of this action MTV moved the show from 7 to 10:30 P.M.

In their analysis, *Time* argued that: "The two cartoon nerds do not encourage stupidity and cruelty to animals: they satirize it." That may well be true—if the program had a purely adult audience. From an adult's point of view the program was clever and often funny. But a significant portion of its audience was children, and children generally do not understand satire. Moreover, due to their imitative qualities, children *are* likely to perceive the characters as "role models," and as a consequence attempt to emulate their actions.

As in chapters 2.1 and 2.4, it is legitimate to question at what point a program like this crosses the line from satirizing or reflecting "reality" to beginning to create a new reality. If the show's intention was satiric, the point it made was basic. Essentially, the joke was over in five minutes. So why the endless repetition? The answer is simple: the show was created as straightforward entertainment, with the unambiguous goal of keeping its viewers enthralled. After all, who are the viewers of MTV? They are certainly not all discerning adults with an interest in social satire.

Over the years, world literature has provided us with many examples of rebellious youthful characters, celebrated and loved for their naughtiness. But nothing quite prepares us for the maliciousness and the complete lack of conscience displayed by the two teenage boys in "Beavis and Butt-head." The show's unashamed depravity presented something that had not been seen before. In terms of "youth programming"—and certainly in the medium of animation—the show set a precedent.

This precedent has since been eagerly superceded by others seeking to capitalize on the show's success. Before long, the delights of "South Park" hit our screens, with plenty more manic, uncontrollable, and delinquent characters to relish. But Beavis and Butt-head were the originals; they set the tone, and in so doing, they set us the challenge of coming to a conscious understanding of them as a modern cultural phenomenon.

So what is being depicted in "Beavis and Butt-head," regardless of the intentions of its makers? It is tempting to view the two central characters as idiotic, demented thugs or fools. Such an analysis seemingly provides a satisfactory and conclusive answer, but it would be lazy and inaccurate to settle for that. While Beavis and Butt-head are not portrayed as especially intelligent, they do manifest an aptitude for self-awareness which, in terms of humanity's evolution, is relatively modern in nature. In other words, they demonstrate certain, very specific aspects of self-consciousness, or egohood, which has parallels to what Jung would refer to as individuation.

Evolving Consciousness

The contention that Beavis and Butt-head represent a consciousness which bears a contemporary quality will be justified and expanded upon below, but first some background for the concept of evolving consciousness.

Jung's notion of individuation has been mentioned, a process leading from collective to individual, integrated human consciousness. Jung was preceded by the independent spiritual researcher Rudolf Steiner, who contributed a comprehensive and coherent picture of evolving human consciousness based on the gradual unification and development of higher spiritual bodies. Steiner rejected completely the materialist position, which sees humanity essentially as an accident of nature, and life as a meaningless phenomenon caused by a number of coinciding factors. He also pointed out the inadequacies of the traditional religious view which, while allowing for a God in creation, perceives each individual life on Earth as an isolated experience.

Most religions teach that humans live, die, and then—depending on our behavior on Earth—enter an afterlife of some kind (its nature determined by the interpretation of one's religious confession). In contrast, Steiner saw each individual human life on Earth as part of a continuum, a process within which peoples and cultures are related and grow out of each other. Individuals have the opportunity to develop in different contexts, over millennia. But most importantly, the consciousness of humanity changes and evolves.

While it is true that the materialist also speaks of evolution, in the sense that modern man has developed technology and scientific understanding that did not exist previously, the critical distinction here is that Steiner saw the human race as involved in a process of evolving *consciousness itself*, rather than simply gaining new technical abilities. The inner nature of people of Egyptian times, for example, was far different from ours. According to Steiner, the ancient Egyptian person was far less material and "earthly," and had an instinctively spiritual consciousness. Egyptians would have known without question, for example, that first and foremost they were spiritual beings, and would have had no doubts about the existence of metaphysical dimensions of reality.

As part of this long developmental process, humanity is presently coming to terms with the birth or incarnation of individualized consciousness, moving from the overriding identification with family, clan, tribe, nation, and race, to the "I"-centered universe of individuality (see chapter 1.5). Whereas previously our identity was tied up largely with these differing kinds of group-consciousness, now we can relate more freely to what we as individuals (as "I") want to become. The ego, or "I," should not be confused with the common, everyday understanding of these terms, which can imply selfishness. Rather, spiritual ego consciousness is a state through which the individual is able to relate freely to others, to be able to act out of responsibility, knowledge, and ultimately love.

So how do Beavis and Butt-head relate to all this? Well, far from being fools, it is apparent that their creators intended them to be clever, aware, and awake. In their critique of music-videos Beavis and Butt-head exhibit a sharp black humor and alert wit, suggesting an ability for close observation. Their immoral inclinations are usually calculated and often have a sardonic, scheming aspect to them; ulterior motives are never far from view. In one episode Butt-head encourages Beavis to fake being hit by a car and then, pretending that his liver has been damaged in the accident, to ask the driver for an instant payment in return for a promise not to sue for damages.

In other contexts, their destructive urges, while sometimes pure hooliganism, often suggest a frustrated creative faculty, an imaginative capacity which enables them to continuously discover new means to counteract their boredom. In the episode "Closing Time," for example, bored of their repetitive jobs, they artistically "decorate" the fast-food restaurant where they work by throwing food and drink at the overhead fan.

Yet, despite demonstrating a close understanding of what they do, Beavis and Butt-head know no remorse or conscience. On the contrary, all their actions are accompanied by the repetitious machine-gun cackle of their laughter: "Huh huh huh—Heh-heh m heh-heh." While they are not simply thugs or fools, neither is there any inherent morality apparent in any of their actions or thoughts.

Evil Relating to "I" Consciousness

An important corollary to the picture of human evolution outlined here is that the different stages of humanity's development also have a negative aspect. The emancipation of individuality is a process which calls ultimately for conscious development. While the objective potential for such evolution exists within each of us—and spiritual forces are correspondingly present to enable such development—this potential has to be taken up and worked on through inner effort. As discussed in chapter 1.7, these forces are made available and they *must be used*. Otherwise those selfsame forces which are intended primarily for individual development manifest in a destructive and malign way.

It is critical to note that the quality of evil in somebody who has the capacity to develop "I" consciousness is different in nature to the quality of evil manifest in somebody who doesn't. Perhaps the most obvious example here is the type of evil apparent in Nazis who devised and implemented a "final solution" of the Jews and other perceived miscreants in Germany in the 1930s and 1940s, based on their theories of eugenics. While in other contexts and cultures the "enemy" has been openly and straightforwardly fought and killed in any way possible, the small groups of Nazis who devised the concentration camps and insidious methods of killing planned and executed their scheme with great precision and secrecy. Their actions were not carried out from sheer rage or uncontrolled violence. Rather, they had a calculating, and perversely "conscious" aspect—which is why, perhaps, the atrocities of the Second World War linger in our memory.

But the Nazi Holocaust was not the only tragedy of the twentieth century which betrayed this new character of evil. Under Stalin, the expulsion of peasants from their land and priests from their churches in Russia and the eventual deaths of millions of people from starvation, exhaustion, and war, suggested the same calculating quality. As with the Nazis, Stalin acted out of a fanatical adherence to an ideology—in his case Marxism—and the implementation of his plans bore the mark of a cold intellect.

Finally, the Allies' dropping of atom bombs on the Japanese cities of Nagasaki and Hiroshima had a similar detached, clinical air of evil. The bombs devastated large areas and contaminated them for generations, killing hundreds of thousands of innocent civilians in the process. Despite the cool justifications of its perpetrators (the questionable arguments that this was the only way to bring the war to a quick end), the dropping of the atom bomb raised the curtain for a new kind of violence and destruction.

In this sense, the twentieth century demonstrates the negative side effects of the birth of human individuality. If the potential that can take humanity forward does not find positive expression, it degenerates and becomes destructive. Of course, such acts of evil have precedents in human history, such as the annihilation of the indigenous population of Tasmania by colonialists, or the slave trade, which, for purely economic reasons, displaced and killed millions of Africans. It is not being argued that such acts are totally unique to the twentieth century. But it is a fact that the twentieth century saw a greater concentration of this new quality of evil.

Conscious development of individuality in our time calls for the nurturing of certain inner qualities, for example, reverence, respect, devotion to truth, tolerance, and objectivity. In "Beavis and Butt-head" we see, *par excellence*, the antithesis of such inner qualities. The cartoon characters are irreverent, sarcastic, cynical, and intolerant. It would be naïve to expect to see representatives of personal development in a contemporary slice of popular entertainment. But what is remarkable about "Beavis and Butt-head" is not that the characters on the screen display zero positive qualities, but that what they represent is diametrically *opposed* to any kind of human evolution.

What we actually see, I suggest, is a substitution of the development processes associated with conscious individuality by degenerate forces which allow evil to be perpetrated with a new "I" consciousness. This is a subtle point. As stated earlier, the forces which humans have been granted to develop self-consciousness *must be used consciously*. If these forces are not used consciously, they fall foul and, in their place, new types of evil manifest. This is a kind of shadow, mirror image of true ego-development. Within it we recognize traits which relate to I-consciousness, but these are now decadent, misplaced manifestations of the qualities of the higher ego.

I have indicated how this new quality of evil was evident on the historical stage of the twentieth century. Of course, I am not suggesting that the manic tendencies of Beavis and Butt-head are in any way directly comparable to the historical evils of Nazism, Stalinism, etc. But in the fictional characterizations of our twin villains we do see qualities which relate to the fallen ego-consciousness I have described.

My essential point is that these are unhealthy and unhappy images. What we are being presented with as (anti) role models are characters who have the self-consciousness of the modern individual, but do not have social, moral, or spiritual awareness of any kind. They are like empty vessels, vacuums, whose capacities for self-awareness are made available to forces of destruction. In other words, "Beavis and Butt-head" gives us a modern depiction of contemporary evil, and great entertainment for the kids to boot!

Of course, the program is not in itself responsible for the many social challenges humanity faces at the present time. It is not the cause, but rather it is an important symptom. As in medical matters, symptoms often point to the root of the problem. In its inspired presentation, "Beavis and Butt-head" offers us prophetic pictures which point to two areas in the individual and society which require immediate and urgent attention:

1. In depicting evil behavior arising from a modern state of consciousness, "Beavis and Butt-head" indicates the dangers which arise as a consequence of greater individualization. As a result of this process of moving from group to individual consciousness, outward norms, laws, precepts, traditions, and prescriptions begin to become secondary to every individual's inner ability to bring to birth their own higher moral ideals, and to find ways of making these socially applicable. But the flip side of this fresh capacity is new and more sophisticated kinds of destructive, morally decadent, antisocial instincts. The need for humanity to begin working consciously and progressively with its ego-forces becomes apparent if we are not to face one social crisis after another.

2. "Beavis and Butt-head" gives us an illustration of how, for their own part, many children and youths will react—and are reacting today—if they do

not find what they need from adult society. In other words, the souls that arrive here on Earth have great expectations, and if all they find is consumerism, materialism, and self-gratification, they will react negatively. The nihilism depicted in "Beavis and Butt-head" is one very obvious reaction. It provides us—and for this we should be grateful—with a clear picture of the abyss looming ahead if we do not, individually and collectively, take up spiritual ideas and find serious, practical ways of applying them to all we do. "Beavis and Butt-head" mirrors society's failings in this respect, showing the response of youth to the spiritual vacuum of modern culture.

The motivation in writing this chapter has not been a desire to express moral outrage at a commercial television entertainment program. In the final analysis, "Beavis and Butt-head" is not the problem. In any case, it is tame in terms of what is possible, and what is likely to come, if our culture does not change. Rather, my intention is to point to an important *symptom* from modern pop culture and to indicate what we can learn from it, and to show that what seems to be a threat can become a challenge posed to every conscious, striving person.

2.6 Between Nationalism and Federalism: Discovering the Meaning of Identity

There are times in a nation's history when it is challenged to its very core, when its identity, purpose, and meaning are brought into question. This happens most dramatically in times of war, when a nation has to decide whether its values are sufficiently threatened for lives to be put at risk. But in modern times, through the increasing consolidation of political life and the all-encompassing nature of the media, it has become easier to manipulate and exaggerate national feelings and, in effect, to create such a crisis situation, often to ill ends. The following is a story of how this was once achieved in connection with the sport of soccer.

To many people, sport is inconsequential. To others, however, it is much more than just a game. The English Liverpool soccer manager, Bill Shankley, famously opined that English football (soccer) was not a matter of life or death, but was "much more important than that." No doubt there was humor in his remark, but it also reflected a genuine passion experienced by many devotees for various types of sport. Such passion is not always healthy. In the face of defeat, and allied with national feeling, it has the potential to metamorphose into a tidal wave of rage. Many instances of this can be

cited, but a single moment in recent British sporting history epito-
mizes the tendency.

"Defining an Agenda"

It was the summer of 1996, and national pride for English sporting heroes was sweeping the country. It began with the Englishman
Tim Henman's commendable and surprising run in the Wimbledon
Tennis Championships. Originally an outsider, Henman caught the
attention of the nation by reaching the quarterfinals of the competition—a feat not achieved by an Englishman for many years. However,
the main focus of sporting attention was soon to turn to the English
soccer team's achievement in the Euro '96 tournament (a knock-out
competition for European teams).

In response to this rather rare national sporting success, the
English press went berserk with the type of jingoism not seen since the
1982 British-Argentinean conflict over the Falkland Islands. The long
media build-up to the tournament began with horror stories of the
potential violence that could occur between organized gangs of hooli-
gans. This was the first major international soccer competition to be
held in the United Kingdom for many years, and—with the British reputation for organized soccer violence—the fear of potential disturbance was great. The press took the stance of defending the nation's
standards, launching a moral crusade against the thugs who enjoy
fighting for the sake of it. But soon the self-righteous journalists were
to be inciting bad feeling and aggression themselves.

Once England had got past the early rounds of the tournament,
the content of many journalists' writing began to take on a xenophobic
quality, with the Dutch being the first targets of the tabloid press. This
initial haranguing of the northern Europeans was followed by the bait-
ing of the Spanish, who England met in the quarterfinals. However, the
treatment that these countries received from the media was mild compared with what was to follow. After all, the English don't bear much
animosity towards the Dutch, and the Spanish are generally tolerated

with mild, condescending amusement. The truly earnest "banter" was saved for Germany, who England met in the semifinals, and the *Sun* newspaper proudly led the way.

Although owned by Australian Rupert Murdoch, the *Sun* is a peculiarly English phenomenon. While there are parallels with other tabloid papers around the world, there is something unique about the lurid blend of sex, sport, national lottery stories, photos of bare-breasted women and ardent right-wing politics that comprises its cultural tone. With a readership of over ten million, it is Britain's best-selling newspaper, influencing more than a fifth of the electorate. Not surprisingly, the *Sun* is not displeased with its political influence. After the victory of the Conservative government in 1992, its front page boasted, in typical subliterate *Sun* style: "It Was The *Sun* Wot Won It." Likewise, its sometimes extreme patriotism is often roughly and crudely expressed. During the Falklands war it delighted in the killing of "Argies" (Argentineans), declaring "GOTCHA" in giant letters on its front page when the retreating Argentinean ship, the *Belgrano*, was sunk by the British with the loss of hundreds of lives.

This time the *Sun* headline shouted proudly: "Let's Blitz Fritz." But in the rush to whip up nationalistic feeling, it was being closely challenged by its rivals. Its editor Stuart Higgins even declared in a rather disingenuous statement to Channel 4 News: "*The Sun* has maintained a jingoistic approach, rather than a xenophobic one." He was alluding to his paper's chief competitor, the once proudly left-wing *Daily Mirror*, whose front-page "joke" featured photos of two of the England team players wearing World War Two helmets, and the declaration: "ACHTUNG! SURRENDER. For you Fritz, ze Euro '96 Championship is over. *The Mirror* declares soccer war against Germany." In the following pages of "coverage" its readers were treated to stories entitled "Filthy Hun" and "*The Mirror* Invades Germany."

Very soon, it became apparent that the "joke" was not very funny. Once England was beaten by Germany in the semifinals (after the game had gone to a penalty shoot-out), London's Trafalgar Square turned into a battleground with up to 2,000 English soccer fans fighting police, smashing car and shop windows, and causing general mayhem. Dozens of police officers and members of the public were injured. Violence also erupted in other parts of the country as England fans vented their fury at their team's defeat. Much of the violence was targeted: A German-owned supermarket was attacked in Shirley, while in Birmingham the window of a German car dealer was smashed. More seriously, in Hove a Russian student was stabbed five times after two youths asked him if he was German.

When German pupils on an exchange trip to London were taunted with Nazi salutes by classmates, the head of Islington Green school said that his pupils were reacting to anti-German sentiment in the press. Police commander John Purnell blamed xenophobic reports in some of the tabloid papers for the violence which took place after the game. And even former England soccer star Bobby Charlton stated: "I really wish they [the press] would think a little bit more before they put out all this print which creates hatred, which for 99 percent of the people is not there."[1] John Williams of the Centre for Soccer Research in Leicester added: "This is about defining an agenda, about setting a tone in which people watch the match."[2]

The Meaning of Nationhood

The Euro '96 semifinal was watched by a record British television audience for sport—26 million, almost half the population! Why do the British invest so much emotional energy in the success of their national soccer team? Interest and enjoyment of sport is understandable, but when this interest becomes a national obsession and a measure of a country's "greatness," then it is time for some serious questions to be asked. The violence which followed the defeat was, ultimately, only a further symptom which pointed to the core problem.

This particular instance of sour nationalism may well have had something to do with the residual effects of British colonial history— the fact that the international influence and power of its once-great world empire has now withered to so very little, to the extent that its people are reduced to looking to sport for major victories. Columnist Matthew Engel of the *Guardian* shrewdly observed that the Germans conceivably might forgive the British tabloids' their xenophobic slander and write it off as another manifestation of the British tragedy— ". . . the fact that we have achieved so little since 1945 and have to hark back [to the world wars of the last century] for solace."[3]

But nationalism is clearly not only a phenomenon based on fading power and glory. On September 11, 2001, the most powerful country in the world experienced attacks on its mainland. In the heated atmosphere which followed, national feeling was raised to fever-pitch level, and the Stars and Stripes were displayed everywhere. The Bush administration rushed through legislation sacrificing certain individual human rights, which under normal conditions would have raised an uproar. Talk of massive military retaliation was applauded by an overwhelming percentage of the population, with relatively few questions asked about the government's underlying strategy and goals.

All these phenomena lead to the fundamental question of what nationhood means today. Is the very concept of nationhood an arbitrary one, or is there some deeper meaning to it? After all, some would justifiably argue that the notion of the nation state is a very recent, nineteenth-century invention and has mostly caused nothing but disharmony and conflict. Is the existence of a nation justified by its ability to play soccer or tennis well? To defeat other countries in war? To outperform other countries economically? Or is nationhood simply based on good old-fashioned sentimentality and a *feeling* of unity with a particular group?

In studying what a nation is, one thing becomes apparent: it has very little to do with *race*. The best proof of this is the United States, which is made up of dozens of different ethnic groups. Each has fading memories, customs, and traditions of its land of origin, but increasingly these are overridden by the emerging homogenous culture of the new homeland. The "melting pot" may have been replaced by the "salad bowl," and serious tensions still exist—particularly between ethnic cliques—but nobody would deny that a general American national identity exists today. A brief look at the recent history of other nations indicates that they are also made up of different ethnic groups. The British, for example, are a mixture of the ancient Celts, Normans, Saxons, Vikings, and others. In recent years, the immigration into Britain of people with different-colored skin has provided a challenge to cultural assimilation, but there is good reason to believe that in time these groups will also be readily integrated into a general British culture. (South American countries offer a precedent for this.)

So if the racial or blood relationship is not paramount, what is it that binds a group of people together and gives them a common element? Is it really, as sometimes suggested by political leaders, the adherence to abstract philosophical concepts such as freedom, justice, democracy, or even capitalism?

One undisputed fact about nationhood is that it is related to land. Under British law a person is deemed to be British if they are born within the physical landmass of Britain. Although this concept does not apply in all national situations—Germany, for example—in general terms people are believed to belong to a certain nation if they have been born, or perhaps have lived most of their life, on its soil. For example, African Americans who visit Africa soon realize that the locals view them primarily as American. Likewise, Asians born in Britain have characteristics which betray their Britishness when they visit their ancestors' country of origin.

So what is the mysterious element inherent in nationhood? Modern sociologists argue the cultural aspect connected with nationhood is simply learned behavior acquired as a result of "nurture." But such arguments do not explain how so many different languages, cultures, and traditions have come to be on Earth. Ancient spiritual teachings add a mystical element to the interpretation of how different cultures have developed. Tribal civilizations, for example, have their manifold gods who, these cultures believe, care for and nurture them. The ancient Hebrews spoke of their god as the one Jehovah, and distinguished him from other heathen gods. Other teachings speak of "folk souls" or angelic beings, spiritual entities that guide and nurture the different peoples. Under the leadership of such beings, the different nations of the Earth have been given various tasks and duties to develop the manifold qualities of human nature, which are eventually to come together in harmony to create a whole and unified humanity.

Britain and Europe

In terms of culture and nationhood, Europe is perhaps one of the most diverse and culturally rich continents. Within short distances exist, side by side, peoples who although in many ways are similar have profoundly different characters. One only has to travel through Europe, from north to south, west to east, to experience how culturally diverse these different peoples are. In the northern countries, for example, a more tranquil, inner quality is evident among the people, whereas in the south a more extroverted, expressive character is encountered. Likewise the variations between the people of the West (Britain) and the East (Russia) are huge. To the unprejudiced observer, it is evident that these different peoples have varying qualities of soul. This is not to imply that any nation is better or worse, or higher or lower—but certainly they are different.

When these characteristics are cultivated side by side, they can, as in Europe, create a beautiful complementary whole, a mosaic of distinct but mutually sustaining qualities. It could be argued that each country is developing different aspects of our *archetypal* human nature. Nationalism does not encourage such harmonious development, of course, but pits one nation against another in a vulgar competition for superiority. Following the two world wars of the last century, Europe has had plenty of experience as to how the differences between nations can be exploited by cynical and destructive forces which have the aim of dragging humanity into an abyss. A specific instance of how the malign forces of nationalism can be stimulated was given in the first part of this chapter. Ultimately, these forces seek to isolate, alienate, and spread hatred against "otherness."

It is a strange phenomenon of human existence that, in situations where such harmful forces are at work, the opposite tendency is also usually apparent. An example of such a circumstance was given in chapter 1.5, where it was shown that twentieth-century Communism sought to drag humanity forward to a goal which could only be properly reached in future times, whereas Nazism pulled people back to an outmoded principle from the distant past. In situations where such opposite tendencies are apparent, it is a natural human trait to want to perceive the one side as simply "good" and the other as "bad." Indeed, it is tempting to think in polarized terms. In reality, as I showed in chapter 1.5, the progressive forces often reveal themselves in the balance of two extremes; i.e., the true "good" is often to be found in the balance of the scales.

Given this principle, it is no surprise that while the forces of nationalism are actively seeking to separate the British from their European neighbors with a wall of hatred, other forces are actively striving to *bind* the British people into a confederation of states which is premature and overprescriptive. The concept of a union of European states—a "United States of Europe"—came about after World War Two. Since then, a caucus of political forces has worked consistently to create a structured European vision. What began initially as an economic alliance metamorphosed into an economic union, and is now working towards a full political, cultural, and economic federation.

A true antidote to the nationalism described above would be a *cooperation* of spiritually developing nations choosing to turn their backs on old hatreds and uniting out of free will. A true and firm union of the various European peoples could only arise out of a voluntary and conscious striving. Regrettably, it would appear that the federal Europe agreed upon at the conference of Maastricht in Holland in 1992 is something of a parody of this archetype. The reality is, rather, a federation planned and executed by small groups of politicians, directed by an unelected commission, and created with little conscious involvement, knowledge, or will of the vast mass of ordinary Europeans. The Treaty on European Union allows for a single European currency, common citizenship, a common foreign and security policy, a more effective European parliament, and a common labor policy.

Virtually none of the British people who voted in a referendum in the 1970s for the European Economic Community had any inkling that they were, in effect, voting for an eventual economic, political, and cultural union of European nations. And yet, within a couple of decades, this economic free trade zone metamorphosed twice, initially to the "European Community" and then to the "European Union." As part of this binding alliance, the introduction of monetary union and a common currency (the Euro) has already taken place at the end of the millennium as scheduled. (Britain, though, has yet to participate in this aspect of the project, although it has committed in principle to do so.) If true unity can only come about through free will, the result of the "forced marriage" of the EU can only lead to a crisis in the future, when the partners finally become aware of the constricting mold that has been created around them.

The English people find themselves caught between this bizarre juxtaposition of coercive energies. From the one side, patriotism excites retrogressive passions and emotions, while from the other direction comes pressure—with seeming "inevitability"—to be part of a coldly calculated federal superstate with pretensions of brotherhood and unity.

Given what many perceive as Britain's subservient gesture to the United States, the European Union appears to offer an attractive alternative to those who don't see an Atlantic alliance/"special relationship" as being in Britain's interest. Whatever the truth about the Anglo-American alliance, the plans for a *federal* Europe do not offer a useful alternative. In the final analysis, both paths—nationalism and federalism—are extremes and unworkable. Only a true middle way can offer lasting peace and security: a free spiritual union of European nations, and beyond that a cooperating family of nations, working together out of a common knowledge, understanding, respect, and love for our different qualities and collective tasks.

As I have suggested, nationhood is more than an abstract notion. Beyond the subjective and often self-seeking forces of everyday politics, territorial ambition, and nationalism, it is possible to envision each group of peoples—or to use the more ancient term "folk"—as encompassing a spiritual reality with a corresponding spiritual entity at its helm. According to esoteric Christian tradition (in which such entities are called Archangels) the various nations find their purpose and task through the spiritual being which leads and inspires them. So long as nations and peoples are seen simply as territory or fodder for geostrategic chess-playing or imperialistic control, or even pieces in a federal jigsaw-puzzle superstate, it is unlikely that peace will ever become a reality.

I suspect that mutual respect and cooperation between nations will only come about once a new picture of the world emerges. To complement the wonderful image of the blue planet seen in photographs taken from outer space, maybe one day we will visualize the globe surrounded by the various spiritual entities seeking to guide the nations of the world.

2.7 The Priest, the Nun, and the Soccer Coach: Reading the Signs of the Times

Occasionally, there are short items in the news that are particularly eye-catching. They are seemingly insignificant, and become "stories" for the media only because of their unusual nature. But if seen for what they truly are, these little episodes are often highly consequential. The following three short items are examples. Although they are all true stories, the actual details of when and where they occurred are not so important. What is significant is that they are signs of the changing times in which we live, signs of a society coming to terms with its evolving consciousness.

What I demonstrate here is that it is possible to gain deeper perspectives which are generally ignored by mainstream media. Such perspectives are not always immediately apparent. They require a new way of looking at the world. Despite the countless sources of news available to us today, the interpretations given by the media are surprisingly one-dimensional and predictable. On reaching adulthood, each of us has absorbed, whether consciously or not, thousands of news stories via television, radio, newspapers, etc. Through the way these stories are presented, we are indoctrinated in how to approach and understand the world around us. And so (as we will see below) a priest who doesn't believe in God is a light-hearted, comic item at which we are supposed to snigger. But perhaps such a phenomenon can teach us something else. Likewise, to the media, a soccer coach who speaks of reincarnation and karma is politically incorrect and probably mad. But what can we learn by studying such a story? Is it possible to transcend a straightforward materialistic interpretation?

1. The Priest Who Didn't Believe in God

Anthony Freeman, the priest in charge of a picturesque church in the small village of Staplefield in Sussex, England, was sacked from his position by the Bishop of Chichester for "not believing in God." Not unreasonable, you might think, given his job description. A year previously the renegade priest had lost his position as director of postordination training, following the publication of his book, *God in Us*. The further dismissal caused a letter of protest to be written by 65 Church of England clerics to the *Independent* newspaper. Only some of the correspondents shared Freeman's views, but, in the grand liberal tradition of the Anglican church, all defended his right to freedom of expression.

In his own words, Anthony Freeman stands for "a new, bracing beliefless Christianity." In his book he declares: "There is nothing out there—or if there is, we can have no knowledge of it." In an interview published in his parish magazine, however, he took a slightly different tack when asked if he believed in God. "Yes," he replied, "and to work out what that means is my life's work." He elaborated further on an ITN television news report, saying: "I believe that when we use the word God we are using it to focus all that's best and highest in our own human hopes and aspirations and ideas."[1] He clarifies this further in his book. God is not an invisible person "out there," but lives in the human heart and mind as "the sum of all our values and ideals."[2]

As witnessed by the above quotations, the truth of this strange story has philosophical subtleties which were ignored or trivialized by the popular press. Further, as the letter by the 65 clergymen to the *Independent* demonstrated, Freeman by no means stands alone in his views. On the contrary, he represents a school of thought within the Church of England, and Christianity as a whole, which seeks to intertwine a humanist philosophy (i.e., a benevolent agnosticism that teaches that people should love one another, etc.) with a materialistic interpretation of the Gospels and Christianity. (The new edition of Freeman's book is subtitled *A Case for Christian Humanism*.)

Such a philosophy usually reveres Jesus the man as a great teacher of social values and an example of right living, but generally dismisses the cosmic or spiritual aspect of Christianity. In holding such views, Freeman and his fellow "disbelievers" personify a materialistic stream of thought within theology which is by no means unique or new. (A contemporary example of such theology is in Don Cupitt's book *Taking Leave from God*; but the tendency can be traced back to the foundation of the Jesuit order, whose teachings centered on "Jesus" as opposed to "Christ.")

Despite all this, it is nevertheless somewhat surprising that a *priest* should publicly represent such opinions, particularly as in Church tradition the priest is regarded as being the mediator between man and a *spiritual* God. From this perspective, the actions of the Church authorities in the case of Staplefield's extraordinary priest were understandable, despite the fact that such a dramatic dismissal was unprecedented in recent times.

Defending his decision, the Bishop of Chichester was forthright about the extent to which internal debate of this kind could be accepted within the Church, stating: "The whole thing is ridiculous, there must be some limits to what the Church of England will tolerate if it is going to stand for anything at all." But not all the people of Staplefield agreed with him. Interviewed in the *Independent*, a 19-year-old girl exclaimed: "[Freeman] is more in touch with what people think than the bishops are. They're all hypocrites and they were wrong to sack him. He's just being brave enough to ask the questions we all ask." A 49-year-old woman added: "He tries to preach how he feels, and he doesn't believe in the resurrection or the virgin birth. He is a good priest and we want him to stay."[3]

From a spiritual standpoint, there are many ways to approach a story like this. Perhaps the most obvious observation to make is that, given the context of the widespread materialism of our times, episodes of this kind are to be expected. But it would be simplistic to dismiss Freeman for his lack of concepts regarding spiritual dimensions. Of course, one can draw the conclusion that events such as these indicate the need, perhaps more than ever before, for a clear, knowledge-based, spirituality. It could also be noted that Freeman's statement "that we can have no knowledge of it [the spiritual world]" is in direct contradiction to the many achievements of those spiritual researchers who have pioneered conscious methods of clairvoyance, or to the thousands of people who have had near-death experiences, the millions who have experienced angels and other metaphysical entities, and so on. But these perspectives are somewhat predictable responses, and on their own do not provide a full picture.

The case of Anthony Freeman takes on a far greater value if seen from an altogether different point of view. Freeman's inner struggle to understand Christianity provides an image of the individual soul—the personal conscience—in its search for knowledge based on direct experience. In his struggle to come to a spirituality which he can understand, as opposed to one he can only believe in, Freeman represents the contemporary person who needs to discover, experience, and *know*. Opposed to this personal exploration stand the established spiritual forms of the past—as portrayed in this instance by the Church—with their dogmas, creeds, and certainties.

Whereas once the priest stood before the altar as an initiate, guiding his flock to an experience of spiritual mysteries, today that role has become largely symbolic. Experienced truths have become creeds, living teachings have become dogmas, and stages of development have become hierarchy. Realizing the inner contradiction of his position, Freeman sought to base his ministry on what he felt he knew. His fight for individual truth may have led him—at that time[4]—to materially bound conclusions, away from an acknowledgement of the spiritual world in all its multifaceted reality, but the process of his personal quest for knowledge is one we can respect deeply as modern human beings—for we recognize within it the striving of the conscious soul.

As his parishioner said, "He's just brave enough to ask the questions we all ask."

2. The Nun and the Comet

As the last fragments of the comet Shoemaker-Levy 9 crashed into the planet Jupiter in July 1994, the London-based Catholic nun, prophetess, and self-styled astronomer Sofia Richmond must have experienced ambivalent feelings. Richmond, who is also known as Sister Marie Gabriel and Sophie Segatis Paprocki Orvid Puciato (she claims descent from Polish aristocracy), had placed a large advertisement in the national English newspaper the *Guardian* a year earlier, in which she warned the world that a "huge cosmic event is due soon, namely the great cosmic explosion of a giant comet in our solar system." According to press reports, Shoemaker-Levy 9 was first discovered by three American astronomers on 24 March 1993. In her announcement, however, Sofia Richmond claimed that she had published a "cosmic forecast seven years ago on 4 July 1986 in all the northwest London press newspapers that a huge cosmic event is due soon."

Following her first notice, Richmond placed several more expensive advertisements in national newspapers in which she gave dramatic warnings to humanity. When the comet hit Jupiter, she stated, it would be a "cosmic day of judgement for all mankind . . . a warning ultimatum from almighty God. . . . Each person will see their life judged by God . . . and each individual will see all the evil they have committed." Various famous celebrities would experience conversions to Christianity, including the American pop star Madonna. Richmond also maintained that the comet was a broken-off fragment of Haley's Comet with a tail which could "grow up to 100 million miles long," and that Jupiter "could look like a second sun in the heavens." In the small print on one of her announcements were the ominous words: "People who persecuted Sister Marie or who ridiculed God's message will suffer direct and instant retribution from God on the day of the cosmic blast."

Richmond's admonitions included the following advice: "Adults and children should wear dark glasses for safety between 15–20 July. . . . It would be advisable to stay in cold cellars or basements to avoid any heatwave. . . . Keep curtains drawn and turn on air conditioning. . . . Buy food for 5 days and keep pets indoors. . . . Don't drive cars, lorries, buses, or trains in case comet/Jupiter affects traffic."

The most interesting part of Richmond's peculiar notices were the "commandments"—supposedly given by God to mankind through her—which, according to her pronouncements, should be adhered to if disaster from the comet was to be averted. In this "warning ultimatum from God to all governments" are included the demands to: "Reduce crime as in Saudi Arabia. . . . Ban all indecency, obscenity, immodesty in public or in films, videos, or television. . . . Replace beers and wines with non-alcoholic drinks to reduce crime. . . . Teach all school children moral laws and the Ten Commandments. . . . Women must obey strict modesty laws in public to reduce sex crimes. . . . All serious crimes to be punished by draconian deterrents." One of the more bizarre commands was that people should "become pure innocent angelic saints overnight."

Sofia Richmond also predicted that: "The warning explosion of the comet will herald a royal *coup d'etat* and a royal revolution in England." In her self-published book *Supernatural Visions of the Madonna 1981/1991* (1993), this prophecy is presented as the solution to the United Kingdom's social, political, and religious problems.

Following the physical collision between Jupiter and the comet, it became clear that the warnings and readings of Sofia Richmond were not accurate. Further, her claim to have forecast the collision in advance of the American astronomers remains questionable. So where did Richmond receive her information? The reclusive Catholic nun, who lives a contemplative solitary life in north London, claims to have regular contacts with the Virgin Mary. Her communications with the Madonna have purportedly been regular since a visit at Lourdes in

1962 when Richmond was told that she would take on the mission of St. Bernadette. Over the past ten years the Virgin Mary has allegedly appeared to Richmond six times. "The Holy spirit gives enlightenment. It is an inspirational flash of light. You have the absolute conviction."[5]

What lies behind Sofia Richmond's "inspirational" flashes? The most revealing part of her teaching, and the aspect which offers most clues to the answer, is to be found in her "warning ultimatum from God," which Richmond gives as a solution to society's social problems. This "ultimatum," which relies, in her own words, on "draconian punishments," seeks to force humans to live an "ordered" and "good" life through outward political and religious repression. Such regimens are not unknown to humanity in recent times. Perhaps the most similar such state was that of the fundamentalist Taliban in Afghanistan, which also sought to make the human being "good" through draconian measures. Whether done under the name of Islam or Christianity is irrelevant; the end result of outer repression and coercion was the same as Richmond's bitter pill.

Although such regimens may be effective in achieving their goals in the short term, in the longer term they provide no real solutions for the problems encountered in humanity's evolution. They betray a degenerate impulse which arises from a thinking more in tune with the medieval stage of humanity's development. This thinking works on the assumption that the human needs to be controlled and redeemed through *outer* means. Such an approach is, in modern times, directly opposed to the development of the awake, *inner* conscious soul which acts out of freedom and love.

Given the complex, pluralistic social context of our millennial culture, it is perhaps not surprising that some people should respond to urgent social questions with outmoded and backward-looking answers. It is somewhat alarming, however, that such a call—it so blatantly harks back to past social forms in which religion controls not only politics but culture, economics, and all aspects of social life—should come in the name of Christianity. After all, Christ's only social law was that we should love our neighbor as ourselves.

3. Karma and the Soccer Coach

As unlikely as it may sound, the coach of the English national soccer team was sacked from his job because of personal beliefs connected with the teaching of reincarnation and karma. It all started when the hapless manager, Glenn Hoddle, spoke to a sports journalist of the *Times* newspaper. Towards the end of the 25-minute telephone interview, the journalist steered the conversation away from soccer and towards Hoddle's spiritual views, perhaps hoping for some choice quotes. Hoddle, innocently believing these questions to be of intimate concern to the journalist Matt Dickinson, was happy to oblige, and discussed his convictions relating to the laws of reincarnation:

> My beliefs have evolved in the last eight or nine years, that the spirit has to come back again. That is nothing new, that has been around for thousands of years. You have to come back to learn and face some of the things you have done, good and bad. There are too many injustices around. You and I have been given two hands and two legs and half-decent brains. Some people have not been born like that for a reason. The karma is working from another lifetime. I have nothing to hide about that. It is not only people with disabilities. What you sow you have to reap. You have to look at things that happened in your life and ask why. It comes around.[6]

Realizing that this could be turned into a sensational news story, the sports editor of the *Times* brought the piece to the attention of the chief editor of the paper, who promptly placed it on the front page of the main section of the newspaper. The interview, which first appeared in the Saturday edition, created a storm. By Monday, it seemed that almost everybody was calling for Hoddle to be fired from his job: sportswriters, mainstream journalists, political and social commentators, even top politicians, all seemed to be in firm agreement that he should lose his position. David Mellor, the Chairman of the Football

Task Force, wrote that Hoddle should "clean out his head or clear out his locker." Rock star and polio sufferer Ian Dury was reported as saying: "I can't stand him and I hope he goes." A 13-year-old, one-legged boy, featured on the front page of the *Sun* newspaper, said of Hoddle's comments: "It was so hurtful. I feel very sad." Many of the tabloid newspapers took the opportunity to interview people afflicted with disabilities, and to survey their views on the story.

From the side of the government, the Minister for the Disabled, Margaret Hodge, said that it was "inappropriate" for Hoddle to stay as the England coach; the Culture Secretary, Chris Smith, said the whole affair was "deeply regrettable"; while the Sports Minister, Tony Banks, asserted that Hoddle had caused "enormous offence." Remarkably, even the Prime Minister, Tony Blair, intervened, stating that: "If he said what he is reported to have said . . . I think that was very wrong." He added that it would be "very difficult" for Hoddle to stay in his job.

The following day, Hoddle tried—in vain—to put the record straight. In an exclusive interview in the *Mirror* he said:

> Certainly, I do not believe disabled people deserve what they get. But I am seeking some reason for their suffering, as I am sure many disabled people do for themselves . . . I will continue to be a Christian in my views, but to look at other theories and ideas which may put a new light on issues like poverty, abuse, and handicap. But I will not judge anyone. I will simply offer them my support and sympathy—and if that is a crime then so be it. . . . I let my guard down and was drawn into a conversation about reincarnation. I made some comments but they have been totally distorted. The person who interviewed me brought up the subject of the disabled; it was his words he wanted me to agree to.

The *Mirror* also revealed Hoddle's long record of charitable work for the disabled. But other newspapers were far less sympathetic. They reported with glee a press conference Hoddle had given on the Monday when, under the pressure of multiple questions and interrogation, he had been less than articulate.

Hoddle spent his entire career in English soccer. Born into an ordinary working-class family, he signed as an apprentice with Tottenham Hotspur Football club at the tender age of 16. Over a career spanning more than 40 years, he worked his way up to the most challenging position within the sport—manager of the national team. Given the often unrealistic and distorted expectations of an ex-colonial people for its soccer team, Hoddle's record as England coach was actually quite good. In fact, his performance compared well with the recently departed— and generally short-lived—incumbents in the job. (The top post in English soccer is famously something of a poison chalice.) In 1998 he took England to the second round of the World Cup finals, in which they battled hard and were unlucky to lose ultimately to old rivals Argentina.

But by Tuesday afternoon all this had been forgotten. The press wanted Hoddle's head on a plate, and were getting impatient. Eventually, the Football Association—employers of the England coach—bowed to the inevitable, unable to withstand pressure from the media, commentators, pundits, and politicians. They sacked Glenn Hoddle for what they called a "serious error of judgment."

The media was triumphant, and virtually no internal voices of dissent were heard. During the ruckus, the Labour peer Lord Ashley had been almost alone in defending the besieged coach, stating: "We need to keep a sense of proportion. He is entitled to express his religious opinions." In the aftermath, soccer player Les Ferdinand reflected: "For someone to be sacked for their beliefs, I'm not sure if that's right."

In the more highbrow press, some alert readers had a similar view of the whole mad charade. In the *Guardian* newspaper, a letter-writer opined: "Hoddle's beliefs may be distasteful to many but it is not possible to establish whether or not they reflect reality. So is not the Hoddle witchhunt a clear example of politically correct bigotry?"[7] In the same context, a Professor of Buddhist Studies pointed out that: "Congenital disabilities can only be viewed in one of a small range of ways: as meaningless facts, arising due to purely natural events; due to the 'will of God'; or as a consequence of actions in a past life. I do not see the last as in any way 'worse' than the others. The Buddhist version is that a disability is an unfortunate natural result of an unwholesome action carried out by an earlier form of the person concerned. It is not seen as a 'punishment' for a past 'sin,' and should not elicit guilt or blame."[8]

Given that the doctrine of karma is accepted by millions around the world and is part of an ancient and respected religious system, what was Hoddle's "serious error of judgment"? Why had the whole nation become so embroiled in an esoteric question more likely to concern theologians than soccer enthusiasts?

Within a few days of making a statement of personal belief in what he naively believed to have been a private conversation with a journalist—a statement which had not been intended to cause offense to anyone—Glenn Hoddle had been fired from his job. Was this an insidious example of the loss of freedom of speech in a once highly tolerant society? Or was it the worst hypocrisy of a culture which feels guilt about its attitude to disabled people? After all, the same society which purported to feel such outrage at Hoddle's theoretical comments supports and finances a medical system which systematically seeks to scan fetuses in the womb for "congenital diseases" (read "disabilities") and, in cases where such irregularities are discovered, puts strong pressure on the prospective parents to have the pregnancy aborted. Why is this done? Presumably because of the financial and other perceived "burdens" such a "disabled" life might create for the individuals concerned and society as a whole. Do such actions indicate a true valuing of disabled people?

Whether Hoddle's particular interpretation of the laws of karma is valid, however, is another question, and open to intelligent debate. When Jesus Christ was asked by his disciples whether a particular man had been born blind because of his own sin or because of the sins of his parents, Christ answered that neither was the case, but "that the works of God should be made manifest in him."[9]

As has been pointed out by exponents of reincarnation, the disciples' question implied a belief in that doctrine. Christ did not discount their assumption, but offered a different interpretation of the situation. His somewhat mysterious answer suggests that the suffering the blind man experienced as a result of his disability was not a "punishment." Rather, it was a preparation for something else in the future, a strengthening of the soul for a glorification to follow, possibly in a future life. Christ's words could therefore be understood to mean that the blind man was inwardly preparing for a future mission, for which his present life was a critical precursor.

But regardless of whether we agree with Hoddle's views or not, there is no question that he should have been entitled to express them—providing, of course, that he was not deliberately inciting hatred or violence (which he clearly was not). Furthermore, his personal views should have had no bearing on his employment situation. Otherwise, what is the meaning of the free speech which we value so highly in Western society?

It is apparent that Hoddle's persecutors were not interested in theological subtleties or spiritual debate. What they demonstrated was the self-righteous, politically correct, and intolerant certainty of the closed-minded, who seek to impose their narrow opinions on others.

Conclusion

We have reviewed three short news stories and seen how deeper perspectives can be revealed through study. In each case, it seems to me, spiritual aspects are right there below the surface. The observer only needs to ponder on these stories for such aspects to reveal themselves. In the case of the priest who didn't believe in God, we were able to see an individual struggling to come to a personal knowledge of truth. He was no longer prepared simply to believe, or to be told what is true and what is not. This is what we would expect from a contemporary person, given humanity's evolving consciousness. Of course the media—who have no interest in concepts of spiritual development—saw the whole thing simply as a joke.

With the nun Sofia Richmond and her dramatically inaccurate predictions, we were able to see beyond what again appeared to be a rather superficially comic news story: a cranky nun who believes she is inspired by the Holy Spirit and can tell the future. Studying her new commandments, it is evident that she was seeking a form of society which belongs to humanity's historical and spiritual past. Her medieval picture of a "good" society is abhorrent to most people of today who—again according to humanity's evolving consciousness—would prefer to find their way forward in freedom.

And finally we saw the brave soccer coach who expressed his views on reincarnation and was then courageous enough to stand by them and try to explain them. But a materialistic society, which actually shows greater inhumanity to the unborn than could be expressed in Hoddle's honest convictions, demonstrated a one-dimensional, self-righteous, and hypocritical attitude. In the end, our apparently tolerant, pluralistic society (which supposedly loves freedom of speech) could not allow his voice to be heard. This story raises the question of what real freedom of speech (and thought!) actually mean.

These examples aim to demonstrate how the reading of simple, everyday stories can reveal spiritual truths. The insights gained do not need to be particularly profound. What is important is that we begin practicing and sharpening our faculties of perception. We can only do this, it seems to me, if we take spirit seriously and understand how it works in the world around us.

2.8 Evil and Freedom: A Perspective on the Case of Mary Bell

With great satisfaction, the *Sun* newspaper in 1998 announced to its readers that it had discovered the whereabouts of a 41-year-old female ex-convict—despite a court order protecting her identity and location. The middle-aged woman had been released from prison 18 years earlier after serving 12 years for murder. Her identity and location had been kept secret in order to protect her daughter's life from press intrusion. "We Find Mary Bell, Killer's Seaside Hideout" screamed the *Sun*'s headline, and the story revealed that she lived in a resort in the south of England, in a cottage one mile from the sea, with an unmarried partner and a 14-year-old daughter.[1] Despite the court injunction expressly forbidding the publication of her daughter's name, and a journalistic code of practice which is explicit in protecting innocent children, the paper's actions were sufficient for the young girl's identity to be revealed. Very soon, the rest of the national press had caught on to the *Sun*'s exclusive, and Bell's house was besieged by journalists and photographers. As a result of this investigative scoop, the family—fearful of lynch mobs—was taken into police custody.

In 1968, 30 years before these events, the name of Mary Bell was notorious in the United Kingdom. The young Mary, a child-killer, was popularly reviled. Not only was Bell herself a child, aged 11, when she committed murder, but her victims were two young boys, aged three and four respectively. At the time, the case had received much attention due to the horrific and troubling nature of the crimes. They were as inexplicable as they were terrible. Why should a girl of 11 kill two young children? Bell was given a life sentence, but released at the age of 23, no longer considered dangerous.

The more recent uproar in April 1998 began with the disclosure that Bell had cooperated with the respected author and journalist Gitta Sereny in the writing of a book, *Cries Unheard*. Sereny's study was a serious attempt to understand Bell's crimes through a detailed examination of her life. The book was based on six months' worth of interviews with Bell. Outrage was expressed by many, including Prime Minister Tony Blair, over the fact that Sereny chose to share some of the advance payment from her publisher, Macmillan, with Bell. In interviews, Sereny expressed the view that had she not done this, she would have been guilty of "doing [to Mary Bell] what was done to her virtually since she was born: to *use* her."

Here, Sereny was alluding to the awful early years of Bell's life, which she revealed in full for the first time in *Cries Unheard*. Sereny catalogued the emotional and physical battering and sustained sexual abuse which, according to Bell's own account, characterized her childhood. Bell's mother was a prostitute specializing in sadomasochism. From babyhood, the young Mary was forced to watch her mother beat clients and made to participate in oral sex. The presence of an innocent child in these activities was evidently sought by her mother's clients, increasing her fees. Her stepfather, a petty criminal, did not intervene, and neither did any other member of her family.

"Understanding" versus "Condemnation"

The sincere attempt by Sereny to comprehend why a child should kill another child was not appreciated by the British tabloid press. Upon hearing of the book's publication, editors and journalists immediately began to reawaken old animosities and incite new hatred towards Bell. Perhaps the cruelest effect of their actions was the fact that Bell's daughter, who had been raised in ignorance of her mother's criminal history, was forced to learn of her mother's true identity in the middle of the night, while their house was barricaded by journalists. (Bell had apparently been planning to tell her the full truth when she was 18.)

Despite the inhumane results of this dubious "journalism," the tabloids have been unrepentant. The justification for their self-righteous wrath is that Bell is an "evil child-killer" and therefore forever deserves society's contempt. The fact that she committed her crimes thirty years ago and is now a middle-aged mother who appears to be reformed, did not seem to be of any consequence. In contrast to the hysterical tabloids, the sober and intelligent writer Gitta Sereny—a woman who has received much praise for her penetrating studies of the Nazis Albert Speer and Franz Stangl—has appeared as the voice of reason and calm. Hers is a struggle to *understand*.

She wrote to the mother of one of Mary Bell's victims: "There had to be a *reason* for the awful pain she caused." The tabloids stuck to the opposite view, deriding Sereny's attempts at comprehension. "Understand what made Mary Bell kill?" the *Daily Express* scoffed in its editorial. Its conclusion was that an understanding was neither possible nor desirable. The tabloid press's explanation of the riddle was unanimous. The answer was plain and simple: Mary Bell killed because she was evil.

A Killer Because She Is Evil?

Before returning to the views of Gitta Sereny and others who seek to *understand* Mary Bell's crimes, it is useful to consider the modern, popular use of the word "evil" in this context. There are philosophical issues here which need to be addressed in order for deeper aspects of this case to be comprehended. These issues involve age-old questions regarding the nature of evil and its causes. For many years the tabloid press has conducted sustained hate campaigns against individuals who have been responsible for terrible murders. The implication of this attitude, along with the repeated use of the word "evil," is that these people committed their crimes out of a conscious knowledge of their deeds and a desire to be wicked. This is the only logical conclusion one can draw from the press coverage.

After all, if these murderers were simply born evil due to their genetic makeup or some other reason, they could not be blamed or held personally responsible for their deeds. It would, effectively, be something they were predetermined to do and therefore would not be able to help. Likewise, if they had acted in an evil way solely as a result of their environment and upbringing, again they could not be held fully responsible for their actions. They would merely be products of the society into which they were born, and hence society as a whole would be to blame.

So if we are to hate violent criminals—as the tabloids clearly wish us to—and hold them fully responsible for their actions, then we must assume that they committed their crimes in freedom and with knowledge and understanding.

It is crucial that there is clarity over this question, as in essence this is the rationale which for decades provided the philosophical basis for the criminal justice system in the United States, United Kingdom, and many other countries. The government of Margaret Thatcher, taking its cue from the U.S., based its policy of *punishment* of crime—as opposed to *reform* and rehabilitation—on this thinking. Why does society send people to prison at such great expense and inconvenience? Is it in order to satisfy a primal urge for revenge and to mete out a painful penalty, or is it to try and bring about a change in that person so that they will not commit further crimes when they are released? There is good reason to believe that politicians have systematically sponsored the former approach in order to gain popularity with an electorate that appears to like the "punishment" alternative. And yet it is well known that prison and punishment on their own—i.e., without programs for reform and rehabilitation—are simply "universities of crime," and lead to the creation of lifelong criminals.

Since the early 1970s, following the publication of an influential U.S. study,[2] prison regimes on both sides of the Atlantic became more brutal, and political efforts were made to extend sentences. Although in recent years thinking and practice within the UK has quietly begun to change towards reform, the philosophy of punishment has dictated prison methodology for some 30 years.

The logical conclusion to that line of thought about punishment is *capital punishment,* when it is considered that the criminal is utterly irredeemable, and must pay with his or her life. In contrast, proponents of reform believe that through education and example a criminal can be completely rehabilitated as a useful and responsible member of society.

Evil and Freedom

So is a murderer "free" when committing a crime? If they act freely, then the present "justice" system with its emphasis on punishment could be shown to be appropriate. But if they are not free, i.e., if we accept that they might have come under the influence of other agencies, metaphysical or otherwise, then surely that individual is in need of help. They are, literally, not themselves, i.e., not fully and truly *human* at the moment they commit a criminal act. From that point of view, reform makes much more sense, as the person can be seen to need guidance and support in order to be healed, and eventually reabsorbed into society.

At the heart of this dilemma is a problem of philosophy. The popular definition of "freedom" is that we have the possibility of choosing between good and evil, i.e., I am "free" to kill that person or not to. A contrasting philosophical standpoint is that an individual is *not* free simply as a function of having choice. Rather, we attain a state of freedom when we act out of our *true* and *whole* humanity. In other words, true freedom is a lofty goal for each individual to aspire to, to act out of our higher selves, our spiritual ego. According to this thinking, we are only fully human when we act out of this higher ego. This state of being is something which can only be achieved through conscious, dedicated work, and for the majority of us that is a distant goal.

Following this rationale, it follows that a murderer or child-killer is so far from acting out of their true humanity that they are, in fact, profoundly sick. In spiritual terms, their ego has been subverted to such an extent that *other forces* are able to enter in and inspire inhuman deeds. In cases like this, then, it is futile to think in terms of crude punishment. Such a person needs help to become whole, and to find their true humanity.

In the case of Mary Bell it is patently clear that she was not "free" in committing her murderous actions. Not only in that sense, but also, as an 11-year-old child, she had not yet matured sufficiently for it to be said that she could act with knowledge and clear intention. While in a superficial sense she may have been aware of "right and wrong," as a child her inner consciousness would not have individualized sufficiently for her to be fully in control of all her deeds. Thus, most criminal justice systems retain an inherent wisdom that does not allow minors to be sent to jail or executed.

Nature versus Nurture

Popular psychology and social science use two methods of interpretation in analyzing crimes such as those committed by Mary Bell. These two approaches form a polarity, characterized by the age-old argument of nature versus nurture. The essential question is this: What forms the human being? Is it inherent in the sense of biology and genetics and/or the person's soul or spiritual nature, or is it environment and upbringing?

In other words, are humans somehow naturally disposed to evil, or do factors experienced through earthly life incline us towards evil? The former view suggests that our nature is somehow predestined, a view in line with modern scientific theories that we are determined by our genes, or that we are affected through the agency of supernatural forming forces and influences. The other perspective suggests that we are simply products of our environment in the sense that we are formed by our cultural surroundings, social position, or family. These theoretical positions have political overtones in that the "nature" argument is generally seen as the conservative, establishment one, while "nurture" is considered the sociological, liberal view.

Towards a Fuller Picture of the Human

If anything, the case of Mary Bell allows us to see beyond the polarized simplicities of the nature/nurture analysis, as both in themselves are inadequate for understanding the wonder and complexity of human existence. Sereny's book advises that Bell had a desperately tragic, abused, and deprived childhood, which might seem to prove the "nurture" argument. But the flaw in this thinking is the implication that her social conditions were somehow deterministic. We cannot assume that a deprived (or depraved) upbringing will of necessity lead to criminality of the type perpetrated by Mary Bell as a child. While it may well be possible to detect certain patterns of behavior in people who are sexually abused as children, the fact is that only a tiny fraction of them will become murderers.

Why is it that one person will react to a set of circumstances in one way, while another person will react to the same circumstances in quite another way? The existence of an individual, human soul/spirit nature would explain why people will behave and respond differently in similar situations. For example, within a single family children will grow up with unique and often contrasting natures, despite the fact that they experience a similar socioeconomic and cultural setting. Given a common set of influences, one child will grow up to love painting and baseball, while another will be a devoted mathematician and chef; one will be academic, and another artistic, and so on. Likewise, it by no means follows that sexual, physical, and emotional abuse will lead a person to perpetrate criminal acts. This is not to pass judgment on Mary Bell, but merely to make the point that nurture is not the only factor in forming a person's character.

In contrast, if nature is seen as a sole determining factor in the formation of the human character, then an individual's personal life situation—what could be called their "destiny"—is in effect overlooked and downplayed. If we see Mary Bell as somehow inherently "evil," then we disregard the importance of her present incarnation, her need, for whatever reason, to come to Earth to such an awful situation and under such a constellation of influences. We would have to assume, as the tabloid newspapers do, that she is somehow eternally "evil" in her inner being. Her upbringing and environment—her karma—become unimportant. (Although this is not to say, of course, that she was "destined" to kill two young boys in this incarnation.)

In reality, the given circumstances within which we find ourselves are critical to what we will become in later life. A person may be born into a wealthy family, have the best education and become successful in business, but who is to say that this same individual might not have become a drunkard who slept on the streets if he were born into other social circumstances. In this sense, it is not possible to judge the actions of another person. As banal as it may sound, we cannot say what we would have done if we were "in their shoes."

Evil and Us

In reviewing a case like Mary Bell's, there is a danger that we externalize the evil tendencies of humanity, seeing them as apart from ourselves. But any person who, with all honesty, looks within will know that the *tendency* to evil is something of an ingrained potentiality, common to each one of us. Evil is not something we can view as apart from ourselves, as the tabloid newspapers encourage us. The evil source of Mary Bell's actions is actually something all humanity is struggling with.

If we continue to absolve ourselves from evil by focusing only on others who for one reason or another have committed inexplicable deeds, we detract from the individual battle to find real humanity in ourselves—to be truly free. On the other hand, if we can begin to meditate upon the individuality (nature) and destiny (nurture) of each human being, we can start to grasp some of the many strands which might lead eventually to a fuller understanding of Mary Bell and others like her, and the appalling tragedy which befell the families of the two young boys who died at her hands.

In relation to the central theme of this book, my purpose in discussing this case is to show how everyday news stories can reveal manifold complexities when viewed from deeper perspectives of soul and spirit. By its trivial coverage of such stories, the media encourages us to take simplistic stances on critical issues. It is very easy to feel anger and rage against somebody who has done something terrible. But it is not so easy to ask *why* that person has committed such an awful crime.

In the relatively rare cases where such investigation *is* made in the media, as I have indicated, one of two polar positions is usually taken. Either it is believed that the person is somehow genetically inclined to act in an evil way, or it is said that they have an inclination to be evil due to their upbringing. But the philosophical positions of nature and nurture are somewhat simplistic and do not provide the whole picture. Essentially, both positions ignore spiritual aspects of life. The nature argument ignores the spiritual individuality of each human being. Who are we? What do we bring with us into our present incarnation on earth? What have we done in the past to influence the way we act in this lifetime? On the other hand, the "nurture" argument ignores our spiritual destiny (karma). Why are we born into a specific family? Why do certain things happen to us in life? Why are we born into a specific country surrounded by specific people, a specific environment, and so on?

Opening up these perspectives creates a far more differentiated picture of each human life. In this short piece I have not speculated as to why Mary Bell did the terrible things she did. What I have indicated, however, is the need to be evermore searching in our understanding of events which take place around us if we are to take a spiritual picture of the human being seriously.

My intention here is not to give easy explanations to what is an incredibly disturbing, complex, and difficult human situation. When we seek cognition of truth, answers are rarely simple. But thoughtful meditation on such themes leads to a more wisdom-filled approach in contrast to the clever, quick-thinking, intellectual arrogance which increasingly characterizes materialistic culture.

2.9 In the Grip of Lizards: The Phenomenon of David Icke

David Icke (rhymes with "like"), now an underground cult author, international speaker, and conspiracy writer, was once a popular sports presenter on British television. In 1991 he made a radical career shift, which is when I first became fascinated by him. Although I missed Icke's now infamous interview with Terry Wogan on his enormously popular TV chat show—during which the audience persistently laughed at Icke—I managed to receive a perception of him, along with much of the British public, through an insidious process of media osmosis. The picture portrayed of Icke was that, overnight, he had turned into something of a lunatic; a madman who believed he was "the Son of God"—Jesus even! The former television sports presenter had set himself up as a spiritual guru, and was now proudly making apocalyptic prophecies. Few people had any time for David Icke during this period, and the thought that he was simply mad was actually, in a strange way, quite comforting. But then I had the opportunity to hear Icke speak for himself, and my image of him swiftly changed.

In December 1991 Icke appeared on Channel 4's "Jonathan Ross Show." On entering the studio, Icke was roundly jeered and taunted by the studio audience on account of his loony reputation. Undaunted, Icke responded with impressive assurance and equanimity. He spoke lucidly about the "growing evidence around the world" for the truths of reincarnation and karma. He shone charisma, and by the time his brief appearance was over Icke left the studio to genuine applause and even loud cheers.

Around this time, I had the opportunity to hear Icke speak in London. Having not been especially inspired by his two books, *The Truth Vibrations* (1991) and *Love Changes Everything* (1992), I was once more pleasantly surprised to hear a coherent, clear, and articulate speaker. He focused on ecological and spiritual issues, although what he had to say about spiritual changes and awakenings was presented in rather general terms. To be fair, Icke's thinking was in a state of constant flux. His perception changed with each book, and because of his prolific output his individual path of development became very public. Looking back, this must have been a painful process for him as well as his readers.

In 1994, Icke published *The Robots' Rebellion*, his most hard-edged book to date and his first to delve into conspiracy theory. It was on his speaking tour promoting this book that I shook Icke's hand after he had given a talk in Glastonbury, and gathered round him while he chatted to a small group. Icke had just talked for almost two hours about secret societies with malicious aims and intentions. A questioner in our group asked Icke whether he was not fearful to speak against such powerful and entrenched forces. "What can they do to me?" he asked in return. He gave his own answer: "They can take away my physical body!"

The implication was that *that was all* they could do to him. He spoke with the conviction of somebody who knows that death is not the end—and that in any case nobody could kill his spirit. These words indicated a tremendous personal courage and dedication to his cause. I knew he wasn't bluffing, and from this experience I was certain that Icke was completely sincere in what he said and wrote.

Other books followed, including . . . *And the Truth Shall Set You Free* and *I Am Me, I Am Free* (in which Icke proved the point by appearing naked on the cover), which expanded on the conspiracy theme. There didn't seem to be much further for him to go. His ideas may have been developing subtly, but the basic parameters were laid out, and there was an awful lot of repetition in the contents of these books. But Icke had one more ace up his sleeve, to be revealed in his new telephone-directory of a book—*The Biggest Secret, The Book That Will Change the World*—published in 1999.

"Are you ready for this? I wish I didn't have to introduce the following information because it complicates the story and opens me up to mass ridicule," Icke states in chapter 2 of this book, before elaborating his theory that humanity has been interbred by a reptilian race, the worst elements of which originated from the Draco constellation. The descendants of this bloodline comprise the power elite who ruthlessly control the world and manipulate humanity for their own selfish ends. They are shape-shifting reptiles, inherently open to possession from "reptilians of the lower fourth dimension." These creatures/people like to take part in diabolical practices which involve murder and the drinking of blood, and their number includes the British Royal Family, George Bush, Henry Kissinger, and many others identified by name in the book.

Predictably, as Icke himself expected, *The Biggest Secret* opened him up to yet more ridicule, although the mainstream media largely ignored the book. Icke continued to develop something of a cult following, but he was no longer considered newsworthy.

"It Doesn't Have to be Like This"

David Icke began his career as a professional goalkeeper with the English soccer team Coventry City. On developing arthritis he was forced to give up soccer at the age of 21, and gradually established himself as a successful sports journalist and television presenter. As Icke approached the end of his thirties, he took an interest in environmental issues and joined the Green Party. In February 1990 he had a booklet published, *It Doesn't Have to Be Like This*, in which he celebrated the Green Party as one which was "not prepared to tell the people what they wanted to hear if that was at odds with the truth."[1] Six months after joining the party he reached a prominent position in its collective leadership, and traveled across Britain furthering the Green cause through speeches, interviews, and press conferences.

Icke's conversion to ecological and environmental politics led him to question the hegemonic materialistic conception of life: "[T]he deeper I traveled into Green politics, the more it became a spiritual journey. I was soon asking many questions about the reason for our existence. Why were we here? What happened next?"[2] His search took him to "medium and healer" Betty Shine. Through this meeting Icke was introduced to spiritual ideas and was "led to a stream of books." Later, he described his meeting with Betty Shine as a turning point: "Through Betty I received some astonishing revelations and predictions of fundamental importance to the future of humankind which set me on a journey of discovery that I would have found impossible to comprehend unless my path had crossed with hers."[3]

As Icke's interest grew, he became convinced that he had an important role to play in helping to alert humanity to the spiritual foundations of its existence. The "spiritual communications" he received led him to believe that, as a public figure, his task was to write and publish influential books which would awaken people to the dangers of materialism.

By March 1991, Icke's book *The Truth Vibrations* was completed, and scheduled for a May publication. As a direct consequence, Icke gave written notice of his immediate resignation as national spokesman of the Green Party in Britain. He warned that the imminent publication of his book would put him "at the center of tremendous controversy."[4] Icke followed this dramatic move by staging a press conference in London, in which he appeared on a platform with his wife, daughter, and follower Deborah Schawsun. All were uniformly dressed in turquoise track suits. Surrounded by cynical newsmen, Icke spoke at some length about the crisis facing humanity and warning of widespread natural disasters if things did not change.

"The biggest threat to the earth is thought pollution," he declared, adding "any imbalance filters up to God. . . . We can balance the earth so the earth will not be destroyed."[5] He explained to his disbelieving audience that natural disasters such as earthquakes, hurricanes, and tidal waves occurred as a cleansing action by the Earth, which desired to "rid itself of energies trapped by evil feelings of anger, hatred, and aggression."[6] Icke also proclaimed: "I channel an energy known as the Christ Spirit."[7] He elucidated to his disbelieving spectators that "Christ isn't a person, it's an energy known as pure love and wisdom and resonates to the same frequency as the color turquoise."[8]

The conference was a personal disaster for Icke, effectively killing his reputation as a respected minor celebrity. The media reaction to his declarations was dramatic: He was attacked, vilified, and denounced as a madman. The tabloid newspapers in particular gave wide coverage to the story, all maintaining that Icke had proclaimed himself to be "the Son of God." The *Sun* asked its readers "Is David Icke off His Bike?" and quoted a psychologist as saying: "He's not mad, but his ideas are certainly crazy."[9] The paper also held a telephone poll in which it inquired: "Do you think Icke has gone bonkers?" The results were published the following day—beneath a story headlined "Icke Is My Son, not the Lord's Says Mum"—revealing, unsurprisingly, that *Sun* readers had voted by more than 4–1 to affirm the charge that Icke had, indeed, "gone bonkers."

The *Daily Mirror* similarly showed little tolerance for Icke's new stand, heading its story "The Loony Gospel of Saint David" and quoting another psychologist as claiming that Icke was probably going through a midlife crisis. According to the *Daily Mirror*, only one man welcomed Icke's words, the chairman of the Raving Loony Green Giant party, who reportedly enthused: "He's the man for us."[10]

The oft-repeated charge that Icke had declared himself "the Son of God" was based on Icke's statement that he was a "channel for the Christ spirit." Although a misrepresentation of his words, the "Son of God" tag stuck, and led to a perception in the mass-consciousness that Icke was simply demented. A few months later, in an interview in *The Face* style magazine, Icke was asked whether he still thought himself to be the Son of God. He replied: "We are all expressions of the infinite energy of Creation, what I call the infinite Mind and others call God. If you look at what I said, it was not *the* Son of God, but *a* Son of God. So I was not saying anything that wasn't symbolically true."[11]

Even in the book Icke was promoting at the time, there is no word of him being "the Son of God." On the contrary, precise indications are given of his supposed—very human—spiritual identity. Icke describes how, with the aid of psychic and astrologer Judy Hall, his previous incarnations had apparently been traced—revealing him to have been most recently a "soldier, spy, and medium." The "spirit messages" which make up the core of *The Truth Vibrations* refer to him as "still a child spiritually."[12] Nevertheless, he does assume the position of a prophet endowed with a sacred mission:

> My role would be to help bring about a spiritual revolution, and I would become a "cosmic parent" to the planet and humanity. . . .[13] I had a job to do in this lifetime that would, in conjunction with other events and other people, change the world forever. I felt a bit isolated and lonely with the knowledge I had been given, but the Grand Plan was soon to take care of that.[14]

In his second book, *Love Changes Everything*, Icke gave a commentary on that ill-fated press conference. Perhaps in a vain attempt to rehabilitate himself, he generously accepted that his behavior was the cause of the disaster, although he stood by the content of his words, saying, "While I was behaving in a way to attract enormous ridicule, I was also speaking the truth." He recalled: "I stood there in my turquoise track suit telling them all this stuff and as I read out the list of 'changes' I remember hearing my rational aspect saying in a distant voice: 'David, what the hell are you saying? This is absolute nonsense.' But my mouth continued to sign its own death warrant. . . . Of course, the reaction of the press was predictable and, let's be fair, understandable."[15]

But in retrospect was the press reaction fair? Few would dispute the fact that Icke's method and style of presentation were greatly flawed. Standing around in a turquoise track suit and lecturing jour-nalists on spiritual concepts and impending catastrophes is hardly the way to endear oneself to the mainstream media. But the willful misrep-resentation of Icke's stance was as malicious as it was dishonest. In par-ticular, the use of the highly emotive term "the Son of God" could be perceived as an underhand strategy to undermine everything he had said. As for the language employed to describe him—"loony," "bonkers," "off his bike"—it simply reflected the press's unintelligent and supercilious approach to alternative and unusual thoughts and ideas.

But it was not just the tabloid papers that adopted such heavy-handed methods to dispose of Icke's arguments. The highbrow estab-lishment paper the *Sunday Times* devoted several pages to analyzing Icke's life and times in an endeavor to expose him as a psychologically unstable and power-hungry megalomaniac. The in-depth piece con-cluded: "He has ostentatiously renounced the entire network of con-sensus and order of concessions by which a society agrees to conduct its business and to regulate its arguments."[16]

What was this "network of consensus" that Icke had so ostenta-tiously renounced? Essentially, Icke had threatened the materialistic sta-tus quo. In spite of his offbeat presentation, the words Icke spoke at his initial press conference amounted to a challenge to the materialistic supposition which underpins modern society. Had Icke been a vocifer-ous priest or spiritual guru, he might have been simply ignored or laughed off. But Icke was an unusual spiritual spokesman: an ex-soccer player, a television presenter, and a respected politician and campaigner. As a popular public figure from the cultural mainstream of society—a celebrity—he would be listened to by ordinary people and given wide access to modern means of communication. Icke would have an advan-tage over the average preacher or spiritual teacher in being able to spread his message to those who might not normally come into contact with such ideas. And so, sadly, he had to be dealt with.

In saying this, I am not implying that there was a conscious media conspiracy against Icke. There didn't need to be! The tendency to hardened, intellectualized, materialistic thinking is so ingrained—particularly in the media—that the fierce retort to Icke was an instinctive, knee-jerk reaction.

So what of Icke's work? It is not my intention to study Icke's now substantial literary output in any detail in this brief essay—only to give a few perspectives.

While far from being the work of a madman, Icke's debut, *The Truth Vibrations*, is not especially profound. The *Sunday Times* magazine described it, not altogether unfairly, as "a belch of semi-digested spiritualist, New Age, and mystic canons of belief."[17] As a populist piece of New Age literature, it is not dissimilar in content to many dozens published each year. Which is not to say that it does not contain many "truths." Icke writes lucidly about reincarnation and karma, guardian angels, the modern spiritual path, etc. But the book contains some straightforward inaccuracies due to poor research. The Grail cup, for example, is described as "a chalice cup made from the cross on which Christ was crucified,"[18] rather than the cup that Joseph of Arimathea used to catch the drops of Christ's blood. Elsewhere, Icke presents bizarre and ill-conceived theological ideas. In relation to Christ, for example, he says the following:

> He [Christ] could have responded to the prospect of death on the cross by unleashing his immense power against the forces of darkness, but such an occult battle would have caused so much damage to the Earth and its people that he decided to go quietly to his physical death. In this sense, you could say that Jesus died to save us all.[19]

How should one assess the content of a book like *The Truth Vibrations*? One way is to analyze it from a dogmatic standpoint and reject anything which does not coincide with one's particular beliefs. A more constructive approach to evaluation would be to assess the methods that the author uses to gather the information presented. So what is Icke's methodology? In *The Truth Vibrations*, he is quite open about the fact that the esoteric content is not the product of his own research. His information is gathered mainly from "spirit messages" conveyed through colleagues and friends whose techniques center on automatic writing, mediumship, and channeling.

How reliable are these methods? With automatic writing, a person places a clean sheet of paper before them and waits for their pen to move without their volition. When successful, a message or messages are received. The information in these messages may or may not be useful—but what is the source? Usually, the entity manipulating the automatic writer will identify itself. But how is the recipient of the message to know that he or she is being told the truth? The experience of using a Ouija board has many parallels. Many teenagers have, at some time or other, played at laying the letters of the alphabet on a table, placing their hands on a glass in the middle, and waiting for someone or something invisible to move the glass and spell out words.

As with automatic writing, the entity involved will often identify itself—but again, who is to say that "it" is telling the truth? Is it *really* John Lennon trying to communicate, or could it be some troubled, discarnate soul longing for contact with the physical world, a mischievous nature spirit, a demonic being, and so on. From the point of view of a precise spiritual science, these are important and critical questions. This is not to say that in individual cases a person might not receive information of great value through automatic writing, but on its own it is an unreliable and imprecise method.

Mediumship is not greatly different. The classic medium goes into a trance and allows a discarnate entity to speak through her. The medium gives over her body to the being, who is then able to give messages to the audience. After the session, the medium is unaware of what has been spoken through her. Mediumship can involve varying states of consciousness, from the completely unconscious to ascending grades of awareness. But again, who can say which or what being has spoken? The information is, essentially, taken on trust.

With channeling, the situation is slightly different. Icke defines channeling as follows: "To channel is to allow a spirit to speak through you. The spirit puts thought forms into the mind, and the channel turns them into words and speaks them."[20] Here, the individual is involved consciously to the extent of translating the thought forms. But once again, the channel is generally not able to identify the entity who is providing the information.

There is an assumption by some New Age practitioners that whatever is received from metaphysical sources is by definition "good" and "true." That position is naïve, to say the least. The problem with all the above methods is the potential for manipulation and distortion from metaphysical entities of various types. Another very real possibility is that nonspiritual entities, i.e., physical people on Earth, may also seek to feed untrue or distorted information through such a medium. By this I mean that individuals with their own agendas can use occult means to give "spiritual" messages to others, which the recipient mistakenly believes is being given by an angel or spirit guide.

So what is a trustworthy technique for gaining spiritual knowledge? As mentioned previously, the most reliable method is a far-reaching and discriminating clairvoyance which, at the very least, enables the individual to perceive the entities involved in delivering messages and information. Even this can be problematic, as spiritual beings can deliberately take on other guises in an attempt to fool the seer. The greatest spiritual initiates develop means to identify precisely who and what they are dealing with. In addition they are able, actively and with full consciousness, to research by "reading" the spiritual records of past, present, and (to some extent) future events. These records, sometimes referred to as the Akashic Records, are available to anyone who has developed the requisite spiritual capacities.

Icke does not appear to be aware of the problems inherent in the methods used by his friends. On the contrary, he repeatedly exhibits a complete faith in the accuracy of his findings: "All the information in these pages has come through psychic communications or been confirmed as accurate by those communications,"[21] and "the vast majority of what you have read and are about to read is absolutely correct."[22]

The Bigger Secret?

By the time Icke got around to writing *The Biggest Secret,* some eight years later, his methods of research had expanded somewhat. Chiefly, he had become expert in utilizing secondary sources, i.e., other people's books! Allegations of plagiarism abounded. In a *Fortean Times* review of *The Biggest Secret,* Jim Keith wrote: "As I read through the book and ran across sections dealing with books I had read, I could almost see them open in Icke's lap while he paraphrased. At one point he quotes me verbatim, without crediting me." The book also includes a fair amount of reliance on psychic communications of various types. In fact, Icke's main proof for the existence of the reptilian race is anecdotal evidence from those who have, apparently, seen them, often in metaphysical form. This includes pages of the most fantastic revelations, inserted just before going to print, given by a psychic "witness" who purports to have seen members of the British Royal Family as "shape-shifting reptiles" carrying out ritual murders, cannibalism, and blood-drinking.[23]

Given the methods of research that Icke uses, perhaps it is no surprise that the central thesis of *The Biggest Secret* is in essence extremely materialistic. His rather dated view—a sort of third-hand *Chariots of the Gods*—suggests that the human race has been interbred by alien races (read "gods") from outer space. The reptilian race—the bad guys—are the ones who now control the planet.

Some have already pointed out that, by its very nature, Icke's latest work discredits serious research into political and occult conspiracies. By suggesting such a seemingly absurd hypothesis, Icke makes the whole raft of independent researchers and writers on this subject appear to be crazy. But the core problem with Icke's work is that, due to his materialistic mindset, he misreads and misinterprets much information. Thus, biblical gods like the Elohim are taken to be physical aliens. Individuals' experiences of horrific monsters or reptilelike creatures—which could be genuine spiritual perceptions of demonic and similar entities—are taken to exist on a physical level and identified with known personalities. And so on.

Interestingly, the same tendency is evident in *The Truth Vibrations* in which Icke has a habit of materializing aspects of the spiritual world. He is preoccupied with changing "vibrations," "frequencies," and "energies," using concepts which are always analogous to the physical world and physical processes. Purely spiritual conceptions of other dimensions are conspicuously absent. Back in 1915, the spiritual teacher Rudolf Steiner made a critique of the theosophist A. P. Sinnett's book *Esoteric Buddhism*, and Steiner's comments are remarkably pertinent to David Icke:

> Sinnett was a journalist and was therefore steeped in the materialistic tendencies of the 19th century. Here, then, was a personality whose brain tended entirely to materialism, but the longing for a spiritual world was also present in him. He therefore had every aptitude for seeking for the spiritual world in a materialistic form. . . . Of course, the teaching about the members of man's being, the doctrine of karma and reincarnation, are truths. But materialism has here been woven into all these truths. In Sinnett's *Esoteric Buddhism* a genuinely spiritual outlook is combined with an eminently materialistic tendency.[24]

In my view, the great tragedy of David Icke is that he has for the time being at least become locked within materialistic conceptions. This articulate and charismatic man could have continued in politics and fought with great resilience and courage for social and ecological change. Alternatively, he could have become an effective populist spiritual teacher. Instead, he is making unfortunate allegations about people being blood-drinking reptiles.

As stated earlier, Icke is nothing if not courageous, if sometimes a little rash in prematurely publicizing his views. In *The Truth Vibrations,* he wrote: "Some of what I have said in terms of detail I will modify in future books." Further, he was generous enough to concede, "there is still an enormous amount I do not know."[25] In any event, the gulf between the content of his debut and *The Biggest Secret,* written eight years apart, is so great that it is almost impossible to believe they have been authored by the same person. Initially Icke wrote about Jesus Christ's incarnation on Earth, asserting that his teaching "had a positive effect on humanity in that it highlighted the values of compassion, peace and love for all things."[26] Eight years later he was busy dismissing the "Jesus myth" altogether, categorically denying that Jesus ever existed.[27]

This does not constitute "modification of detail." The truth is that Icke's whole worldview has turned on its head. So who is to say what he will be thinking and writing about in another eight years' time? We wait with anticipation, interest, and hope.

2.10 The Tragedy of Charles and Diana: Death in Paris and the Struggle for the Throne

In this chapter, I will make a study of events involving the British Royal Family around the time of Princess Diana's death in a car crash in 1997. Readers may wonder why I am asking them to look at the pomp and circumstance of British monarchy. Many Americans will understandably view monarchy as a European anachronism; an entertaining but ultimately vacant soap opera. I don't dispute that assessment in principle, but the fact remains that at the present time Britain has a monarchy—albeit a symbolic one—and the queen or king still has an influence on public life and thought. He or she performs the function of a figurehead, and therefore the person in question is of consequence.

There are certainly many people in British society who recognize the importance of the monarch's identity. Among them are individuals and groups who work in secret. The aim of these people is to manipulate public opinion in favor of their intentions, and thus project their will on the British people. Often they will influence or pressure others to carry out their wishes. In relation to the monarchy, I suggest that these hidden (occult) forces are seeking control over the succession of the present Queen Elizabeth.

In a remarkable series of interviews with the *Daily Mirror* in November 2002, Princess Diana's former butler Paul Burrell revealed details of a conversation he had with the queen two months after Diana's death in 1997. Burrell claims the queen gave him a strong warning to remain alert to possible danger. He quotes her as saying: "Be careful, Paul, nobody has been as close to a member of my family as you have. There are powers at work in this country which we have no knowledge about." Burrell said that the queen did not qualify her words or offer any further explanation, and that he himself had "no idea who she was talking about." However, it was clear to him that she was deadly serious and was warning him "to be vigilant."

Who was the queen talking about? We will never know for sure because the queen herself will never comment publicly on such matters. Some have interpreted her words as referring to the secret services such as MI5 and MI6 (well known to moviegoers through the fictitious James Bond), but I suspect that it is more likely she was speaking of the many established secret societies which are at the heart of British power. These societies are not the stuff of paranoid fantasies, and neither are they nebulous and unknown cabals. On the contrary, their existence is well known and their practices copiously documented. Although their proceedings are private, the grand tradition which they represent forms part of British cultural history. These secret brotherhoods are usually known by the name of the Freemasons, or simply the Masons. Their members hold key positions in British society in politics, business, the arts, and cultural institutions. (For more on the goals of such brotherhoods see chapter 3.2.)

This chapter shows how hidden interests work through the media to influence public opinion for what are usually undeclared ends. The goal of such forces in this case was to discredit the most intelligent, cultured, and spiritual member of the Royal Family, Prince Charles, in an attempt to usurp his position as the future king. Possibly, they seek also to destabilize or overturn the monarchy as a whole. These groups also seem to have as an objective the sanctification of Princess Diana. I suspect that their purpose in this respect is to create a further means of demeaning her ex-husband. As indicated, I have linked the anti-Charles agenda with Masonic brotherhoods, and I suggest later why they may have an interest in targeting him.

I advise that this chapter be read not as a piece of British history, but as an example of how public agendas are set and how they are carried through. But first, back to those heady days of 1997 when the death of a single person caused a massive emotional stir around the world, and perhaps the biggest media frenzy of all time.

For many years Princess Diana was the popular face of the British Royal Family. Her style and glamour, charismatic beauty, and her intuitive grasp of high-class fashion led the media to follow her every step. Prince Charles, on the other hand, represented in many people's minds something of a dowdy contrast, seemingly a conservative steeped in tradition with a penchant for religion and neoclassical architecture. The Princess's tragic death in Paris, and the subsequent coverage of the event by the media, brought this polarization in the public mind to a climax.

In the many tributes that were written to her, Diana was presented as something of a modern icon; one mourner in Paris described her as representing "the spirit of the age." In contrast, many will remember the television pictures of her divorced husband Charles walking behind her hearse with an anguished look on his face. He was—or so the media story went—the villain of the piece: the guilt-ridden culprit in a fairy-tale marriage that went desperately wrong.

The Mourning of a Princess and Media Saturation

Nobody who had the chance to witness the remarkable sea of flowers, gifts, and tributes in front of the gates of Kensington Palace—the Princess of Wales's former residence—could question the devoted affection for her by a large portion of the British public. In the days following her unexpected and sudden death, it become the chief site of pilgrimage for what rapidly became a Diana cult. A reverent mood—a quasi-religious air—hung over the palace. Trees in the surrounding park were turned into places of worship; their branches festooned with bunches of flowers and cards carrying fond messages of condolence, and hiding burning candles placed before pictures of the princess. The atmosphere of a holy shrine permeated the area.

To what degree this remarkable display of public devotion—unprecedented in modern times—was encouraged by the avalanche of words and pictures which came from the world's media in the days following the princess's death is open to debate. One could argue that there was a reciprocal effect, with the vast media coverage sparking greater feelings of bereavement in the public—and the media in turn responding to such feelings with more stories, pictures, and analysis.

Whatever the cause, the British public's open display of sadness was stunning, as witnessed by the pained cries of grief which followed Diana's hearse during the September funeral procession along London's streets. Similarly, the media's interest in the story was overwhelming. Most television channels devoted the whole of the Sunday following the car crash to reports and discussion of the story. Newspapers followed suit, particularly the tabloid press, which allocated most of their pages to stories arising from the tragedy for weeks after.

In the context of this awesome outpouring of feeling, the coverage of Princess Diana was, perhaps not surprisingly, profoundly reverential. Pictures of her with landmine victims in Africa, walking in war-devastated Bosnia, and with AIDS and other patients in hospitals, dominated. Many words were spoken and written about her love and compassion for the suffering and the victims of war and disease. This is not to say that Diana did not have her critics in Britain—but they were largely silenced in the emotional climate generated in the wake of her death. Her detractors would claim that the princess was stage-managed by expert public-relations consultants who knew exactly when to bring her in front of the cameras, and briefed her on which causes she should fight for.

Whatever element of truth there might be in the above contention, the many personal testimonies which emerged since her death from people with whom the princess kept close private contact through letters, telephone calls, and visits—long after the television cameras had gone—prove that her love for the suffering was much more than a public relations stunt. Her melancholic temperament, after all, so evident in her famous BBC television *Panorama* interview in 1995, was perfectly suited to understanding and relating to other people's pain. In the light of the extant evidence, it would be churlish to suggest that she did not feel genuine compassion towards her constituency of the suffering.

A Prince with a Tarnished Image

While the representation of Princess Diana was staggeringly sympathetic, the picture given through the media of her ex-husband Charles, the Prince of Wales and heir to the throne, was quite the opposite. For many years the prince had been presented as a dabbler in the weird and wonderful, and the press relished its role mocking and vilifying him. In the early 1980s, as a result of his personal interest in ecology and the environment, the tabloid press initiated a campaign to portray him as the "loony prince." The *Daily Mirror* imagined the future king sitting "cross-legged on the throne wearing a caftan and eating muesli." One tabloid paper even claimed that he had used a Ouija board to make contact with his dead relation Lord Mountbatten![1] Even the broadsheet press joined in the attacks, using slightly more reserved language by referring to him as "eccentric" (the *Guardian*) or a "hermetic, mystical crank" *(Time)*.

In the years previous to the public announcement in 1992 that the Prince and Princess of Wales were to separate, the tabloid press unanimously held Charles responsible for the breakdown of the couple's marriage. Many stories were published which presented him as a cruel, cold, and uncaring husband whose behavior made his wife ill and led her to stage several suicide attempts. When Andrew Morton's book *Diana, Her True Story* (which, it later emerged, was written with the full cooperation and blessing of the princess) was first published in 1992, this criticism reached a crescendo, and the idea was introduced into the public consciousness that the prince might not be fit to take his role as the next king. (*The Prince of Wales, A Biography*, written by Jonathan Dimbleby with the cooperation of the prince, gives the other side of the story regarding their unhappy marriage, and as you might expect paints quite a different picture.)

While the princess received sympathetic and appreciative coverage of her charity work, the prince's work was largely ignored. Diana was consistently portrayed as a great force for compassion and goodness, who faced resistance from the conservative and traditional Royal Family led by the queen and Charles. The irony, however, is that her ex-husband shared many of her concerns, and had a long history of working extraordinarily hard for charitable causes.

The organizations he has founded over the years include: the Prince's Trust, which reaches many thousands of individuals each year with a program of grants and training for the unemployed; the Prince's Youth Business Trust, which helps disadvantaged young people set up in business; the Prince of Wales' Committee, which provides grant aid to thousands of voluntary groups working on projects to improve the environment of Wales; Business in the Community, which promotes partnership between business, government, and the community; the Business Leaders Forum, which encourages international cooperation for regeneration through education, training, and environmental projects; as well as Scottish Business in the Community and several other similar organizations. These are successful and productive initiatives, often with turnovers of millions of pounds, and continue to be intimately associated with the prince.

In addition to this work, Prince Charles has proved himself to be a powerful thinker and leader, speaking consistently and with great courage and passion in support of progressive causes (which were usually highly unfashionable when he took them up). His BBC television documentary *The Earth in Balance*, a significant contribution to the debate on the environment, was made in the late 1980s when the issue had not entered mainstream thinking. His pioneering speeches on complementary medicine and the need for "human," aesthetic architecture were made in front of audiences comprising the very establishment he was criticizing, facts requiring great fortitude and courage. And he consistently sought to practice his own teachings. His interest in organic agriculture, for example, led the prince to convert his 1,050-acre Highgrove estate into one of the largest and most admired organic holdings in the country.

A Prince with Spiritual Leanings

Schooled by his mentor, the South African-born writer, explorer, and mystic Laurens van der Post, Charles took an early interest in spirituality. His rapport with van der Post grew especially close around 1975, when the two began to organize expeditions together. During these trips van der Post would teach the prince esoteric ideas. Charles responded with a vigorous interest and began his own in-depth study, which included an immersion in the work of C. G. Jung and the doctrine of reincarnation. His preoccupation with these subjects grew and matured over the years, to the point that Charles has become a serious and authoritative force for a new and contemporary spirituality.

As early as 1981, in a speech to celebrate the centenary of the Salvation Army, in which he criticized the doctrinal disputes which divided Christendom, he urged that "what we should be worried about now is whether people are going to become atheists; whether they are going to be given an idea of what is right or wrong; whether they are going to be given an awareness of the things of the Spirit and of the meaning and infinite beauty of Nature."[2] In 1986, in a speech at the 350th Anniversary of Harvard University, he stated: "Never has it been more important to recognize the imbalance that has seeped into our lives and deprived us of a sense of meaning, because the emphasis has been too one-sided and has concentrated on the development of the intellect to the detriment of the spirit."[3]

In 1996 he published an article in the magazine *Perspectives in Architecture* which reflected on British plans to celebrate the millennium.

Something of a *tour de force*, it was the first effort by any public figure to encourage deeper thought on the millennium. Charles observed that "the rather limited public discussion so far in Britain about the millennium has not focused on its spiritual importance and the potential it holds for personal and national renewal." It was "depressing," he went on, "that there is so little one could describe as transcending the merely material in the projects which have so far been submitted to the Millennium Commission." He encouraged his readers to "see and sense the spark of the spirit in everything," but warned that "this sense of spiritual renewal is something which has to originate in our hearts and not our heads. . . . But it cannot do so until we recognize the need to renew the way in which we educate people, so that we do not educate out those intuitive powers of the heart which lie at the root of all spiritual experience."

He continued: "The millennium is, therefore, both a celebration and a challenge. Few people expect, unlike a thousand years ago, that the year 2000 will usher in a new and just world ruled by wise politicians, and from which violence and turbulence will have been eradicated. But there is, I believe, a resurgence of spirituality across the world; small beacons of civilizing values in the face of the all-pervading materialism of recent times, which represent a yearning to improve the deeper quality of our lives and to restore those enduring cultural priorities which represent a moral foundation in a world dominated by consumerism. If the millennium can be used to respond to those feelings and emotions, it will last well beyond the year 2000, and add immeasurably to the quality of our lives."[4] One might expect to hear such penetrating thoughts from a spiritual or religious leader—but to hear such incisive words from a royal prince, indeed the man destined to be the future king of Britain, is a surprise.

Monarchy Today?

Despite the resurgence of interest and support for the British Royals following the Queen's Golden Jubilee in 2002, the image of the

British Royal Family has been tarnished. During the 1980s and 1990s, the House of Windsor appeared to be closer to a grandiose soap opera—its members indulging all too publicly in affairs, scandal, and divorce—than true nobility. In other words, they have appeared to be what they of course are: *all too human.* Given this fallibility, contemporary individuals may well be tempted to back the antimonarchist cause. After all, can "the divine right of kings" have any meaning in an age of individual autonomy and potential freedom from ties of rank, class, nation, and race? In the face of increasing individuation and personal empowerment, the notion of royalty may well appear to be a relic from former times. After all, the new aristocracy, respected and worshipped by millions of ordinary people, are celebrities; often very ordinary people who might earn their social status from simply appearing on a television "reality" show. In the modern world, it is not necessary to be great in order to be famous, sought after, or even fabulously wealthy.

The original conception of monarchy, an institution which is thousands of years old, was quite different. The monarch, it was believed, was established and inspired by God to lead his people. The king or queen was perceived to be the highest authority—the divine mouthpiece—and their mission was to govern with justice and wisdom. Today the British royal family has no real political power, although it still retains a constitutional role. At best, it is something of a symbol of leadership, deriving from a heritage of pomp, ceremony, and tradition. In many people's eyes it offers continuity with the past, giving guidance to the present and future.

Given the present state of affairs, what chance for the monarchy? Although Diana was popular with the media partly because she embodied many characteristics of the modern celebrity—she was beautiful, took exotic holidays, was photographed with handsome men—the long-term future of the monarchy is surely dependent on less transient fascinations. Enduring qualities of depth are called for: courage, sacrifice, intelligence, spirituality, culture, etc. Although at present there is little likelihood that the monarchy is about to be toppled—opinion polls consistently show more than 70 percent of the British population in favor its existence—sooner or later people will tire of the soap opera and demand substance. In this respect, Prince Charles represents the best hope for the monarchy, and the finest argument for the existence of an institution which is beginning to feel antiquated.

With God's inspiration, the monarch was traditionally the spiritual head of a country, and had the task of leading and inspiring an entire people. Although in the modern age there could be no question of a monarch having political power, there is no reason why a modern king or queen could not embody genuine spiritual qualities of leadership. As has been discussed, Charles is the best candidate for such a position. He works tirelessly for the social good against unemployment, homelessness, and inner-city decay, and yet (despite his active engagement of politicians and ministers) stands above party politics. He fights for the environment, progressive medicine and agriculture, a human architecture, morality in science, the preservation of literary heritage, among countless other worthy causes. And, perhaps most significantly, he argues with great force and eloquence for the necessity of a renewed and vibrant spirituality.[5]

Could it be mere chance that such an individual is born with a destiny to be the monarch—whether symbolic or not—of a country with such an incisive historical past and critical cultural heritage as Britain? And could one not expect that, as the figurehead of Britain, such an individual might be a real spiritual power for Britain's development and evolution?

The Royal Family and an Unsympathetic Press

Unfortunately, however, Prince Charles has influential enemies. Despite great pressure during his twenties, he adamantly refused to join the secret brotherhood of the Freemasons, partly at the behest of the Queen Mother (his grandmother) and Lord Mountbatten.[6] (One could reasonably assume that Laurens van der Post would also have strongly advised him to keep away from "the Brotherhood" and its specialized occult interests, which manifest adversely in politics, economics, and culture.) If Charles ascends to the throne as intended, he would become the first monarch in centuries who has not been the titular head of Freemasonry in Britain. Is this the cause of his troubles? Whatever the truth, it is certainly a fact that many in the establishment are strongly opposed to him.

One unexpected consequence of the princess's death was the subsequent antimonarchist mood stirred up by the British press, particularly the tabloids, which used every opportunity to attack the grieving father and his family. The *Daily Mail*—its proprietor Lord Rothermere also owns the London *Evening Standard*—ran a relentless campaign against the Royal Family, asking questions such as "Has the House of Windsor got a heart?" remonstrating the queen for not mourning publicly ("Let the Flag Fly at Half Mast"), and further berating the royals for not addressing the grieving nation ("Your People are Suffering").

The paper claimed that there was "mounting concern that the Royal Family was not adequately responding to the national mood of grief over Diana's death." The clamor was for a display of public emotion—something wholly alien to the dignified composure and discipline of the Royals. Prince Charles was also targeted, with a wholly unsubstantiated story ("Charles Weeps Bitter Tears of Guilt"), which had the prince tramping over his Scottish estate in remorse for his past misdeeds to Diana. The *Daily Mail* was joined by the antimonarchist Rupert Murdoch's *Sun* and a number of the other tabloid papers.

In response to this pressure, which was said to have "caught the public mood," Buckingham Palace issued a statement in which it was announced that the queen had been "hurt by suggestions that they are indifferent to the country's sorrow at the tragic death of the Princess of Wales." However, in something of a concession, the queen also took the unprecedented step of addressing the nation over the incident of the princess's death, and Charles and his sons met mourners outside Kensington Palace.

Once the funeral of the princess was over, however, the press continued their anti-Royal campaign, with Charles now being much more clearly targeted. This was done by reintroducing the notion that the monarchy should "skip a generation" and that Prince Charles's son William, the 15-year-old William, should be the next king. The *Sun* began the onslaught by publishing a MORI survey which asked the slanted question: "If Prince William were to become the next monarch, would you favor a republic or a monarchy," in response to which 82% favored a monarchy.[7] The question was ridiculous.

Many people had watched with sympathy and admiration as the young William had conducted himself with astounding dignity at his mother's funeral. In the circumstances, it would have been highly unlikely for the public not to state their support for William as a king. However, the slyly worded question allowed the *Sun* to announce: "Where there's a Will there's a way ahead." And through this insidious method, the idea that William should become the next king was actively encouraged.

A couple of days later, the broadsheet *Daily Telegraph*—its editor Charles Moore is a graduate of the top establishment public school Eton—published a similar Gallup poll in a leading front-page story, under the headline "Half favor William as next King."[8] "For the first time, an opinion poll has indicated that more than half of the British people believe Prince William should succeed to the throne in place of his father," it claimed.

This time, Prince Charles fought back. One of his aides stated: "This form of muck-raking is causing anger, hurt, and distress not only to Charles but also to William. Nothing could be more intrusive for William at a time when he has just lost his mother, than days later seeing his father being vilified. The monarchy is hereditary, not something that can be passed over on a whim. Charles *will* succeed to the throne." A Buckingham Palace spokesman added: "Charles is heir and will become King. After him will come William."[9] These strident words were not mere rhetoric. After all, there is no constitutional or other reason to set the bizarre precedent of the throne skipping a generation. But unfortunately that does not mean that Charles's enemies—of which he has many—will not continue to work for his downfall.

The death of Princess Diana caused unprecedented grief and upset around the world, and many mourned the loss of her independent role as a campaigner for charities and worthy causes. But if her untimely death were to lead to difficulties for Prince Charles in his future role, the tragedy would be compounded. In 1993 Prince Charles made a statement in a letter to his friend Tom Shebbeare of the principles and intentions which guided his public life. At the end he stated: "Having read this through, no wonder they want to destroy me, or get rid of me . . . !"[10] Several years later, the death of his ex-wife gave those who wanted to "get rid" of Charles a chance to cynically exploit a tragic situation. Simultaneous to these attacks on Charles, the unofficial canonization of Diana was begun.

Despite the findings of the French official enquiry into the princess's death in Paris, many questions remain. Was she indeed seriously considering marriage to the Muslim Mohamed Al Fayed's son Dodi? If so, it was conceivable that she might have a child; a half-Egyptian, Muslim brother or sister to the future King of England. Could such a situation be tolerated by the highly conservative British establishment? Because of the suspicious circumstances surrounding Diana's death, these questions will not go away. Malicious forces may well have been involved in her untimely demise. What is unquestionable, however, is the fact that malevolent forces used her death to further their own goals in relation to Charles.

Admittedly it has not been possible to prove conclusively that hidden brotherhoods are behind these attacks. The evidence, by the very nature of the case, is bound to be purely circumstantial. But who else would be after Charles, and more importantly what would be their motive? The fact that he has taken a firm stand against joining the Masons is a key reason to suspect their involvement. The other motivation, as will be elaborated in chapter 3.2, is that these brotherhoods are essentially antispiritual and work against human evolution. They do not want aware, highly conscious, and progressive individuals like Charles who are prepared to stand against their agendas. They much prefer puppets, driven by greed and ambition.

In the current climate of post-Jubilee, promonarchy euphoria, the attacks on Charles have subsided somewhat. But there is no reason to think that they will not begin again at an opportune moment—especially when the present queen nears the end of her reign. Prince Charles's supporters and spiritual allies should be vigilant and awake, for the struggle is not yet over. The potential prize, however, is great: a worthy figurehead for the 21st century.

2.11 Gods, Devils, and Human Beings: The Remarkable Story of Malcolm X

As U.S. resources were being poured into fighting Saddam Hussein and the Gulf War in 1991, a very different kind of war, largely hidden from the public eye, was being played out on the streets of Los Angeles. With little warning, an incident was to bring that conflict to the forefront of public consciousness. In March of 1991, an amateur video, relayed repeatedly by the media, showed a man being kicked and beaten with batons for over two minutes by three police officers while eleven others looked on. The victim was a black, an unemployed laborer. His injuries included nine skull fractures, a broken leg, concussion, a shattered eye socket, damage to his knees, and partial paralysis of his face.[1] His antagonists were white, members of the Los Angeles Police Department. They had chased the suspect after a California Highway Patrol car team had reported that his car was speeding.

The beating of Rodney King would probably have gone unnoticed had it not been for a bystander, trying out his new video camera, who filmed what was going on. King was on parole for robbery, and without material evidence was unlikely to have any recourse against the police through the courts. But the dramatic film changed everything. Minority groups suggested that the beating was not unusual, and only differed from many other similar incidents because of the filming. The Los Angeles chief of police, on the other hand, described the event as "an aberration" and refused to resign.

Anger exploded into violence just over a year later when a jury acquitted the policemen of all charges, despite the graphic evidence of the video tape. Some members of the black community responded with rioting and looting in many cities, particularly Los Angeles, where dozens of people were killed and thousands arrested.

Following the riots, in a special edition of *Oprah* entitled "L. A. Talks Back," a young black man exclaimed angrily: "I'm looking at the news and they are telling me my life is not worth a nickel. They are telling me they can beat me, they can do whatever they want to me whenever they feel like it."

Where did all this leave the American dream of the racial "melting pot"? Contrary to expectations, as time has gone on there has been a growing consciousness among U.S. citizens of ancestry and ethnic identity, rather than a gradual forgetting of their background. Terms such as "African-American" and "Italian-American" came into common use in the 1990s. Along with them came something of a revival of chronic racial tensions, as expertly depicted by Spike Lee in his film *Do the Right Thing*, with its dramatization of the polarization of urban blacks and whites.

Throughout the 1990s, popular culture, in the form of a string of popular black-made films and an increasingly mainstream rap music, brought the issues surrounding the social situation of many African-Americans (drugs, ghetto housing projects, and territorial armed gangs) to wider public consciousness. The growth of a black middle-class, which gradually gained more strength and political influence, seemed to make little difference to the plight of this disadvantaged sector of society. A typical study showed that a third of U.S. blacks were born into poverty, with two-thirds raised by single mothers. Only 12 percent received university degrees (compared to 23 percent of whites), while a third of black males in their twenties were in prison, on parole, or on probation. Black men were eight times more likely to be murdered than white men, black unemployment was twice the rate of whites, and life expectancy for blacks was 69.6 years compared to 76.5 years for whites.[2]

In this context, with the background of the Rodney King trial and the subsequent riots, African-American attitudes contrasted strongly to the mood of the Civil Rights movement of the 1960s. While that generation had been dominated by the pacifist leadership of Martin Luther King, the new generation, raised on hip-hop attitude, was much more likely to lean towards the radical approach of Malcolm X. In his view, freedom was a right to be won "by any means necessary." Linked with this attitude was a stress on affirming African identity, rather than seeking integration with white society and its European roots. Afrocentricity, as opposed to Eurocentricity, became the keyword.

It was into this incendiary atmosphere that Spike Lee released his film biography of Malcolm X. For added potency and to show its immediate relevance, Lee spiced up the introduction of his film by including clips of the beating of Rodney King alongside a burning star-spangled banner. Based on Malcolm X's autobiography,[3] Lee's film portrays the life of a complex individual with a remarkable life path. It is a unique story which contains within it something of an archetypal spiritual journey of great relevance to our time.

The Course of Malcolm X's Life

Malcolm X was born Malcolm Little in Omaha, Nebraska in 1925. One of his earliest memories was of his family's home being burned down by a white supremacist group, the Black Legion. His father, a Baptist preacher who followed the "back to Africa" teachings of Marcus Garvey, was killed two years later, apparently by the same group. His mother, a Seventh Day Adventist, struggled to raise her children in conditions of poverty, but was declared insane and committed to a state mental hospital in 1939. The young Malcolm was placed in a juvenile home, moving later to various foster homes.

Leaving school early, Malcolm made his way to New York where he worked as a waiter in Harlem. He soon became a hustler, selling drugs and bootleg whiskey, and became addicted to cocaine. In 1946, following involvement in a string of thefts, he was arrested on charges of larceny, breaking and entering, and possession of firearms, and was sentenced to ten years' imprisonment. While in prison he was introduced to the teachings of the contemporary Elijah Muhammad, leader of a religious sect named the Nation of Islam. The Honorable Elijah Muhammad, he was told, was "the Messenger of Allah."

At this critical point in his life, Malcolm X became immersed in the Nation of Islam's extraordinary theology. He learned that in July of 1930, Elijah Muhammad—then called Elijah Poole—had been attracted to a lecture by somebody calling himself Master W. Fard Muhammad. Fard identified himself to Elijah Muhammad as "a brother from the East" who had been born into the Koreish tribe of Muhammad ibn Abdulla. Elijah was immediately impressed and became a follower. Later he described "the Master" Fard—a.k.a. Wallace D. Fard—as "God in person."[4]

Fard apparently taught that the black people of America were "the Lost-found Nation of Islam." The first human beings on Earth— "Original Man"—emerged on the continent of Africa and were black. They had built great empires, civilizations, and cultures while the white man was still "living on all fours in caves." The "devil white man"—as he was called by Elijah Muhammad—was responsible for pillaging, murdering, raping, and exploiting all the nonwhite races.[5] But the greatest crime in human history was the white man's forcible traffic of blacks out of Africa in the slave trade. The effect of this, as Malcolm X reports, was to cut them off "from any knowledge of their own language, religion, and past culture, until the black man in America was the earth's only race of people who had absolutely no knowledge of his true identity."[6]

According to Elijah Muhammad, the Christian religion, "the white man's religion," taught the Negro to hate his color, and to believe that "everything white was good." It further brainwashed the black race to be humble, turn the other cheek, grin, pray, and to look for Heaven in the hereafter, while the slavemaster (white man) enjoyed Heaven on Earth.

On this point, the Nation of Islam instruction was clear: No Heaven was in the sky, and no Hell was in the ground. Instead both Heaven and Hell were conditions in which people lived on Earth. "Also on earth was the devil—the white race which was bred from black Original Man six thousand years before, purposely to create a hell on earth for the next six thousand years. . . . The black people, God's children, were Gods themselves. . . . And he taught that among them was one, also a human being like the others, who was the God of Gods: The Most, Most High, the Supreme being, supreme in wisdom and power—and His proper name was Allah."[7]

Near the Last Day, or the End of Time, God would come to resurrect the Lost Sheep and separate them from their enemies. According to Malcolm X, Master Fard taught that prophecy referred to this "Finder and Savior of the Lost Sheep as The Son of Man, or God in Person, or The Lifesaver, The Redeemer, or The Messiah, who would come as lightning from the East and appear in the West. He was the One to whom the Jews referred as The Messiah, the Christians as The Christ, and the Muslims as The Mahdi."[8] Elijah Muhammad is unequivocal that the Master W. D. Fard represented the fulfillment of this prophecy. When he had asked Fard who he was, Fard had apparently replied: "I am The One the world has been looking for to come for the past two thousand years. . . . My name is Mahdi; I am God, I came to guide you into the right path."[9]

To the young Malcolm X, incarcerated in a small cell, this teaching had a potent effect. Although he was later to accuse Elijah Muhammad of "religious fakery," in his autobiography Malcolm X states that at the time he felt something close to St. Paul's experience on the road to Damascus. His conversion to the Nation of Islam was swift, and coincided with him being relocated to an experimental liberal reformatory. Here he began an intensive self-education with the help of the prison's extensive library. His studies convinced him that the white race had "brought upon the world's black, brown, red, and yellow peoples every variety of the sufferings of exploitation." Whites had never, he believed, practiced the humility and meekness of the Christ that they professed to follow. Rather, the white man was nothing but "a piratical opportunist who used Faustian machinations to make his own Christianity his initial wedge in criminal conquests."[10]

In 1952 Malcolm X was let out on parole and immediately became closely involved with the Nation of Islam. He changed his surname from "Little" to "X" in a symbolic gesture to represent the loss of the African-American's heritage and culture. Malcolm X was soon appointed as a minister for the Nation of Islam, and rapidly ascended to the number two position in the organization. Through appearing on television shows such as "The Hate that Hate Produced," he was almost single-handedly responsible for raising the profile of the Nation of Islam around the world. A fiery, articulate, and convincing speaker, he won respect among whites, despite the radical opinions he expressed.

The Nation of Islam, an autocratic organization, expected extreme discipline from its adherents. The use of tobacco, alcohol, narcotics, and certain foods such as pork were strictly proscribed. Fornication, dancing, gambling, cinema visits, sporting activities, or even long holidays from work were absolutely forbidden. The "Black Muslims," as they came to be called, were expected to sleep "no more than health required," to be courteous, lead a harmonious domestic life, and be honest and truthful. Life in the "Temples" of the Nation was regimented, with different classes, trainings, lectures, discussion, and services held each evening.

At the core of the Nation of Islam was a political program which instructed that blacks should separate themselves from white society. The program included a demand "to be allowed to establish a separate state or territory," and called for the prohibition of intermarriage between races. In the meantime, African-Americans should be exempt from all taxation "as long as we are deprived of equal justice under the laws of the land."[11] As Malcolm X recalls, Elijah Muhammad instructed that Western society was deteriorating, and had become overrun with immorality. As a consequence, God was going to judge it and destroy it. Thus, the only way the black people could be saved from this doomed society would be "to *separate* from it, to a land of our *own* where we can reform ourselves, lift up our moral standards, and try to be godly."[12]

In 1963 the *New York Times* reported that Malcolm X was the second most popular speaker in colleges and universities across the United States. He began to command as much admiration in academic circles as he did on the streets in rallies and demonstrations. By December of that year, however, he was to be suspended from ministry and "silenced" by Elijah Muhammad, apparently for remarks made about the assassination of John F. Kennedy. Following this decision, his relationship with Elijah Muhammad became strained, and on March 8, 1964, Malcolm X announced his break from the Nation of Islam and formed his own "Muslim Mosque Inc." in New York. Two months later, he embarked on travels to Mecca and Africa that were to change his life.

His pilgrimage to Mecca brought him for the first time into close proximity with mainstream Muslims. Malcolm X was overwhelmed by their natural hospitality and brotherhood. "All ate as One, and slept as One. Everything about the pilgrimage atmosphere accented the Oneness of man under one God,"[13] he recalled. He also met white Muslims who extended the same warmth and friendliness towards him as he had experienced from members of his own race. "The brotherhood! The people of all races, colors from all over the world coming together as one! It has proved to me the power of the One God." He also felt, contrary to his previous separatist convictions, that "the earth's most explosive and pernicious evil is racism, the inability of God's creatures to live as One, especially in the Western world."[14]

He wrote home to friends and family:

> For the past week, I have been utterly speechless and spellbound by the graciousness I see displayed all around me by people of all colors. But on this pilgrimage, what I have seen, and experienced, has forced me to re-arrange much of my thought-patterns previously held, and to toss aside some of

my previous conclusions. . . . I have been always a man who tries to face facts, and to accept the reality of life as new experience and new knowledge unfolds it. I have always kept an open mind, which is necessary to the flexibility that must go hand in hand with every form of intelligent search for truth.[15]

His letter was signed El-Hajj Malik El-Shabazz, his newly acquired Muslim name.

Malcolm X now began a complete reassessment of his previous ideology. "In the past, yes, I have made sweeping indictments of all white people. I never will be guilty of that again—as I know now that some white people are truly sincere, that some truly are capable of being brotherly toward a black man."[16] Back in America, while in his car at a traffic light, a man called over to him, "Malcolm X, do you mind shaking hands with a white man?" to which he replied: "I don't mind shaking hands with human beings. Are you one?"[17]

While Malcolm X continued campaigning uncompromisingly for the black man's cause, establishing the Organization of Afro-American Unity, his philosophy was now more open: "I'm for truth, no matter who tells it. I'm for justice, no matter who it is for or against. I'm a human being first and foremost, and as such I'm for whoever and whatever benefits humanity *as a whole*."[18] He also began drawing deeply on his spiritual and religious understanding: "Mankind's history has proved from one era to another that the true criterion of leadership is spiritual. Men are attracted by spirit. By power, men are forced. Love is engendered by spirit. By power anxieties are created . . . no government laws ever can force brotherhood."[19]

His analysis turned strongly against the political system, leading him to conclude that it was not the white man who was inherently evil, but America's racist society which influenced him to act in an evil way. In his view, that society was responsible for producing "a psychology which brings out the lowest, most base part of human beings."[20]

On February 21, 1965, Malcolm X was assassinated as he began a public lecture. He died from several gunshot wounds. He had been prophesying his own death for months, indicating that the Nation of Islam could not tolerate his continued teaching outside of their group. However, the mystery of his death has never been fully explained. Alex Haley, author of *Roots,* recalls that near the end of his life Malcolm X became convinced that other agencies apart from the Nation of Islam were involved in the harassment he was experiencing. "Things have happened since that are bigger than what they can do. I know what they can do. Things have gone beyond that."[21]

Alex Haley also recounts that the police would not take Malcolm X's requests for protection seriously. Although twenty policemen had been assigned to the meeting where he was killed, and even agents of the Bureau of Special Services were in attendance, "these men were nowhere in evidence during or after the assassination."[22]

In the months before the assassination, Alex Haley had visited "a very high government official" who was interested in Malcolm X. Haley also records that when Malcolm X arrived at the airport from his visit to Africa, "white men with cameras were positioned on the second level, taking pictures of all the Negroes who entered, and almost as obvious were Negro plainclothesmen moving about."[23] The Nation of Islam's website claims that a declassified memo reveals that the U.S. government "played a role in the 1965 assassination of Brother Malcolm X."[24]

Whoever was responsible for Malcolm X's murder, there is little doubt that they were motivated in their crime by his thinking. Malcolm X himself felt frustrated that the development of his ideas could not be accepted by either liberals or extremists: "They won't let me turn the corner!" he exclaimed exasperated to Haley. "I'm caught in a trap!"[25] To the end, however, he remained courageously open to new concepts. Shortly before his death he remarked to a reporter: "I'm man enough to tell you that I can't put my finger on exactly what my philosophy is now, but I'm flexible."[26]

In the last year of his life, after denouncing the Nation of Islam, Malcolm X developed an uncanny ability to walk a tightrope between the conflicting demands of different constituencies and party loyalties.

He gave speeches in all sorts of contexts, from black nationalist rallies and religious meetings to Marxist conferences. Yet he did not join any group or organization (apart from his own), or develop a coherent program himself. To the end he was a true independent, trying to find a way forward between the conflicting demands made on him. Thus at times he appeared to contradict himself.

On the one hand he was a firebrand protector of his race, willing to use "any means necessary" to defend his people's cause against the wily "whitey," while on the other hand he spoke of tolerance for all races and nonviolence. At one point he declared in desperation: "For Muslims, I'm too worldly; for other people, I'm too religious . . . for militants, I'm too moderate; for moderates, I'm too militant."[27] Although some have viewed this dichotomy as a sign of Malcolm X's weakness, a psychological consequence of the traumas of his life, it can also be seen as his unique strength: his aspiration to fight, as an individual, for a truth which could only be determined by himself through his personal struggles and experiences.

Today, only the most hardened racists would deny the justice of Malcolm X's cause. But Elijah Muhammad's philosophy, as Malcolm X was later to discover, offered no real solution; it only encouraged a polarization of the black and white races. This is not to say that the Nation of Islam did not a proffer a helpful influence in the lives of some, i.e., in giving an outer structure, discipline, and hope. However, in general terms it offered nothing for humanity's further evolution. Rather, it harked back to a consciousness based on what is physically—racially—inherited, supposing this to be of paramount importance.

Malcolm X, however, was to discover that the color of a person's skin did not determine that person's inner nature. And so, to his surprise, when he was free of the influence of the Nation of Islam during his pilgrimage to Mecca, he found that white people could also be loving and sincere towards him.

The significance of Malcolm X's remarkable path of destiny is the fact that, based on the phenomena he observed and what he learned from experience, he was able to develop and evolve his thinking.

Within a single lifetime, he was able to metamorphose racial prejudice into a tolerant philosophical and spiritual questioning. After spending 17 years in a pseudo-religious sect, he discovered the mainstream version of Islam, which enabled him to enter upon a path of spiritual discovery. This awakening led him to support, in his own words, "whatever benefits humanity."

Within this transformation shines the spirit of our age—the spirit of cosmopolitanism, of the overcoming of exclusive national, ethnic, and racial loyalties, and the birth of the self-determining, individualized, and free human being.

Elijah Muhammad's Inspiration

Following Malcolm X's murder Elijah Muhammad commented: "We didn't want to kill Malcolm! His foolish teaching would bring him to his own end! I am not going to let the crackpots destroy the good things Allah sent to you and me!"[28] Indeed, Malcolm X's awakening recognition of the individual human was a threat to the views Elijah Muhammad represented.

In his central work *Message to the Blackman in America*, Elijah Muhammad's racial teachings are clearly articulated: The "whole Caucasian [white] race is a race of devils."[29] On the other hand, "Allah has decided to place us [the black race] on the top. . . . We are the mighty, the wise, the best."[30] He continues: "Surely, if the Father of the two peoples, black and white, were the same, the two would love each other because they are of the same flesh and blood. It is natural then for them to love each other. Again, it is not unnatural then for a member or members of a different race or nation not to love the nonmember of their race or nation as their own."[31] Integration is "opposed by God, Himself. It is time that the two people should separate."

According to Elijah Muhammad, God made the black race, whereas the white race was created by an evil scientist named Yakub. Sixty-six trillion years ago a great explosion caused the Earth to separate from the moon. This was initiated by God, who, frustrated by the fact that the people on Earth did not speak one language, decided to kill humanity by destroying planet Earth. He did this by packing the center of the Earth with dynamite and lighting it. He failed in his endeavor to eradicate humanity, and the black tribe of Shabazz continued to live on in Egypt and Arabia.

The creation of the white race, however, occurred relatively recently. Six thousand and six hundred years ago a man named Yakub, a member of the black race, was born in Mecca.[32] Through discovering the science of genetics, Yakub learned that he could create a white race which would rule the black people. At the age of 18 he began preaching on the streets and gathering adherents by promising those who listened to him that he would make others work for them. The authorities in Mecca began to be concerned by this teaching and started arresting his followers, but the numbers of Yakub's people continued to grow. Eventually the jails were full of Yakub's devotees and Yakub himself was arrested, but his popularity continued to increase. And so finally the king struck a bargain with Yakub, who agreed to take his 59,999-strong retinue to live on the island on Patmos in the Aegean in return for 20 years of funding for his new community.

By controlling marriages and procreation, and a secret genocidal policy towards black babies, Yakub ensured that after 200 years only brown babies were born on the island. After another 200 years only yellow or red babies were born; and finally, after another 200 years there was a pale, white race of people on the island. Yakub had died after 150 years, but left instructions to his people which they observed. "When you become unalike (white), you may return to the Holy Land and people, from which you were exiled," he told them. This "devil" race was pale white with blue eyes, and called Caucasian (which, according to Elijah Muhammad, means a person whose evil is not confined to one's self, but affects others).

The devil white race then returned to live among the black people, where they created strife and disturbance. The king realized the problem and instructed his people to drive the devil white race out from "Paradise" and across the Arabian desert to Europe. There they were exiled for 2000 years and became savages living in caves. After this period, Allah sent Moses to recivilize the white race. However, this was a difficult task as this race was so barbaric. Elijah Muhammad describes one incident when Moses became so upset with the white race that he tricked 300 of its members to stand on a mountainside where he had hidden sticks of dynamite and, lighting the fuse, killed them all. When the religious leaders complained to Moses about the immoral nature of this deed, Moses protested that if they knew how much trouble the devils gave him, they would do the same as he!

Eventually, as had been prophesied, the devil white race gained control of "Original Man" (the black race) and subjugated them until the present time. Elijah Muhammad explains that the white race is called "mankind" because they are in the image and likeness of a human being (i.e., a black man). However, their pale skin and blue eyes prove that they do not warrant sincere love and friendship. For the black people have hearts of gold, love, and mercy, while the whites are typified by qualities of treachery, evil, and wrong-doing.

To round off this potent teaching, Elijah Muhammad gives a picture of the coming Judgment and Apocalypse during which the white devil race will be destroyed and the black race will remain on Earth in a physical paradise. This destruction of the "present world of the enemies of Allah" (the white race) will be carried out by a giant "wheel-shaped plane," known as "the Mother of Planets," which carries 1,500 bombing planes with the most deadly explosives.[33] After the annihilation of the white devil race and his world, the Earth will become a "heaven of the righteous forever." The black race will be clothed in silk interwoven with gold and eat the finest of foods.[34]

From one perspective it is apparent that Elijah Muhammad's exposition on race is an extreme reaction to contrary theories of racial superiority, such as those developed by Adolf Hitler in his *Mein Kampf*. These (more common) racist theories put the white race at the top of the hierarchy, and the black people at or near the bottom. Elijah Muhammad does the opposite, of course. And while in the context of white racism and the oppression and enslavement of black people over the last several hundred years such a reactionary philosophy is understandable, to tolerate it for that reason would be patronizing and inconsistent.

Elijah Muhammad also brings a new twist to racist teaching with his detailed theology and demonology, which is embodied in the black and white races respectively. But it is the vehement materialism of this teaching that is most portentous. Thus, together with the descent into base matter of the concepts of "God," "Devil," "Heaven," and "Hell," spirit is relegated to an insignificant status: "God is a man and we just cannot make Him other than man, lest we make Him an inferior one; for man's intelligence has no equal in other than man. His wisdom is infinite; capable of accomplishing anything that His brain can conceive. A Spirit is subjected to us and not we to the spirit."[35] He urges us therefore to see the coming of the "Son of Man" as a physical man "and not the coming of a 'spirit.' Let that one among you who believes God is other than man prove it!" At another point, referring to the Last Judgment, he asks: "How can a spirit be our judge when we cannot see a spirit?"

This crudely materialistic revelation is presented as a glorious gift to the black peoples of the Earth. "The belief in a God other than man (a spirit) Allah has taught me goes back into the millions of years . . . because the knowledge of God was kept as a secret from the public. This is the first time that it has ever been revealed, and we, the poor rejected and despised people, are blessed to be the first of all the people of earth to receive this secret knowledge of God."[36] An integral part of this teaching is a rejection of Christ as a divine being. As with the instruction of traditional Islam, Jesus is respected as a prophet, but Elijah Muhammad vehemently dismisses the idea of any spiritual entity connected with Jesus or Christ. Thus, he urges his followers to rid themselves of "the old slave teaching" that Jesus is still alive and listening to their prayers. Moreover, "Christianity was a religion organized and backed by the devils for the purpose of making slaves of black mankind."[37]

What are the origins of Elijah Muhammad's teaching? According to official Nation of Islam information, Elijah Muhammad received his knowledge from Master Wallace Fard Muhammad. For three and a half years, Fard taught and trained the Honorable Elijah Muhammad, night and day, about "the profound Secret Wisdom of the Reality of God." As we have already seen, Fard had supposedly identified himself to Elijah Muhammad as the Messiah, Christ, Jehovah, the Son of Man, God, etc. In other words, in Elijah Muhammad's opinion, Fard was an incarnation of the greatest divine power.[38]

While this view of Master Fard is well established and accepted within the Nation of Islam, it is not given much credence elsewhere. In his exhaustively researched biography of Malcolm X, George Perry claims that the Master Wallace Fard Muhammad was originally named Wallace Dodd Ford, and was a traveling door-to-door raincoat and silk salesman who also sold drugs. At one point Ford was even imprisoned in San Quentin for selling heroin. According to Perry's version of events, Ford did not claim to be God. Rather, he told his followers that he was from the same tribe as the prophet Muhammad and was Allah's messenger. Having set up a temple in Detroit, Ford registered its members and, for a fee, replaced their given slave names with their "original" names. In 1933 Ford was arrested in Detroit because one of his followers had killed another during a "religious sacrifice."[39]

In 1934, Ford is said to have vanished. Elijah Muhammad states that he "chose to suffer three-and-a-half years" in America, after which he returned to Mecca, having appointed his pupil Muhammad as head of the North American branch of the Nation of Islam. Unconfirmed rumors at the time suggested that Elijah Muhammad—having taken Ford's position at the top of the organization—may have had something to do with his disappearance.

Ford reportedly looked white, but maintained that he was a "light-skinned Negro" and "a brother from the East." Elijah Muhammad said that he was of mixed race, half black and half white, in order for him to go about "without being discovered or recognized."[40] The photograph, purported to be of Fard and used by the Nation of Islam, portrays a Caucasian-featured man with neatly combed and parted shiny hair; his hidden eyes solemnly focused on an open book which he holds in his hands.

It is probably fair to say that, like Perry, most researchers into the Nation of Islam suspect that Ford (or Fard) was a fraud who was using his political/religious teaching to extort money from the black community. But there is yet another possibility which has, perhaps understandably, been overlooked by conventional historians. Could it be that Ford really was from the East, and was even a "master" of sorts, albeit one with a hidden agenda?

On the surface, Fard was, seemingly, promoting and strengthening the identity of the black race. By telling them that they were gods and that the white race were devils he was promoting their self esteem at the expense of the "opposite race." In reality, though, his philosophy was divisive, materialistic, and spiritually impoverished. While it may have had some short-term positive effect in internal community-building and the development of some African-American business and cultural infrastructure, in the long term it compounded the injustice done to African-Americans by attempting to lead them away from a genuine spiritual knowledge of humanity. But what could be the motivation for developing such a teaching which took white supremacist philosophy and turned it on its head?

According to the spiritual teacher and researcher Rudolf Steiner, in recent times certain Eastern adepts have sought to take revenge against the West "for the suppression of Eastern occultism, and for the conquest of the East by the materialistic resources of the Western world."[41] In the early part of the twentieth century, the East was exploited by Western colonialists and had much to be aggrieved about. The West had not only been triumphant against countries like India, exploiting them for its own purposes, but had also exerted its own socio-political and religious influences. Steiner claimed that in retaliation occult groups—in particular Indian adepts—sought to take "revenge" against the West by corrupting Western esoteric teaching with their own form of "egotistic national occultism."

An example of an Eastern master with such an agenda can be found in the theosophist H. P. Blavatsky's travel diary *From the Caves and Jungles of Hindustan*. There she speaks of an Eastern master named

Gulab-Lal-Singh who accompanies her party on its travels. This figure—her colleague Colonel Olcott spoke of him as "a real Adept . . . with whom I have had to do"[42]—is described by Blavatsky as belonging "to the sect of raja-yogins, initiated into the mysteries of magic, alchemy, and various other occult sciences of India."[43] At one point in the narrative she reports that Gulab-Lal-Singh "hates and despises" the white race.[44]

If Gulab-Lal-Singh was a tangible Eastern initiate of the type that Rudolf Steiner refers to, could Fard similarly have been a genuine master from the East? Like Gulab-Lal-Singh, Fard's pupil Elijah Muhammad seemed to "hate and despise" the entire white race, calling them devils, regardless of who they were or what they had done. Parallels to "egotistic national occultism" can also be found in Elijah Muhammad's invectives against Christianity, his presentation of Jesus Christ as one prophet among many others, and his materialization of spiritual concepts.

In his important work, *The Masters Revealed*,[45] K. Paul Johnson attempts to identify the adepts and "mahatmas" of H. P. Blavatsky, revealing them to have been actual historical personalities. Johnson associates Blavatsky's master Gulab-Lal-Singh with the Maharaja Ranbir Singh of Kashmir. Whether similar research could prove that "the Master" Fard was truly a historical personage from the East remains to be seen. Certainly, his possible identity as an initiate with the specific mission of creating racial division and enmity as a "revenge" against Western society, would provide a good explanation for his racially orientated philosophy.

What is without question is that, in carrying out his work and helping to establish the Nation of Islam and its teachings, Ford (or at least Elijah Muhammad) helped further a view of the human being which is ultimately retrogressive in nature. At its heart, this philosophy lacks a holistic, integrated vision of the universal human spirit with the power to shine through all creeds, nations, and races. In contrast, Malcolm X struggled towards such an outlook in the final year of his life. In the following chapter, a spiritual picture of the human being will be explored in greater detail.

2.12 Race Against Time: Humanity, Group Consciousness, and the Individual

In the last chapter, we followed the remarkable course of Malcolm X's life and the transformations he underwent on his journey. From a perception that humans are determined by their race, he came to recognize the *individual* living beneath the skin color. In this chapter, I will make some observations about the issue of race in our time, and relate this to questions of group and individual consciousness.

We live in a time of extreme positions on the matter of race. Various viewpoints and tendencies exist, many of which are distant and not reconcilable. On the one hand we have the mostly well-intentioned phenomenon of "political correctness." From this perspective, humans are born "equal." Our differences are perceived to be purely cultural, and largely as a result of conditioning and influence through upbringing. Underneath this learned behavior, we have capacities and capabilities of equal value. At the other extreme of the spectrum is the notion that humans are determined by physical makeup, i.e., that we inherit our intellectual capacities, our character, our physical health, etc., from our ancestors.

The politically correct view veers towards the philosophy of "nurture" (see chapter 2.8), and thus no judgments can be made about anybody from external qualities. Male, female, gay, straight, black, white—all are essentially the same in the broadest sense. On the other hand, scientists and others who believe we are somehow genetically determined lean towards the "nature" argument. According to such thinking, we are given everything at birth and little of what we do in life can change our essential nature.

Racists also adhere to this view, believing that a person is defined and limited by his physical make-up. Black racists think that the black man is superior to people of all other races, while white supremacists believe that the white man is greater. Racist viewpoints may differ subtly, but the essence of such belief is that we are predetermined by our inherited physical organism. As I intend to show, both the politically correct and the scientific-deterministic positions are fairly useless, as they are both based on dogma and belief rather than true observation. More importantly, they are partial and incomplete views. Truth is more complicated than is allowed for by such fixed and rigid parameters.

I will attempt a phenomenological approach—observing what is apparent to our senses and thinking—and complement it with spiritual concepts, which together allow for a more elaborate, and hopefully truthful, picture of the modern human being. However, it is not my intention here to study modern scientific theory and research into race. Suffice it to say, that much of the earlier views which categorized people neatly into racial formats have been discredited and discarded. Today the concept of race is altogether more controversial and chaotic than the comfortable, nineteenth-century colonial view of the world. There is a good deal of argument as to what "race" means, and whether it is a useful and meaningful term at all. But for the purposes here, I use the common definition of race as defined in the Oxford Dictionary as a "group of persons connected by . . . distinct ethnical stock."

A walk down a main street in New York, London, Paris, or Berlin today will reveal a remarkable cross section of humanity, wholly different to what one would have observed walking down a similar street one hundred years ago. In the past, these Western cities would have been dominated by people of a Caucasian (white) appearance. Today, one is confronted by humans of all races. It is apparent that what we are experiencing now is an intermingling of people of different racial backgrounds. In the past there were also international cities with cosmopolitan populations, such as ancient Rome or Greek Alexandria. But although these places would also have teemed with a diverse humanity, no period of history matches the present time in terms of a worldwide convergence of races.

So why is this happening? Naturally, there are fundamental political and economic factors that on the surface appear to adequately explain the present situation—and on a certain level these are absolutely correct and true. We are all conversant today with the terms "asylum seeker," "economic migrant," "refugee." But it is also conceivable that these external factors are facilitating something else: a hidden evolutionary principle which is conspiring to bring about a new situation. These new circumstances offer a differentiated context for human development within which people are encouraged to meet what is outwardly different from themselves. This phenomenon will be examined in relation to varying traditional groupings of people.

A consequence of the dramatic movements of peoples across the globe is that the original races are becoming more diffuse and gradually intermixed. However, "race" in its broadest sense is still representative of the largest groupings of peoples around the world. Thus, in a superficial sense, a Caucasian can outwardly identify with other members of his race across national boundaries, as can a person of African origin, or Semitic, Oriental, or Native American.

In terms of such extensive classifications of people, the next largest group with which individuals identify are the various nations. Nations can include people of different races—the United States being the best example—and constitute a grouping of people who inhabit a certain land mass and often speak the same language. Thus, people born within the political territory of Italy are usually considered to be Italian, and so on.

A step down from nations is the concept of tribe, although these are no longer found (in their original form) in the Western world. But we know from history that tribal groupings did exist in the West, and are still to be found in Africa and South America. A tribe is a closely connected group, usually by blood, with a common way of life and culture. In the West, young people often seek to recreate the experience of the tribe through music fashions which have strong cultural and ideological bonds (punks, metal fans, ravers, etc.).

Finally, the smallest of the traditional groupings are families. Although these are far less strong than they were in the past, they are of course still significant. In Southern Europe, for example, the family still dominates life and is the focus of many activities. The "extended family" still provides an extensive support system. On the other hand, in countries like Britain the family is disintegrating so quickly that increasing numbers of houses are having to be built because more and more people are choosing to live alone or are forced to live alone due to separation and divorce.

Overall, it is an observable phenomenon (at least in the Western world) that these groupings—race, nation, tribe, and family—are gradually losing their power. Migration is beginning to dilute the concept of race, nations are becoming less significant in the globalized world, tribes are disappearing, and families are shrinking. In their place, what we are witnessing is a birth of new networks of people who create their ties out of free choice, be it a common interest, cause, belief, faith, or passion. Thus we have environmental and political groups like Friends of the Earth and Amnesty International, religious and spiritual organizations such as the Western Buddhist Order or the Baha'i faith, international soccer fans who follow the fortunes of multicultural teams such as Manchester United, and so on.

These new networks are not based on any of the old relationships. The old connections worked largely through the ties of blood. People were related either closely through a family, clan or tribe, or more broadly through a nation or race. Their relationships were inspired by a principle which came from something that was *given*; from a past kinship. We are now witnessing a fragmentation of these old relationships based on forms of group consciousness. Arising in their place are networks of individuals who come together through freedom and choice. This is not to say that the old connections are in any way "bad" or to be discouraged. On the contrary, they are real and should be honored. But it is becoming apparent that the trend of human development is taking us in another direction—towards the birth of the autonomous individual self, forging its own path to the future, free of the traditional bonds of the past.

This new situation is not always easy, however. As we know from experience, the ties felt through race, nation, tribe, and family are to a certain degree inherent. They arise from the human being's constitution, and—although they can of course also be difficult—they are to a certain extent *given*. The new relationships to be forged between individuals, richly rewarding as they often are, sometimes require far greater inner effort, at least initially. These connections, almost by definition, appear to be calling for a new exertion of creative human energy. The force which is produced by this inner effort is also known by the more familiar name of *love*.

What is revealing itself through these new pictures of human interrelations is an evolutionary process of development from the group soul nature (connected by blood) to a process of individualization and separation. Through the forging of new connections, new communities are born on Earth; communities which are increasingly based on soul and spirit instead of physically inherited traits.

Many people instinctively feel that racism—the notion that one person is less than another because of his race—is a retrogressive and pernicious phenomenon in modern life. What I intend to show here is that it is also unscientific. However, the sort of science (or knowledge) I will apply encompasses a spiritual conception of the human, and in this sense can be referred to as a *spiritual* science. From this perspective, the human is formed and developed under the influence of manifold spiritual and physical forces. Racism as a philosophy takes a single factor—essentially the physically inherited body—and makes it an all-important principle. It therefore ignores, in effect, the multitude of other shaping and forming influences on human consciousness. I will consider a few of these below.

As stated earlier, whatever influence the factor of race has on the human—it is not my intention to try to define that here—it derives from the physically inherited body. In other words, racial characteristics are received from the outer, physical organism. It is a fact that we recognize people's racial origins from the way they look. In this sense, race is connected to *the body*.

Moving from race to nation, it has already been discussed that nations can—and do—consist of different races. This is illustrated in an excellent way by international soccer competitions such as the World Cup, in which national teams of dozens of countries play each other in a knock-out tournament. While many countries, particularly African and Asian, still field racially homogeneous teams, most European teams are racially mixed. At the 2002 World Cup, for example, the England team had a core of five black players. Nobody except the most racially prejudiced questioned the "Englishness" of those players.

So if nationhood is independent of race, how does it work? What is the binding force of the nation? As discussed earlier in chapter 2.6, the phenomenon of nationhood is associated with a geographical region, and often also with language. A person belongs to a certain nation through being born and/or raised on a certain land mass and within a certain culture, and usually speaking a certain language. If one considers the strong national characteristics of racially mixed nations—people actually born or raised on the same soil—it is apparent that subtle binding forces are at work. Materialists would describe such forces as being purely cultural, "learned behavior." Certainly it is learned, but what are the influences at work molding the national character? From where do the multiplicity of national cultures arise?

Spiritual researchers have added mystical dimensions to the concept of nation, suggesting that the binding force works through the subtle, metaphysical bodies. According to such perception, the physical landmass is encompassed by an invisible aura, which works on and modifies the individual subtle bodies of the people living there. This national aura is sustained by the spiritual entity associated with that nation.[1] Whereas the racial aspect works through the physical *body*, the national influence works on the individual *soul*.

The above may seem like a fantastic theory to many readers, but it gives an important alternative understanding to the phenomenon of mass migration in our time. What is it that drives a person to want to live in another part of the world and to have their children brought up there? Of course there are the outer economic and political entice-ments, but perhaps unconscious impulses are also at work, impelling such people to live in areas of the world to which they have a special, hidden affinity. This largely unconscious impetus could be interpreted as the force of individual destiny.

In the first part of this chapter, I spoke of the forces of fragmen-tation and individualization at work everywhere in modern culture, and the evident emergence of individual consciousness. To this pat-tern can be associated an actual psycho-spiritual phenomenon which people like Jung had an inkling of: the higher ego, or "I." This core spiritual aspect of each human being is, as described earlier, the element which has allowed for the human being's increasing individ-ualization from the previous racial and other types of group consciousness.

The "I" carries the essence of our being, our identity, our personal "individuality." According to the Western tradition of reincarna-tion, it is the "I" which travels from incarnation to incarnation into different races, nations, tribes, and families. The individual "I" incarnates over time into varying physical bodies, experiencing the fruits of different peoples and cultures. Therefore, if race is con-nected with *body* and nation with *soul*, the higher self or "I" is connected with *spirit*.

From this broader perspective, it is not possible to make any judg-ments about an individual human being based on their outer physical appearance. Any pre-judging (prejudice) of a person becomes mean-ingless. Take as an example a woman who is racially of African origin but was born and is living in France. Firstly, the woman's racial aspect is visible from her physical appearance. Secondly, however, having been born into the French nation, she also embodies the geographical and metaphysical reality of being French. Thirdly, and most importantly, this woman carries a core spiritual identity—her universal "I"—which is neither African nor French, but human.

This study could be perpetually deepened and extended, because our limited perception—based on the five commonly known senses—provides only a partial picture of reality. In our present state of materialistic denial, Western humanity is rather like the proverbial man born blind who denies the existence of sight. Today, the increasing numbers of first-hand testimonies from individuals who have broken through to advanced states of consciousness suggest that we only have a glimpse of the many dimensions and cosmic influences which work on human consciousness. Here I will give only two more examples of circumstances which influence our individual character, one of a cosmic, the other of an earthly nature.

Apart from the spiritual beings associated with nations, spiritual researchers talk of an entity connected to humanity as a whole. This can be referred to as the *Zeitgeist*, or the spirit of our time, which represents a force transcending nation and race, working uniformly on humanity as a totality. This being has an influence which is characterized by the concept of "epoch." Its subtle authority molds the different periods of human history.[2]

In contrast to such a cosmic influence, spiritual investigators have also identified metaphysical energies—telluric forces—which arise from the various geographical regions of the Earth. These forces, popularly known as "Earth energies," work independently of ethnicity, but have a powerful effect on the inner nature of the human being.[3] Such an influence can work on any person, depending on their geographical movements.

A truly advanced and all-encompassing science could go further and identify many other influences which work on human consciousness. When humanity has begun to overcome the superficial emotions and thoughts which lie behind racism, nationalism, sexism, and all the other negative "-isms," it will be possible for these manifold spiritual influences to be studied widely and seriously, and for a greater picture of the human being—a knowledge which is at once spiritual and scientific—to emerge.

Postscript

As the bonds of family, tribe, nation, and race begin to dissolve, and as people begin to meet each other through their individualized consciousness, retrograde elements within society seek to divide humanity up into new forms of group-consciousness. Such groups have little to do with the new networks of free individuals mentioned earlier, and have much more in common with the character of a tribe.

An example of this is the notion, much discussed since the events of September 11, 2001, of the "clash of civilizations." This idea, first put forward by Harvard University Professor Samuel Huntington in an article in the American foreign policy periodical *Foreign Affairs* in 1993, envisages a post-Cold-War world divided no longer by ideology (Capitalism versus Communism) but by civilizations and cultures. The attacks on U.S. soil in September 2001 appeared to confirm this thesis, i.e., that somehow the "Islamic world" had declared war against the West.

As the Egyptian-born author Ahdaf Soueif wrote in a moving essay, most Arabs are bewildered by the "clash of civilizations" theory and "marvel that the West wastes any time on it at all. Can't they see, people ask, how much of their culture we've adopted?"[4] She goes on to list the enormous Western influences in Egyptian culture, arts, and education. As others have argued, the "clash of civilizations" idea may well be a front for the "need" for an enemy following the collapse of the Soviet Union. Just as in the visionary novel *1984*—in which the great continental political blocks were constantly at war with each other—so it appears that our contemporary political masters envision a twenty-first-century war without end against undefined enemies—what the historian Charles A. Beard called "perpetual war for perpetual peace." This is necessary, from the point of view of a shadowy elite, in order to keep populations under control through the repressive conditions of wartime and a generally pervasive and debilitating sense of fear.

Whatever the full truth of the political situation, the attempt to categorize people according to their "civilization" is ultimately retrogressive. Civilizations are made up of individuals. To characterize large groups of people according to abstract notions is to ignore the emerging autonomous self within each individual. Any attempt to push people into new tribal blocks is contrary to the evolutionary principles described here, and is something we should be awake to.

Part 3

Concepts: Signposts for the Weary Traveler

Introduction to Part 3

In my general introduction, I spoke of this section as providing a backdrop to the rest of the book. Here is what I mean by this.

In the last section, I gave examples of how a person might begin to view aspects of modern culture from a spiritual perspective. In some instances I introduced spiritual ideas which threw light on the phenomena observed in the essays. In this section, I present concepts which have an important bearing on present times, but I do not always connect these directly to particular events or situations. Rather, I introduce these ideas here as essential background information to the overall theme of overcoming materialism in modern culture.

In chapter 3.1, I seek to explain why *people* appear to be changing so much today. I relate this to an idea derived from Rudolf Steiner's research about humanity crossing a threshold in personal consciousness, and show how this might relate to behavior and human interrelations. The essays in part 2 are about what is happening now. Central to current affairs are people. I believe that we are all undergoing changes in consciousness, and in the broadest sense are experiencing an initiation, i.e., a rebirth to a new way of being. The people we have studied—David Icke, Malcolm X, Charles and Diana, Mary Bell, etc.— all demonstrate in different ways this rebirth to a new consciousness. They reflect the modern experience of struggling for selfhood in the midst of confusion and changing times. As I show in this chapter, we are all having to find our essential selves—our "I"—in the context of radical soul separation. Our thinking, feeling, and will are being torn apart.

In chapter 3.2, I discuss further a concept introduced briefly in chapter 1.6: the notion that there exist groups of individuals who work secretly towards the goal of pushing human history and development in a certain direction. The idea of "conspiracy theory" is of course not new. What is significant in Steiner's view of the matter is his explanation of why specific groups are seeking to gain global control. Steiner speaks of groupings who represent what he calls "Anglo-American" interests. Post 9/11, the special relationship of Britain and America has taken center stage, and the fact of the Anglo-American alliance is there for all to see. Steiner's research explains why these hidden "Anglo-American brotherhoods" are working to control human destiny, and specifically why they want to see the continuing dissemination of materialism. As this book is all about overcoming materialistic tendencies in contemporary culture, this chapter is important in showing why we face the challenges we currently do.

In chapter 3.3, I give a brief survey of the concept of the "Antichrist" in popular culture, the Bible, and in a short story by a Russian mystic. Finally, I relate this to a prediction by Steiner about the imminent physical incarnation of a particular spiritual being on earth. This entity, who Steiner calls Ahriman, after the Persian god of the same name, is also intimately associated with materialism. I present this idea here because, once again, this theme is closely connected to the materialism which is so omnipresent in the people and situations described in this book. The preparations for the incarnation of a being who is said to be the chief representative of materialistic thinking are inseparable from the continuing materialistic nature of Western culture itself.

Are we really about to witness the birth of a figure who, although Christlike in appearance, is actually a kind of Antichrist? There is already a vast fundamentalist Christian movement in the U.S. which is awaiting the End Times of the biblical Apocalypse. I do not wish to relate the concepts I present here with that movement's interpretation of the Bible. If Steiner is correct in his descriptions of the incarnation of Ahriman, it is quite likely that some of those fundamentalist Christians will greet the Prince of Materialism as their long-awaited Second Coming (i.e., they will be deluded into believing he is the Christ). I felt it important to present Steiner's view of Ahriman as an aid to developing a differentiation between these various interpretations of how evil might incorporate itself in a physical form on Earth.

3.1 Crossing the Threshold of No Return: Waking to a Changing Consciousness

It is a fairly common experience today that time appears to be speeding up. Despite all our labor-saving devices and our higher standard of living, there never seems to be any *time* for anything. Concurrently, we are faced with new antisocial phenomena, from the uncontrollably violent behavior some people exhibit while in an airplane (so-called "air-rage") to the anger that can erupt while people push a shopping cart around a crowded supermarket. Tempers seem to have a shorter fuse, and many people betray signs of a ruthless self-interest. Looking back one hundred years to the beginning of the twentieth century, life appeared to be slower, calmer, and altogether less competitive.

This situation can be analyzed and explained to some extent from a socioeconomic viewpoint: people working longer hours, families without a homemaker having to contract out child care, greater levels of stress, etc. But do these factors truly explain what is going on? From a different perspective, it has been suggested that the life conditions on Earth are changing, that the context of life is being altered and inner consciousness is undergoing an enormous transformation.

Steiner spoke about changes in human consciousness and how these affect life. The concept of evolving consciousness is central to his work, the idea that humanity changes with the development of supra-sensible (spiritual) bodies. In our time, according to him, a two-thousand-year process of the incarnation of the individual spirit—the "I," or eternal part of ourselves—is undergoing an intensification. This new sense of individuality, which emerged markedly in the twentieth century (see chapter 1.5), has had significant consequences which include our gradual emancipation from ties of the blood (family, tribe, nation, race) and traditional roles based on gender, social class, and so on.

Steiner also spoke about supplementary changes which would occur in our present time. The whole of humanity, he predicted, would experience an unconscious crossing of an inner threshold around the turn of the millennium.[1] This change would not entail any choice; it would, essentially, happen to everyone, like it or not! In spiritual terms, this process amounts to an "initiation," and in effect demands an acceleration of personal development. I will discuss the implications of such an *unconscious* initiation for humanity as a whole, implications which Steiner did not spell out.

In what amounts to his basic meditation manual, *How to Know Higher Worlds*, Steiner describes sound methods for obtaining evolved modes of consciousness and the ability to perceive hidden dimensions—clairvoyance. During the process of achieving such higher consciousness, a division occurs in what Steiner calls the "soul forces"—the abilities to think and feel, and in the will. Previously, these forces had been held in a harmonious unity by a kind of cosmic grace. Cosmic laws guided their interconnections.

What did he mean by this? Let's take an example. Under normal conditions, most people seeing an accident would try and help those affected. This is an instinctive human reaction. On seeing a person needing help, our feelings and thoughts connect with our will to act. Such a reaction, for most people, is largely unconscious.

However, a person who is an initiate experiences such an event in a different way. In the course of consciously directed personal development, a point is reached when an inner spiritual threshold is crossed.

At that point, our forces of thinking, feeling, and will become more independent of each other. To return to the example of the accident, in contrast to the (unconscious) human instinct to help in such a situation, an initiate would experience complete inner freedom as to what actions he or she could take. The instinct to automatically help would no longer be there. Rather, the initiate makes a decision to help out of a truly free, conscious resolve.

Outwardly, the actions of an ordinary person and an initiate may appear identical. Of course the initiate would still help the affected person, but the inner processes preceding these actions would be different in the sense that one is carried out in full consciousness and freedom while the other is largely instinctive. Through the course of higher development, the cosmic grace which held together the initiate's forces of thinking, feeling, and will would have withdrawn. In its place, the initiate has given birth to a new higher consciousness which now has the role of controlling thinking, feeling, and will. The central guiding factor that has now been given full power to make free choices is the evolved self—the individual nature or "I." (It goes without saying that this presumes that the initiate had followed a sound path of development.)

However, Steiner warns of the dangers involved if the forces of thinking, feeling, and will become emancipated before the self has been sufficiently strengthened. One can imagine here an image of a carriage with three horses, the carriage representing the higher self and the horses representing the forces of thinking, feeling, and will. Previously, the horses were kept in check by an experienced driver. Now, the newly born "I" has to take the reins and gain mastery over these forces. If allowed, each of these horses would like to go its own way.

If we are not sufficiently prepared to take on this process, if we cross the threshold of consciousness prematurely, there is a danger that one or more of these soul forces could overpower another. Steiner gives examples of what can happen:

1. The will predominates and runs rampant, leading to a violent character, and the tendency to "rush from one unbridled action to the next."

2. Feeling predominates, so that a person who reveres others can become dependent on them; or an individual can be lost in raptures of religious self-gratification.

3. Thinking predominates, which can lead to a boundless desire for wisdom, or general indifference and coldness.

Many other possibilities exist, of course, but this gives some indication of the inherent dangers of what can happen if the forces of thinking, feeling, and will become emancipated before the self is sufficiently strong enough to take hold of "the reins" and keep them in balance.

The spiritual entity which Steiner calls "the Guardian of the Threshold" (known as "the Dweller of the Threshold" in other traditions), warns the initiate: "[Y]our own wisdom must be great enough to take over the task previously performed by the hidden wisdom now departed from you . . . do not try to cross this threshold until you are completely free of fear and feel yourself ready for the highest responsibility."[2]

Steiner says that everything that has been instilled in us, all the influences of our upbringing and life-experiences up to this point, are now dissolved. The individual becomes truly free from all previous constraints, and must take full responsibility for her thoughts, feelings, and actions.

From the above account, initiation may appear to be an unattractive and frightening prospect. But what Steiner is talking about is a process of becoming cocreators with the divine world—the same goal to be achieved in Christian and other religious traditions. Man is no longer a subservient creature, but an autonomous, free individual. This is the path of human development and evolution.

To counter the dangers unearthed on the path of inner development, conscious initiation involves a strengthening of the self through specific exercises. Steiner shows how, already in everyday consciousness, the "I" can gain control over the thinking, feeling, and will through meditation and other inner activities. To gain control over the will, for example, a person might resolve to carry out a simple but specific, perhaps meaningless, task at a given time each day. To develop the power of thought, an individual should direct their thinking to a particular concept and keep it from deviating for a period of a few minutes.

The problem humanity faces today, assuming Steiner is correct, is that it is being taken through this process *unconsciously*. Humanity is being taken over the inner threshold of consciousness to achieve initiation without being given any choice in the matter, so our forces of thinking, feeling, and will are losing their harmonious balance. People are bereft of their inherent ability to find inner equilibrium, and are driven by one or another of their soul forces. Feelings get out of hand, thinking becomes cold and detached, or an unruly will drives crazed actions.

What does this mean for us today? Each person is called upon to intensify their selfhood, to strengthen their consciousness and take greater responsibility, to develop control over their thinking, feeling, and will.

I believe that the symptoms of an emancipated thinking, feeling, and will are there for all to see in our present culture. Life is potentially more extreme and dangerous. But the flip-side of these changes in human consciousness is a fantastic possibility for conscious freedom: for true knowing, real feeling, and noble action.

3.2 Brothers of the Shadows: A Perspective on Conspiracies

In his recent book *The Last Empire*, Gore Vidal suggests that the American public has been conditioned to respond to the word "conspiracy" with a smirk and a chuckle. Conspiracy, in other words, is for the nuts and the loners, and is not to be taken seriously. In this way, Vidal argues, through the media's association of the concept of conspiracy with fringe or extreme elements, the real conspirators go unnoticed. It is a vital point, and Vidal courageously chases and exposes real conspiracies by politicians, the FBI, and lobbyists for the tobacco companies.

But the flip-side of the conspiracy coin is the proliferation of fanciful and fantastic theories which now crisscross the globe in seconds with the help of electronic media. The spread of the Internet has democratized conspiracy theory. Millions of people now have the ability to publish their own unique analyses of what is going on. A necessary consequence of this massive growth in personal publishing is that it is much more difficult to find pearls among the rubbish. Someone even observed, humorously, that in the Internet age if you want to keep something secret make it public! (For example, how can anyone today make a reasonable assessment of who was responsible for plotting the assassination of John F. Kennedy? Simply reading the reams of material on this subject alone would take weeks.)

Amidst the more fantastic theories of UFOs and intergalactic lizards, certain core themes persistently reoccur in the mass of "conspiracy theory" material now available. Principal among them is the idea that a shadowy elite is seeking to enslave humanity under the auspices of a single, centralized world government. The name of the mysterious "Illuminati" is most often associated with such a group, although what is meant by it is usually ill-defined. The Illuminati are, supposedly, a cabal of top bankers, politicians, and businessmen seeking to create the aforesaid all-powerful government.

What is the truth of all this? I do not propose to give a full answer here, but would like to introduce a perspective on the theme, one which has generally not been given serious consideration, taken from the research of Rudolf Steiner. Why Steiner? Because, if for no other reason, his pronouncements and indications on practical areas have borne such remarkable fruit, testimony to which are thousands of Waldorf schools offering a new kind of education, farms successfully practicing bio-dynamics, clinics dispensing anthroposophic medicines, and so on.

As a profound clairvoyant, Steiner claimed to be able to investigate other dimensions of reality for insight into the human condition. His legacy is hundreds of volumes of published talks and written works on a cornucopia of themes. However, as mentioned above, his work—in contrast to that of many other spiritual teachers and gurus—has shown itself to have practical applications in all areas of life. This in itself does not provide ultimate evidence for the truth of his work, but it does correspond to the biblical dictum: "[B]y their fruits ye shall know them."

In 1916 and 1917, in the midst of the catastrophic First World War, Steiner gave a series of 25 lectures to a group of his followers who gathered together in their center in Dornach, in neutral Switzerland. These lectures, since translated and published in English,[1] offer a unique reading of contemporary events. Behind the outer façade of world affairs, suggested Steiner, the machinations of occult groups or "brotherhoods" were at work. Certain of these brotherhoods had wanted the

Great War to take place, and had manipulated events to bring it about. In doing this, they sought to protect the dominant economic position of the English-speaking world, and in turn to crush the "mediating" role of Central European powers such as Germany, the Austro-Hungarian empire, and so on.

These occult brotherhoods—small groups of men who met together in "lodges" and practiced ceremonial magic as a means of achieving certain goals—originated from the English-speaking world and were allied, in particular, with Anglo-American interests. Their aim was to extend Anglo-American influence across the globe, and to ensure the predomination of Anglo-American culture. Furthermore, they sought to extend its superiority into the distant future, essentially to ensure that the present state of affairs continues evermore.

According to Steiner's research, human evolution goes through "great periods" of development. During each of these periods, a particular people is given the task of leading humanity in a spiritual sense. Over the millennia, it has been the destiny of different peoples to bring specific qualities, in a benevolent way, to the whole of humanity. Particular periods of history are thus "led" by particular nations. This does not imply a form of political control or empire—and it is certainly not a theory of national or racial superiority—but refers to a spiritual form of authority.

Steiner suggested that the Western world, and in particular the English-speaking peoples, has been given the task of coming to grips with the material world—of becoming comfortable on Earth and developing a harmony with it. In this specific sense, the West was to introduce a certain kind of (beneficial) materialism into human development. But this materialism was only meant to be developed up to a certain point. As we saw in part 1, materialism in human evolution was necessary for humans to become fully part of the earthly world, and to help incarnate our individual "I" nature. But beyond that it has the potential to be destructive. Materialism as a *philosophy*, which shuts out the possibility of soul and spirit, is retrogressive, and works as an evil in human evolution. The Anglo-American brotherhoods who seek

239

dominion over mankind know this, and hence today are deliberately sponsoring various kinds of materialism in the hope of halting and trapping humanity at the present stage of its development. They don't want humans to progress beyond the present stage of immersion in the material world. In other words, they don't want us to reconnect in a free way with our spiritual "I," because they know that their grip over humanity would then be lost. Human progress is dependent on spiritual knowledge, and thus the occult brotherhoods work against it.

Steiner explained further that the brotherhoods were aware that the Slavic peoples were to be given the task of leadership on behalf of humanity during the next great period of history. For this reason, the Anglo-American brotherhoods not only sought to dominate the present "great period" of human development, but—knowing that the Slavs had an important mission in the future—sought to gain control over the Slavic peoples (Russia in particular) in the present, in order to interfere with or even put a halt to their coming task.

In this way, the Anglo-American brotherhoods could extend their control over human development into the distant future. Steiner later claimed that the Bolshevik Revolution in Russia, which led to the later USSR and the 72-year cultural, intellectual, economic, and political repression of the populations of its various peoples, was masterminded and sponsored by these same brotherhoods as a means of controlling the region and its peoples.[2]

What is the evidence for Steiner's analysis? Apart from anything else, it is interesting to note the present state of world affairs, and how since 1916–17 Anglo-American culture has come to dominate the globe in tandem with American economic and political influence (with the enthusiastic support of British politicians). However, this observation admittedly does not offer "proof" in a strict sense.

Another source of evidence is the remarkable research of Prof. Carroll Quigley (1910–1977) who wrote two substantial volumes, *The Anglo-American Establishment* (1949) and *Tragedy and Hope* (1966),[3] on the secret network which emerged from the enterprise of Cecil Rhodes. Quigley characterized the power of this group through its influence in politics, culture, and social life as "terrifying." It is important to note that Quigley was no crazed and paranoid conspiracy nut, but a respected Georgetown professor, and a teacher of Bill Clinton.

Other authors have followed Quigley's lead and complemented his studies with contemporary observations. A few have even related Steiner's ideas to Quigley's research.[4] In this context, however, I would like to mention two "symptoms" which, at the very least, offer circumstantial evidence for Steiner's diagnosis.

In chapter 1.2, I mentioned C. G. Harrison and cited his remarkable book, *The Transcendental Universe*, a record of six lectures given in 1893 to a mysterious group of "Christian esotericists" named the Berean Society. Little is known about the Berean Society or Harrison, although he wrote two more books in his lifetime. What is clear is that Harrison, who speaks in defense of the "high" Church, had access to a phenomenal store of esoteric thought, and was privy to a certain amount of "inside" knowledge. In his second lecture, he speaks not only of "the next great European war," but also of the "national character" of the Slavic peoples and its ability to "enable them to carry out experiments in Socialism, political and economical, which would present innumerable difficulties in Western Europe."[5] Remember that these lectures were given in 1893, 21 years before the First World War and 24 years before the Bolshevik Revolution!

While Harrison claimed to be a "theoretical occultist" as opposed to a "practical" one—he did not practice magic or ritual, with the implication that he was not a member of a "lodge" himself—from his work it is evident that he represents an esoteric train of thought which is clearly in defense of the English establishment. How did he know about the forthcoming war, as well as the "experiments in Socialism" which would take a grip on Russia and its surrounding states for most of the twentieth century? If he was not, as he claimed, a "practical occultist" himself, it is reasonable to assume that he had contact with people who were, and who had access to the malign plans of such secret groups.

The second significant piece of evidence which offers some backing for Steiner's claims of occult interference in world politics is to be found in a special edition of the satirical weekly *The Truth*, published at Christmas 1890. Under the heading "The Kaiser's Dream," the magazine featured a cartoon map of Europe together with a humorous commentary. Many observations can be made of the map, but the most pertinent is that all the countries of Europe are shown as republics with the exception of Russia and its neighboring states, over which are written the words "Russian Desert." In addition, Germany is identified with the words "German Republics."

This map signifies not only a foreknowledge—similar to Harrison's—of the fate of Russia to become a cultural and economic "desert," but also of the future splitting of Germany into "republics." The magazine's editor, Henry Labouchère, was a Freemason.

Was his remarkable foresight luck, or did he have inside knowledge of plans to shape the world? Is it possible that the above examples are coincidence and happy flukes? Perhaps it is possible, although it is unlikely. Do these examples offer evidence for the existence of occult brotherhoods with pernicious plans for political manipulation? We may never know for sure, but it is evident that Steiner's perspective offers much food for serious thought, and opens up important new vistas for understanding current world events.

3.3 The Real Omen: The Incarnation of Evil

The concept of Antichrist—a being who is the antithesis of Christ—is well established in popular culture. The 1970s film trilogy *The Omen*, about the orphan Damien Thorn who is capable of the utmost evil, probably did more than anything else to introduce the concept into the public mind. Although marketed today as an "all-time great," to the modern eye the *Omen* films appear naïve and relatively tame, even comic. But their theme is as enduring as it is archetypal.

A young boy loses his mother and father in mysterious and strange circumstances and is adopted by his wealthy uncle. Slowly, he eliminates all who stand in his way as he establishes a powerful position in corporate business. He is perceived as a creative thinker and an attractive, charismatic individual. But he embodies Satan, and his goal is the pinnacle of earthly power: the Presidency of the United States. In the final film of the trilogy he is deposed, but only after he has deceived a large portion of humanity.

The earliest echoes of this tale are to be found in the Bible. Although the word "Antichrist" is only used by John in his epistles to the faithful,[1] the apostle Paul refers to "that man of sin . . . the son of perdition," who will put himself in place of God, "shewing that he is God . . . with all power and signs and lying wonders."[2] Paul's brief account bears all the keynotes of the Evil One.

Biblical scholars argue about the origin of the idea of "Antichrist," some believing it derives from the Old Testament, principally the book of Daniel, while others claim that Paul received original inspiration. Whatever the origin of Paul's passage, Christ himself refers to the idea of evil masquerading as good when he speaks of the arising of "false Christs and false prophets" who would show great signs and wonders with the potential to "deceive the very elect."[3] But perhaps the most famous references to such an evil entity are to be found in St. John's visionary book, Revelation. Although this section of the Bible is written in quite a different style—pictorial and symbolic as opposed to realistic—it also tells of a "Beast" who deceives humanity through miracles and wonders. Here, the evil being forces all people to receive a mark on their right hand or forehead without which they can neither buy nor sell.[4]

Many fundamentalist Christian tracts take all the above references and create a composite narrative out of them. In particular, much is often made of the reference from Revelation in relation to a possible future in which the world's population would have microchips inserted into their skin. Without such a "mark of the Beast," it is said, nobody would be able to buy or sell. But whether the Beast of the book of Revelation is the same entity as the Antichrist figure in the other references given above is questionable. Nevertheless, the often enigmatic language of the Bible leaves plenty of room for continuing conjecture, controversy, and lively debate.

One literary depiction of the concept of Antichrist which has not received nearly as much attention as the references in the Bible is to be found in the work of the nineteenth-century Russian philosopher and poet Vladimir Solovyov. In his *War, Progress, and the End of History* is a remarkable "Short Story of the Antichrist."[5] This concise tale is set in contemporary times, with the following scenario. A "Pan-Mongolian" movement has resulted in the Japanese leading a unified Eastern Asia, comprising Japan, Korea, China, and Indochina. Creating a colossal army, the Pan-Mongolians march across Russia, Eastern Europe, and into Germany, France, and England. Here they create a great empire which lasts for half a century until it is eventually deposed by a unified Europe. This painful colonial experience causes the European nations to create a United States of Europe.

It is into this context that a great man is born. By the age of 33, many recognize him as a "superman": spiritually brilliant, a great thinker, a genius of exceptional beauty and nobility of character, a philanthropist, ascetic, etc. Solovyov tells us that although the great man believes in God, he truly "loved only himself." He respects the Christ of the Gospels, but in reality he believes that he has a more important mission.

One night, the great man is contemplating the nature of Jesus Christ, when he feels great fear followed by a burning envy, and eventually an intense hatred. In a fit of madness he attempts to take his own life, but is saved by a supernatural force which speaks to him in his desperation. This force incorporates itself into the very being of the great man, and thus is he possessed by the Antichrist himself. The great man is now changed, and displays a supernatural, inspired brilliance that surpasses even his previous state. With this newfound genius he writes a great work, *The Open Way to Universal Peace and Prosperity*, which is soon translated and published in all the major languages of the world. The book, which is received with great acclaim, appears to answer all the main questions people have, and is accepted as "the revelation of the complete truth."

Eventually, he is elected lifetime president of the United States of Europe, and finally "emperor." Very soon, all the nations of the world voluntarily come under his dominion, and he begins a great reign of peace. Indeed, in the very first year of his reign he promises and manages to establish peace around the world. In the second year he promises and again delivers universal prosperity, with all the world's social and economic problems solved. In his third year, understanding that people want amusement in addition to peace and prosperity, he appoints a mysterious magician from the East, Apollonius, who—as the emperor's constant companion—gives the nations of the world "the possibility of never-ending enjoyment of most diverse and extraordinary miracles."

Finally, having resolved all other major problems, the emperor seeks to address the religious question. Beginning with Christianity, he calls a great congress of all its representatives, consisting principally of the Catholic, Protestant (Evangelical), and Orthodox churches. In an immense temple created in Jerusalem for the unification of all religions, the Antichrist attempts to impose his will on the Christian representatives by asking them to accept him as their "sole protector and patron." Many of the gathered Christians are enticed by his entreaties and temptations, and only a small band from each of the major confessions hold out against him. Two of their leaders are eventually killed by lightning after they recognize and proclaim the emperor to be the Antichrist. The remaining small group of dissenters are sent away from the city. In contrast, the other groups of various Christian denominations cement their relationship with their new leader by accepting his magician Apollonius as their common pope.

The story ends with a great apocalyptic battle followed by an enormous earthquake and the eruption of a great volcano which swallows up the great emperor and his forces. The Antichrist is defeated, principally—one assumes—because he has been recognized by at least a small group of people.

Solovyov's story is significant for many reasons. For one, he creates an epic narrative out of the biblical prophecies which is far more convincing and insightful than Hollywood's *Omen* trilogy. Solovyov, a mystic and devout Christian himself, clearly takes these prophecies seriously, and attempts to show how such a scenario could actually develop on earth in modern times. But more than that, his "Short Story of the Antichrist" is instructive because of its treatment of evil itself. Solovyov shows us that the presence of evil in the world is a far more complex phenomenon than we are accustomed to believe. He challenges our very perception of evil by demonstrating how easily it can appear to be "good." As one of his characters observes, "all that glitters is not gold."

Solovyov's tale is particularly relevant to our day (and the theme of this book) in that it offers a schooling for ways of perceiving the world and interpreting contemporary events. Do we always distinguish between glitter and gold? Solovyov's story challenges us to ask ourselves sincerely whether, amidst the fog of media hype and digitally bedazzling technology, we would be awake to the manipulations of such a "great man" today.

This chapter's final link to the theme of Antichrist comes from Steiner, who also spoke on the incarnation of evil, in this case a being he referred to as Ahriman. For Steiner, Ahriman was synonymous with the biblical Satan (although distinct from Lucifer), and represents materialism. His task is to convince human beings that soul and spirit do not exist. In contrast to Lucifer, who is a majestic, ethereal being, Ahriman seeks to harden, densify, and materialize human nature to turn us away from any conception of metaphysical dimensions. Ahriman, Steiner claimed, would incarnate in a human body in the near future. However, while Steiner described Ahriman as an entity who opposed Christ, he did not see him as "the Antichrist" as such. His picture of Ahriman is closer to St. Paul's "son of perdition" referred to earlier.

It is important to note that, as we have seen, Steiner was not a mere interpreter of biblical texts, nor a theoretician or hypothesizer. Rather, when speaking on spiritual matters, he was gleaning his knowledge directly from spiritual sources. Using a highly developed clairvoyance and advanced methods of verification, Steiner was purporting to convey highly accurate information. At the same time, he did not ask for anybody to believe what he said, but to treat it as spiritual-scientific research: to be thought about, meditated upon, and where possible compared with other sources. The following material is therefore presented not as dogma, but as a relevant investigation into the theme.

It is interesting to note that in a speaking career spanning some 6,000 lectures, Steiner spoke only six times about the earthly incarnation of Ahriman.[6] From his various statements, it is clear that he believed this incarnation would take place in the West, probably in an English-speaking country, and in the near future. Steiner rarely spoke in a prophetic mode, which probably explains why he did not give specific indications of time and place for Ahriman's incarnation. He would also have been conscious of the dynamics of spiritual events, and the fact that an occurrence of such import was liable to be affected by human free will and how it manifested on Earth.

What he was very specific about, however, were the conditions that would allow the being of Ahriman to carry out his mission. For one, Steiner spoke about the human intellect becoming "very inventive in the realm of physical life," through which "it will be possible for there to be a human individuality of a kind in which Ahriman will be able to be incorporated." As commentator Hans Peter van Manen points out, this reference can bring to mind modern fertilization techniques as well as the more recently developed technology of genetic engineering, the implication being that such methods could create a physical body into which Ahriman could successfully incarnate.[7]

Other trends and symptoms which would signal the coming of Ahriman's incarnation include the prevalence of the modern scientific, mechanical conception of the universe; the tendency to view social life and society solely from the economic point of view; the acceptance of the principle of nationality as the solution to the problems of humanity; the popularity of the system of party politics; the spread of fundamentalist and simplistic evangelical interpretations of Christianity (in particular the emphasis on Jesus as a "simple man" of good ethics as opposed to the principle of the cosmic Christ); and the spread of a purely intellectual cultural life. As all of these phenomena can be observed in modern life, one could expect that, from Steiner's point of view, the incarnation of the being of Ahriman is imminent.

Finally, one should note that Steiner was not suggesting that human beings should attempt to avert such an event, or even agitate against it in an external way. This incarnation is meant to happen, and could be for the good of human evolution. The critical thing for Steiner was that people should recognize Ahriman for what he is. In other words he should be unmasked; and in this respect one can think of Solovyov's tale. Under such conditions, Ahriman's incarnation would have positive results. Only if Ahriman were to go unrecognized would this event be wholly calamitous for earthly and human development.

3.4 Closing Thoughts

In the first section of this book, I spoke of the philosophy of materialism as an all-pervasive destructive force in modern life. Overcoming it in a healthy way calls for consciousness of other dimensions of reality—of soul and spirit. In this sense, it is apparent that the process of overcoming evil can be a positive, transformative experience.

We are in the belly of the beast of materialism, and are called to work within its skin. As we have seen, the Manichean path is about transforming from within the skin of the dragon. In the context of this book, it is specifically about transforming through cognition. The devil does not like to be detected. In Solovyov's "Short Story of the Antichrist" (see chapter 3.3), the Antichrist is essentially defeated at the point when he is recognized for what he is. What this tells us is that an act of inner understanding can work like magic in bringing about outer change and transformation.

The path outlined here is about bringing spiritual understanding to materialistic culture, entering into a conscious, ongoing process of engagement. As we have seen, this means taking an interest in the culture we find around us, but at the same time not being compromised by it. Rather, we seek to comprehend it at deeper levels of meaning. It may also be necessary to take on broad new concepts (see part 3) which might seem fantastic or even crazy. But if we are to think beyond the box of the materialistic paradigm which is currently constraining our culture, open-mindedness is an essential requisite.

In truth this is an enormous task, and a little bit of humor is required to maintain a sense of humility and perspective. It is unlikely that any one person can change the course of human development, but as individuals we *can* and *do* have an effect. The important thing is that we work, perhaps in the smallest of ways, to understand the things that happen around us. Our insights may not always be very profound, but our effort and intention are significant.

In part 2, I presented a few examples of my studies. My aim there was not to provide exhaustive insights into any one subject. I am well aware of my own limitations, and make no claim to special understanding. Rather, I wanted to show how one can make a beginning. As mentioned earlier, I have always begun study because I was drawn to or fascinated by a certain subject. Then, through research, thought, and meditation, I have tried to reveal deeper perspectives and layers of meaning.

If you see a film and are struck by certain aspects of it, try to understand what is behind the phenomenon. What are violent movies telling us? What are behind the images of sci-fi? Why does a cartoon like "Beavis and Butt-head" emerge at a certain time? When confronted with news stories about striking individuals and events, dig a little deeper and try to see what is working in the background. Why did Malcolm X do what he did? Why are Charles and Diana depicted in certain ways through the media? What is going on with David Icke? Why on earth did Mary Bell do what she did? These are some of the questions I asked in part 2. Tentative understandings emerged. Some of my commentary and insights may be true; some may prove to be false and misguided. But the important thing is that one is engaging with a process that seeks to understand life beyond the outer layer of material appearance. I am convinced that the effort and energy exerted in this exercise is always nourishing for our culture and human development as a whole.

Here, as a closing summary, is the essential message of this book:

We live in changing times. Humanity is undergoing a transformation. Our consciousness, which has a vast potential for further development, is beginning to reawaken to other dimensions of reality.

This is a period of both great danger and tremendous opportunity, a time to be fully awake, and to observe and know what is going on around us. More than ever we should try to see beyond the material veil of illusion, and begin to understand contemporary events and phenomena at deeper levels.

Know that your thinking is a tangible spiritual force. An act of true cognition can have a tremendous effect on the world and life around us. Strive to be aware of retrogressive powers which are seeking to retard our evolution as a human race. At the same time seek the good, the true, and the beautiful.

Spiritual understanding of life is called for today to enable metamorphosis of the dead philosophy of materialism. Your effort to interpret and perceive events at ever deepening levels of truth is never wasted. It works into the future as a force for the good.

A spiritual movement with the task of transforming evil into good is destined to grow in strength and influence. Be part of it. Begin in small ways to breathe in some of the materialism around us, and in turn breathe out spiritual thoughts and concepts to enliven our culture. Know that in the process you are contributing to the health and well-being of humanity and our planet.

Endnotes

Introduction

1. Osip Mandelstam, *Journey to Armenia*, George F. Ritchie, San Francisco, 1979.

Chapter 1.1

1. "Welcome to the Terrordome," from *Fear of a Black Planet*, CBS, 1990.

2. Maggie O'Kane, "The Lies that made the Gulf War," *The Guardian*, London, 16 December 1995. Her film "Riding the Storm, How to Tell Lies and Win Wars" was shown on Channel 4 television (UK) in 1996.

Chapter 1.2

1. C. G. Jung, *Modern Man in Search of a Soul*, Ark Paperbacks, London, 1984, p. 226–7.

2. The idea of applying scientific methods to researching spirit derives from the work of Rudolf Steiner (1861–1925), whose comprehensive philosophy and "spiritual research" remains the most complete and far-reaching legacy of its kind available today. Significantly, Steiner was able to apply the results of his research to practical areas such as education, medicine, and agriculture. His path of spiritual development is outlined in *How to Know Higher Worlds*, while the systematic results of his research are given in *Theosophy* and *An Outline of Esoteric Science* (all Anthroposophic Press, New York). Apart from several other written works, dozens of volumes of his published lectures are also available.

3. C. G. Harrison, *The Transcendental Universe*, Lindisfarne Press, New York, 1993, page 92.

4. A book which gives detailed descriptions and commentary on such exercises and makes a good starting point is Florin Lowndes, *Enlivening the Chakra of the Heart*, Sophia Books, Sussex, 2000.

Chapter 1.3

1. "Working Class Hero," from *John Lennon/The Plastic Ono Band*, EMI, 1970.

2. "Retail therapy will not buy you happiness," *The Daily Telegraph*, London, July 4, 2001. The research among 1,400 people was carried out by Dr. Shaun Saunders of the University of Newcastle, New South Wales, Australia.

3. See Samuel Hahnemann, *Organon of Medicine* (5th edition, 1833) and J. T. Kent., *Lectures on Homeopathic Philosophy* (1900), both B. Jain Publishers, New Delhi.

4. Fernand Niel, *Albigeois et Cathares*, Presses Universitaires de France, Paris, 1959.

Chapter 1.4

1. Richard Seddon, *Mani, His Life and Work*, Temple Lodge Publishing, London, 1998, page 7.

2. Rudolf Steiner, *Correspondence and Documents*, Rudolf Steiner Press, London, 1987, the "Barr Document."

3. Ibid.

4. A. W. Besant and C. W. Leadbeater, *Thought Forms*, Quest Books, 1969.

Chapter 1.5

1. *Parzival*, Random House, New York, 1961, page 422.

2. To my knowledge, this important connection was first made by George Adams in his *Mysteries of the Rose Cross*, Temple Lodge Press, London, 1989.

3. *The Nicene and Post-Nicene Fathers, Volume IV, St. Augustine*, T&T Clark, Edinburgh, 1996, page 237.

4. His actual words are: "For my part, I should not believe the gospel except as moved by the authority of the Catholic Church." *The Nicene and Post-Nicene Fathers*, ibid., page 131.

Chapter 1.6

1. From an interview with Anne A. Simpkinson entitled "What I Would Say to Osama bin Laden," *Caduceus* magazine, Warwickshire (UK), Winter 2001–2.

2. See for example *The Karma of Untruthfulness*, volumes 1 and 2, Rudolf Steiner Press, London, 1988 and 1992, and *From Symptom to Reality in Modern History*, Rudolf Steiner Press, London, 1976.

3. For many examples of how "PR" influences and distorts the content of reported news see Stauber & Rampton, *Trust Us, We're Experts*, Tarcher/Putnam, 2001.

4. This idea is spoken of and developed by Sergei O. Prokofieff in his book *The Occult Significance of Forgiveness*, 3rd edition, Temple Lodge Publishing, London, 1995, p.124. I am also indebted to Prokofieff for his basic concept of seeing "layers" of reality in interpreting outer events—although I have developed this for my own purposes.

Chapter 1.7

1. Rudolf Steiner speaking to the German Foreign Secretary Richard von Kuhlman in 1917, quoted from *The Birth of a New Agriculture, Koberwitz 1924*, ed. A. von Keyserlingk, Temple Lodge Publishing, London, 1999.

2. *Metro*, London, 20 February 2001.

3. *The Heat is On: The High Stakes Over Earth's Threatened Climate*, Addison-Wesley, 1997.

4. Ibid.

5. I should make it abundantly clear here that I am not suggesting that those who suffer from outer evils "deserve" to find themselves in such a situation, i.e., that a person or group of people suffering from an outer calamity are of necessity receiving karmic retribution of some kind. Such a presumption can never be made without exact clairvoyant insight. The reality could be quite the contrary. It is possible, for example, for a person or even a nation to absorb the karmic consequences of another person's actions as an act of sacrifice. Or perhaps through a period of suffering in a present incarnation an individual is developing a positive quality for a future incarnation.

6. Dannion Brinkley with Paul Perry, *Saved by the Light*, Piatkus, London, 1994.

Chapter 2.1

1. *The Guardian*, London, 10 June 1995.

2. *Time*, New York, 12 June 1995.

3. *The Guardian*, op. cit.

4. For a penetrating history of rap see David Toop, *The Rap Attack: African Jive to New York Hip Hop*, Pluto Press, London, 1985; and S. H. Fernando, Jr., *The New Beats, Exploring the Music, Culture, and Attitudes of Hip-Hop*, Payback Press, Edinburgh, 1995. Toop attempts to trace the roots of rap to the West African Savannah Griots.

5. See, for example, Public Enemy, *It Takes a Nation of Millions to Hold Us Back*, Def Jam Recordings, 1988; The Jungle Brothers, *Done By the Forces of Nature*, Eternal, 1989; BDP, *Edutainment*, Jive, 1990; and Gangstarr, *Step in the Arena*, Cooltempo, 1991.

6. "Don't Believe the Hype," from *It Takes a Nation of Millions to Hold Us Back*, op. cit.

7. *The Source, The Magazine of Hip-Hop Music, Culture and Politics*, New York, October 1991.

8. *The Source*, December 1990.

9. *Melody Maker*, London, 26 November 1994.

10. *The New Beats*, op. cit, page 101.

11. *The Source*, December 1990.

12. *The Source*, June 1994.

13. *The Guardian*, G2, London, 14 June 2001.

14. *The New Beats*, op. cit., p.85.

15. *NME*, London, 25 November 1995.

16. "Jesse James," *The Diary*, Rap-a-Lot Records, 1994.

17. *The Source*, June 1994.

18. *The Source*, December 1990.

19. *Select*, London, April 1994.

20. Nathan McCall, "My Rap Against Rap," *Reader's Digest*, May 1994.

21. Ibid.

22. *The Source*, October 1993.

23. Ibid.

24. *The Guardian*, January 24, 2001.

25. *The Source*, June 1994.

26. *The Source*, December 1990.

27. *NME*, London, 26 February 1994.

28. *Select*, April 1994.

29. *The Source*, December 1990.

30. *Time*, 12 June 1995.

31. Ibid.

32. *NME*, 3 December 1994.

33. *The Source*, June 1994.

34. *The Observer*, London, 18 March 2001.

35. *NME*, 6 August 1994.

36. *The Guardian*, 13 August 1994.

37. *The Guardian*, 3 February 2001.

38. *Time*, 12 June 1995.

39. *The Face*, London, February 1994.

40. For a modern exposition see Nicanor Perlas, *Shaping Globalization, Civil Society, Cultural Power, and Threefolding*, CADI/GlobeNet3, Philippines/USA, 2000. The system was first elaborated by Rudolf Steiner; see his book *Towards Social Renewal, Rethinking the Basis of Society*, Rudolf Steiner Press, London, 1997.

41. Ibid., Perlas.

Chapter 2.2

1. Factual information regarding Tibet and quotations are drawn from the literature of the Tibet Society of the United Kingdom, Tibet Support Group UK, and the Tibet Foundation.

2. See Peter Tradowsky, *Kaspar Hauser, The Struggle for the Spirit*, Temple Lodge Publishing, London, 1997, p. 18. This book contains an excellent description of Kaspar Hauser's life (see pages 9–67), and quotes much valuable source material by first-hand witnesses. A remarkably comprehensive study, profusely illustrated, is published only in German: Johannas Mayer/Peter Tradowsky, *Kaspar Hauser, Das Kind von Europa*, Verlag Urachhaus, Stuttgart, 1998.

3. For a detailed look at Stanhope and Kaspar Hauser's opponents see Johannes Mayer, *Philip Henry Lord Stanhope, Der Gegenspieler Kaspar Hausers*, Urachhaus, Stuttgart, 1988. The attacks continue to the present day; see the article in *Der Spiegel* referred to by Tradowsky (pages xv–xviii).

4. See Tradowsky, page 57.

5. See, for example, Hermann Pies, *Kaspar Hauser Dokumentation*, Ansbach, 1966.

6. See Tradowsky, Mayer, etc., above.

7. The tragic case of the Russian Tsarevich Dmitri, who was murdered at the age of eight and a half years in 1591, bears a still closer resemblance to the case of the missing Tibetan boy. Dmitri also bore great spiritual impulses which would have benefited the evolution of Russia and the East-Slavic peoples, but—through the malevolent work of antagonistic groups—was murdered and replaced by the "false Dmitri," who sought to introduce a retrograde element in Russian history. See further in S. O. Prokofieff, *Das Ratsel Demitri*, Verlag am Goetheanum, Dornach, 1992.

Chapter 2.3

1. www.epsltd.com and cyberatlas.com.
2. "Discomfort and Joy," *The Ecologist*, October 2000.
3. "Logging on to love," *The Observer*, London, 21 January 2001.
4. Ibid.
5. *The Ecologist*, op. cit.
6. Ibid.

Chapter 2.4

1. *Vox* magazine, London, January 1995.
2. Ibid.
3. *Moviewatch*, ITV (UK), February 1995.
4. Ibid.
5. The Guide, *The Guardian*, London, 27 May 1995.
6. *Vox*, op. cit.
7. *The Guardian*, 29 October 1994.
8. *Time Out*, London, 1 February 1994.
9. *The Guardian*, 19 November 1994.
10. *Vox*, op. cit.
11. Ibid.
12. Ibid.
13. Ibid.
14. Ibid.
15. Quentin Tarantino, *Pulp Fiction*, Faber and Faber, London, 1994. For a detailed analysis of Tarantino's allusions in *Pulp Fiction* see www.godamongdirectors.com.
16. *The Guardian*, London, 24 January 2001.
17. *Metro*, London, 1 May 2001.
18. *Time*, New York, 12 June 1995.
19. *Time Out*, op. cit.
20. Ibid.
21. *Moving Pictures*, BB2 (UK), February 1995.
22. *Time Out*, op. cit.
23. *Film Guide*, London, May 1996.
24. See for example, Jostein Saether, *Living with Invisible People*, Clairview Books, Sussex, 2001.

Chapter 2.5

1. MTV Books/Callaway/Boxtree, New York/London, 1994.
2. *Time*, New York, 25 October 1993.

Chapter 2.6

1. *The Guardian*, 25 June 1996.
2. Ibid.
3. Ibid.

Chapter 2.7

1. *The Independent*, London, 29 July 1994.
2. *God in Us*, Imprint Academic, second edition, 2001.
3. *The Independent*, op. cit.
4. Freeman was ordained in 1972, and was dismissed from his parish in July 1994. He went on to become the managing editor of the *Journal of Consciousness Studies*, and lectures and writes on theology and consciousness. His published work also includes the books *Gospel Treasure* (1999) and *The Volitional Brain* (co-edited, 1999).
5. *The Sunday Telegraph*, London, 14 February 1993.
6. *The Times*, London, 30 January 1999.
7. Letter by Ivor Annetts in *The Guardian*, London, 3 February 1999.
8. Letter by Peter Harvey, Ibid.
9. John 9:3 (King James Version).

Chapter 2.8

1. This news story was published on 27 April 1998.
2. In 1974 the American criminologist Robert Martinson and two colleagues published a report which analyzed the rates of reconviction for released prisoners who had undergone various rehabilitation schemes. Their dour conclusion was that "nothing works." Although Martinson later tried to recant, it was too late. His research had been appropriated by conservative thinkers and used to justify harsh prison regimes.
    Robert Martinson, "What Works? Questions and Answers about Prison Reform," *The Public Interest*, Spring 1974, pages 22–54.

Chapter 2.9

1. *The Sunday Times* magazine, London, 13 October 1991.
2. David Icke, *The Truth Vibrations*, Aquarian Press, London, 1991, page 13.
3. *The Sunday Times*, 31 March 1991.
4. *The Times*, London, 20 March 1991.
5. *The Sun*, London, 28 March 1991.
6. *The Daily Mirror*, London, 28 March 1991.
7. Ibid.; see also *The Sunday Times*, op. cit.
8. *The Daily Mirror*, op. cit. Some ten years later, Icke was apparently proved right. Researchers from John Hopkins University in Baltimore calculated that if all the visible light in the universe was mixed together, it would glow in the shade of a "pale turquoise." See "Scientists find universal harmony of God's blue period" in *The Times*, 11 January 2002.
9. *The Sun*, op. cit.
10. *The Daily Mirror*, op. cit.
11. *The Face*, London, November 1992.
12. *The Truth Vibrations*, page 17.
13. Ibid., page 32.
14. Ibid., page 37.
15. *Love Changes Everything*, Aquarian Press, London, 1992, page 142.

16. *The Sunday Times* magazine, op. cit.

17. *The Sunday Times* magazine, op. cit.

18. *The Truth Vibrations*, page 86.

19. Ibid., page 116.

20. Ibid., page 109.

21. Ibid., pages 10–11.

22. Ibid., page 120.

23. *The Biggest Secret*, Bridge of Love Publications, Arizona, 1999, pages 453–456.

24. Rudolf Steiner, *The Occult Movement in the Nineteenth Century*, Rudolf Steiner Press, London, 1973, page 65.

25. *The Truth Vibrations*, page 119.

26. Ibid., page 117.

27. *The Biggest Secret*, page 80.

Chapter 2.10

1. Prince Charles's great uncle and Commander of the Royal Navy. He was murdered by IRA terrorists in 1979.

2. Quoted from Jonathan Dimbleby, *The Prince of Wales, A Biography*, Little, Brown and Company, London, 1994, page 255.

3. Ibid., page 390.

4. Quoted from "A Time for Renewal," *Positive News*, 1996.

5. In the light of all this, Earl Spencer's veiled criticism in his eulogy at Diana's funeral, over Charles's raising of his two sons was misguided. Spencer asserted that the two boys should not be "simply immersed by duty and tradition," but allowed to "experience as many different aspects of life as possible to arm them spiritually and emotionally for the years ahead." Charles, as we have seen, hardly represents the conservative "tradition" that Spencer spoke of, but is a true radical who indeed seeks to experience "many different aspects of life."

6. See Stephen Knight, *The Brotherhood*, Book Club Associates, London, 1984, pages 212–14. Newspapers have also reported this as a fact.

7. *The Sun*, London, 9 September 1997.

8. *The Daily Telegraph*, London, 11 September 1997.

9. *The Daily Mirror*, London, 15 September 1997.

10. *The Prince of Wales, A Biography*, op. cit., page 494.

Chapter 2.11

1. *The Times*, London, 19 March 1991.

2. "Second Class from Cradle to Grave," *The Times*, London, 17 October 1995. In 1998 the U.S. Census Bureau reported that the number and poverty rate of African Americans was 9.1 million and 26.5 percent, compared with 24.4 million and 11.0 percent for Whites. In 1997, African-American households had a median income of $25,050, compared to $38,972 for white households (see www.census.gov/hhes/www/income97.html). Similar statistics can also be found in many secondary sources, for example Michael Moore's humorous but politically radical *Stupid White Men*, ReganBooks, New York, 2001 (see chapter "Kill Whitey").

3. *The Autobiography of Malcolm X*, with the assistance of Alex Haley, Penguin Books, Harmondsworth, 1968. The following account of Malcolm X's life is based on his own account, and Thulani Davis, *Malcolm X*, Stewart, Tabori & Chang, New York, 1993. For a more critical account, see also Bruce Perry, *Malcolm, The Life of a Man Who Changed Black America*, Station Hill, New York, 1993.

4. See Elijah Muhammad, *Message to the Blackman in America*, Muhammad's Temple No. 2, Chicago, 1965.

5. *The Autobiography of Malcolm X*, op. cit., page 256. For confirmation of Elijah Muhammad's teachings see *Message to the Blackman in America*, op. cit. (Fard's teachings are exclusively reported by Elijah Muhammad.)

6. *The Autobiography of Malcolm X*, op. cit.

7. Ibid., page 306.

8. Ibid.

9. *Message to the Blackman in America*, op. cit., page 17.

10. *The Autobiography of Malcolm X*, op. cit., pages 267–277.

11. "The Muslim Program," reproduced in *Message to the Blackman in America*, op. cit.

12. *The Autobiography of Malcolm X*, op. cit., page 348.

13. Ibid., page 443.

14. Ibid., page 452.

15. Ibid., page 454.

16. Ibid., page 479.

17. Ibid., page 480.

18. Ibid., page 483.

19. Ibid., page 321.

20. Ibid., page 489.

21. Ibid., Alex Haley's foreword, page 57.

22. Ibid., page 62.

23. Ibid., page 44.

24. See www.noi.org/information/history-elijah.html.

25. *The Autobiography of Malcolm X*, op. cit., page 48.

26. Ibid., page 53.

27. Bruce Perry, *The Life of a Man Who Changed Black America*, op. cit., page 338.

28. *The Autobiography of Malcolm X*, op. cit., page 73.

29. *Message to the Blackman in America*, op. cit, page 23.

30. Ibid., page 32.

31. Ibid., page 24.

32. Ibid., the chapter entitled "The Devil" (pages 110–122) where the whole creation story of the white race is described.

33. Ibid., page 291.

34. Ibid., page 304.

35. Ibid., page 6.

36. Ibid., page 9.

37. Ibid., page 18.

38. See Nation of Islam website www.noi.org.

39. *The Life of a Man Who Changed Black America*, pages 143–144.

40. *Message to the Blackman in America*, op. cit., page 20.

41. Rudolf Steiner, lecture of April 11, 1912: "Address given to the Russian members of the Theosophical Society" (manuscript available from Rudolf Steiner House Library, London).

42. H. P. Blavatsky, *From the Caves and Jungles of Hindustan*, Theosophical Publishing House, Wheaton, 1975, page xxxv.

43. Ibid., page 49.

44. Quoted from Sergei O. Prokofieff, *The East in the Light of the West*, Temple Lodge Publishing, London, 1993, page 108, where it is translated from the original Russian. In *From the Caves and Jungles of Hindustan* (page 462) this phrase is rendered into English more demurely as "the hated and despised white race."

45. K. Paul Johnson, *The Masters Revealed, Madame Blavatsky and the Myth of the Great White Lodge*, State University of New York Press, Albany, 1994.

Chapter 2.12

1. See, for example, Rudolf Steiner, *The Mission of the Individual Folk Souls*, Rudolf Steiner Press, London, 1970, lecture of June 9, 1910. These "Folk Souls" are the Archangels spoken of in the Bible and elsewhere.

2. According to Rudolf Steiner, the being who represents the current *Zeitgeist*—Michael, referred to in the Bible as "the Countenance of God"—has the goal of introducing a cosmopolitan element over the whole of humankind. See Rudolf Steiner, *The Mission of the Archangel Michael*, Anthroposophic Press, New York, 1971.

3. See for example the books of Marco Pogacnik (Findhorn Press), who works extensively with earth energies.

4. "Nile Blues" from *Voices for Peace*, Scribner, London, 2001, page 62.

Chapter 3.1

1. See Rudolf Steiner, *Problems of Our Time*, Rudolf Steiner Publishing Co., London (n. d.), lecture of September 12, 1919, page 30.

2. Rudolf Steiner, *How to Know Higher Worlds*, Anthroposophic Press, New York, 1994, page 187.

Chapter 3.2

1. *Karma of Untruthfulness* Volumes I & II, Rudolf Steiner Press, London, 1988 and 1992.

2. See further in Sergei O. Prokofieff, *The Spiritual Origins of Eastern Europe and the Future Mysteries of the Holy Grail*, Temple Lodge Publishing, London, 1993.

3. *The Anglo-American Establishment* was only published in 1981, Books in Focus, New York. *Tragedy and Hope* was published in 1966 by Macmillan, New York.

4. See Terry Boardman, *Mapping the Millennium, Behind the Plans of the New World Order*, Temple Lodge Publishing, London, 1998, and Amnon Reuveni, *In the Name of the "New World Order," Manifestations of Decadent Powers in World Politics*, Temple Lodge Publishing, London, 1996.

5. *The Transcendental Universe*, Lindisfarne Press, New York, 1993, pages 98–99.

Chapter 3.3

1. I John 2:18–22.

2. II Thessalonians 2: 3–10.

3. Matthew 24:24. See also Mark 13:6 and 22; Luke 21:8; and John 5:43.

4. Revelation 13.

5. Vladimir Solovyov, *War, Progress, and the End of History*, Lindisfarne Press, New York, 1990.

6. I am grateful to Hans Peter van Manen for his excellent summary of Steiner's remarks in his essay "When Did Rudolf Steiner Expect the Incarnation of Ahriman?" See *The Future is Now*, edited by S. E. Gulbekian, Temple Lodge Publishing, London, 1999.

7. Ibid., page 229 (also for the quote from Steiner).

Index

About the Author

Sevak Gulbekian was born in London in 1964. A publisher and writer, he is presently Chief Editor of Clairview Books, Temple Lodge Publishing, and Rudolf Steiner Press. His spiritual outlook is informed by the ancient heritage of his Armenian ancestry, the more modern esoteric research of Rudolf Steiner, as well as the many contemporary accounts of spiritual experience available today. Over the past decade he has sought to find ways of relating spirituality to present-day culture, a path he has elaborated through essays, talks, and workshops, and finally in this volume. In his professional work he publishes books which challenge the "received wisdoms" of the media and the materialistic dogmas of the age. Sevak is also a qualified and registered homeopath. He lives in Sussex, England.

Hampton Roads Publishing Company

. . . for the evolving human spirit

Hampton Roads Publishing Company
publishes books on a variety of subjects,
including metaphysics, health,
visionary fiction, and other related topics.

For a copy of our latest catalog, call toll-free
(800) 766-8009, or send your name and address to:

Hampton Roads Publishing Company, Inc.
1125 Stoney Ridge Road
Charlottesville, VA 22902

e-mail: hrpc@hrpub.com
www.hrpub.com